CARMAGEDDON

CARMAGEDDON

HOW CARS MAKE LIFE WORSE AND WHAT TO DO ABOUT IT

DANIEL KNOWLES

ABRAMS PRESS, NEW YORK

Copyright © 2023 Daniel Knowles

Jacket © 2023 Abrams

Published in 2023 by Abrams Press, an imprint of ABRAMS. All rights reserved. No portion of this book may be reproduced, stored in a retrieval system, or transmitted in any form or by any means, mechanical, electronic, photocopying, recording, or otherwise, without written permission from the publisher.

Library of Congress Control Number: 2022946038

ISBN: 978-1-4197-5880-5
eISBN: 978-1-64700-537-5

Printed and bound in the United States
10 9 8 7 6 5 4 3 2 1

Abrams books are available at special discounts when purchased in quantity for premiums and promotions as well as fundraising or educational use. Special editions can also be created to specification. For details, contact specialsales@abramsbooks.com or the address below.

Abrams Press® is a registered trademark of Harry N. Abrams, Inc.

ABRAMS The Art of Books
195 Broadway, New York, NY 10007
abramsbooks.com

To my parents, who had child bike seats decades before it was cool, and to my wife, who has still not passed her driving test

CONTENTS

Introduction	1
1. When Cars Win	15
2. Hello, Mr. Toad	25
3. Motorway Cities of the Future	39
4. Detroit Breakdown	51
5. Jane Jacobs and the Fight Back	67
6. The Next Frontier	79
7. Electric Delusions	91
8. Bionic Duckweed	101
9. Why You Can't Beat Traffic	113
10. Free Parking, Do Not Pass Go	121
11. Evil Carmakers	133
12. Gas Guzzler Nation	145
13. What Causes Traffic Accidents?	157
14. Bring in the Bikes	169
15. Go East: Lessons from Japan	187
16. Winning the Argument	201
17. Peak Car	215
Conclusion	227
Acknowledgments	237
Index	239

INTRODUCTION

Around three miles away from where I live in Chicago, southeast from my apartment in Wicker Park, is the most congested stretch of road in the entire United States. Just west of Union Station, once one of the busiest railway stations in the entire world, is the intersection between I-90 and I-290, otherwise known as the Kennedy and Eisenhower Expressways. Named the Jane Byrne Interchange, this junction occupies an entire city block. From it, the Kennedy runs northwest while the Eisenhower runs west. Most weeks I cycle across one of the many bridges that cross these two highways into the city. At most hours of the day, the traffic beneath me is thick, with every lane full of vehicles of all sorts. The speed limits posted show that drivers are allowed to go at 55 miles per hour. But except occasionally late at night, almost none do. They move along at 30 mph or less, and often sit almost completely still, bumper-to-bumper, hooting at each other.

These roads came long after much of the rest of Chicago was built. The building I live in was constructed in 1890, on a street built for the new upper middle class produced by the late Victorian industrial revolution. My neighborhood is full of these houses, and it is one of the loveliest places I have ever lived. You can walk almost anywhere you need to, and there is a stop on the L train, Chicago's subway system, around a five-minute walk away, which I use to get around when I don't feel like cycling. Most of the houses are beautiful, solid brick buildings, with grand porches, high ceilings, and huge windows. I only rarely use the freeway that runs less than a mile away from my front door, because, unlike most of the residents of Chicago, I do not own a car.

And yet living in Chicago, it is hard not to wonder what the city might be like if it and the other roads that cross the city had never been constructed. The expressways were built in the 1950s and '60s. Some parts replaced factories and warehouses. But they also were built by demolishing lots of homes much like the one I currently live in—the Eisenhower led to 13,000 families being relocated—and now they run like a scar through the city. If you are on foot or on a bicycle, when you cross over or under them you go through whole blocks of what is essentially wasteland—half-used parking lots, derelict buildings, and a lot of awful big-box stores surrounded by acres of tarmac. Just a fifteen-minute walk from some of the most expensive real estate in Chicago, it can feel like an outer suburb. If you travel by car, you will probably miss the colossal waste of space, but if you walk or cycle around, it is impossible to ignore.

When the freeways were built, West Town, the neighborhood Wicker Park is a part of, fell into decline. The population of the neighborhood, mostly the descendants of Polish and Ukrainian immigrants who had moved to Chicago decades earlier, moved out to the suburbs in droves. The landlords who had housed them, often subdividing the older homes to squeeze more people in, stopped investing in their properties. Many buildings were simply abandoned, or worse, set on fire for insurance fraud. In one three-year period, from 1976 to 1978, Chicago firefighters were called to more than 350 suspicious building fires.

Living here now, eating at the fancy restaurants, and shopping at the boutiques that have opened in recent years, it is hard to imagine. Houses like mine have refilled with well-off yuppies like me, as people realized that cheap real estate still had value and began to come back. And yet it happened. Indeed, not long after arriving in Chicago, I was given the chance to interview Mayor Lori Lightfoot. When I told her where I was living, she smiled and gently told me about how much it has gentrified since she lived in the same neighborhood in the 1980s.

Not everywhere in the city has recovered in quite the same way. Chicago's population is still 25 percent lower than it was in 1950, before the highway construction began. Many neighborhoods elsewhere in the city did not rebound in the way West Town eventually did. Whether because their populations started poorer, or because they contained more industry, or because their housing stock was less pretty, they were abandoned. Many neighborhoods continue to lose population to the present day, particularly on the South and West Sides, the centers of Black Chicago, where the freeway projects were often most destructive. Depressingly large parts of the city, which is still one of America's greatest metropolises, and is now the only true economic center of the Midwest, are now characterized by huge windswept parking lots and overgrown fields where houses once stood.

This process was something that began fifty years before the freeways, with the plan developed for the city by Daniel Burnham, who first proposed the widening of streets and the creation of highways in 1909. Burnham's plan was meant to be an attempt to re-create a "beautiful city," modeled on Paris, with wide boulevards and the like. It was also, however, as the historian Clay McShane writes, explicitly a blueprint for "providing roads for automobility." When it was finally implemented, rather than creating a new Paris, it set Chicago onto the pathway toward suburbanization that the city has struggled with ever since. Seemingly nobody anticipated that the roads would do this. In 1955 the city's planners were still anticipating that the population would grow to six million, rather than falling from 3.5 million.

The idea of all this road building was, simply put, to make it easier for people to get around. In the 1950s and '60s, car ownership was soaring, not just in America, but all over the rich world. And with it came extraordinary traffic jams. Motorways were meant to be the way to solve it, as part of a general rebuilding of cities. But what Chicago proves, however, is that it does not really work. When you build an enormous road through a neighborhood, it is like putting a tourniquet on a healthy limb. It creates a barrier that people do not want to cross, at least not on foot. Parts get cut off from oxygen and die. Roads—especially big, wide, car-only ones—are barriers, and while they make it easier to get around in a vehicle, they make it harder to get anywhere else. The city spreads out, as everyone gets into cars.

Today, drivers spend almost as long trying to get anywhere in the city as they did before the roads were built. According to INRIX, a traffic consultancy based in Washington, D.C., Chicago now has some of the worst traffic of any city in America, and not just on those two freeways. Drivers in the city spend roughly four full days a year stuck in traffic jams. To alleviate them, the state of Illinois wants to spend $2.7 billion to widen the Eisenhower, and more still on the Kennedy. The idea is that more lanes will mean that cars move through more quickly. But that was the idea behind building the roads in the first place.

The aim of this book is to persuade you of something that is antithetical to the development of most of the world over the past 140 years. Ever since Karl Benz invented the first internal combustion engine, we have been making our world revolve around our wheels. But the car is not an unalloyed good. (Indeed, they are generally very much alloyed.) Thanks to the car, our cities are uglier and more dangerous to get around, our air is less breathable, and our lives are interrupted more by traffic jams. The planet on which we live, the only one we have, is warming unsustainably, and vehicle emissions contribute at least a quarter of all CO_2 emissions globally, a share which is growing rapidly. The fortune we spend on producing, fueling, and maintaining cars leaves us poorer. And the more we try to accommodate the car, the more it will come to dominate our lives. Car manufacturers want us to believe that driving is freedom. But in fact, we are trapping ourselves in an enormous prison made up of moving metal cells.

What happened to Chicago has happened all over the rich world. I grew up in Birmingham, the second biggest city in the United Kingdom and another inland city which, much like fellow "Second City" Chicago, was also a global center of manufacturing built on canals and railways in the nineteenth century. In the 1950s, Birmingham was one of the wealthiest cities in the entire world, largely thanks to its manufacturing industry. It was, together with its smaller neighbor, Coventry, the hub of the British car industry, which grew out of World War II aircraft factories. And like Chicago, it too embraced the motorway in the aftermath of the war.

In the city center, along Bristol Road, are stretches where the council (local government) held the Birmingham Superprix through the 1980s, letting Formula 3000 cars zoom around city streets. On the way out is Spaghetti Junction, Britain's first multilevel interchange, named for the hectic strands of overlapping roads. And all around the city center is a tight inner ring road, designed not only to move cars around but to delineate a "central business district," a bit like an American downtown. It is known now as the "concrete collar," cutting off the larger city from the oxygen of the city center. Birmingham, not unlike Chicago, has more than its fair share of derelict buildings, empty plots, and soul-destroying big-box retail stores.

We have come to think of this—the idea that everyone ought to get around in their own personal vehicle—as normal, or even desirable. Drivers, cable news anchors, and popular newspapers sometimes like to argue that there is what Rob Ford, the crack cocaine–smoking former mayor of Toronto, once named a "war on cars." Fox News hosts love the phrase. *Bild*, a German tabloid, laments a culture that it says is "against the car and people who rely on four wheels." It is, in a way, easy to see why. In many parts of the industrialized world, driving is getting ever more miserable. The traffic on the Eisenhower and Kennedy Expressways is a case in point. So too is the ever-growing difficulty of finding free parking, or of dropping off your kids at school. Yet the reality is that it is not a war on cars causing this. It is their proliferation. The main reason driving is getting more miserable is because more and more people are doing it.

In America, there are now 290 million vehicles on the road, or more than one for every single adult. Three-quarters of Americans get to work by driving alone. The only city in the entire country where more people continue to walk, bike, or use public transit to travel to work than drive is New York. Even before the COVID-19 pandemic cut the bottom out of it, the use of public transport had been gently declining for decades. Traffic congestion, meanwhile, has been soaring, as more and more cars fill the roads. The average American driver drives thirty-nine miles every single day. The total amount driven increased every year from 2011 to 2020, and it is increasing more now.

And what applies to America applies elsewhere. According to data from the US Department of Energy, there is no region on the planet where the number of cars is not increasing. There are more registered cars than ever before on the roads in Britain now, some thirty-eight million in total. That is five million more than there are people with driving licenses. The UK Department for Transport estimates road traffic will double by 2050. Public transport in most of Britain is in decline too. If you assume a standard-size parking space for each one, that means that cars occupy around 170 square miles of land. That is more than the entire land area of the Isle of Wight. And of course, a car needs far more than one parking space on average to be useful. In America, the amount of land given over to roads and car parking spaces is the same size as the entire state of West Virginia. A whole state worth of tarmac.

The car was not just a technical invention. With it came a new idea, about how people should live. In the middle of the last century, architects and planners connived with the car industry to reimagine the city. The Futurama exhibition at the 1939 New York World's Fair, sponsored by General Motors, depicted a vision of the future in which everyone had a car, living in megacities dominated by expressways and suburbs. And architects like Le Corbusier, the father of Brutalism, and planners like Robert Moses of New York City, perhaps the most powerful unelected bureaucrat in American history, leapt to try to make it a reality, using all the power of the post–World War II state to acquire land, move people, and replace homes, offices, and factories with roads. These decisions were not made casually. They happened because of the political lobbying of the car industry and because of the power of rich people who owned cars. What was good for General Motors was good for America, said General Motors' executives, and politicians believed it.

They still believe it. What happened in Chicago and Birmingham in the mid-twentieth century is still happening now all over the world. In cities from Cairo to Houston, Berlin to Lagos, whole neighborhoods—often maligned as slums because poor people insist on living there—are still being demolished to make way for new expressways to move those with cars around. In poorer countries, the world's rapidly growing new upper middle class believes in the dream of suburban automotive life too—and once again they are getting their way, whatever it means for the poor and for the cities they are leaving behind.

I discovered that living in Nairobi, as I did for three years as *The Economist*'s Africa correspondent. In Swahili, the lingua franca of most of East Africa, *uhuru* means "freedom." Knowing that, I always thought that whoever named the main road going into the city center of Nairobi Uhuru Highway must have had an acute sense of irony. I never felt more trapped in Kenya than when I had to drive down Uhuru Highway. The road, four lanes of traffic in each direction broken up by roundabouts, is almost perpetually clogged by traffic. Cars move at a snail's pace, and sometimes not even that. It is hot, smelly, and unpleasant. The hooting of horns continues almost the entire time. And most journeys via it mean staying stuck there for hours.

I came to plan my life around the vicissitudes of Nairobi's traffic. More than once I misjudged how long it would take me to get to the airport and ended up climbing out of a taxi and hailing a motorbike to get me there on time, luggage clutched tight to my chest. And yet the funny thing about living in Nairobi is that while the rich are obsessed with traffic, in fact, almost nobody owns a car. There are fewer than four million cars in the whole of Kenya, a country with a population of more than fifty million people. For much of the population, even taking a *matatu*—a shared minibus taxi, costing something like twenty Kenyan shillings, or around twenty US cents, for a ride—is a luxury. The main way in which most people get to work is on foot, or sometimes by bicycle.

Walking in Nairobi is even more miserable than driving. The pavements are cracked, or often nonexistent. Safety is almost nonexistent too: The new highways cut clean through neighborhoods without pedestrian crossings. Driving at night, I would often see people in my headlights clamber over a barrier and sprint across the road. Hundreds die every year. And the pollution, much of it created by ancient vehicles, is appalling. A generation ago, from a tall building in the city center it was possible to see the snowcapped peaks of Mount Kenya and Mount Kilimanjaro, each roughly a hundred miles north and south. Now the smog clears so infrequently that locals do not believe it is possible. East Africa's air quality has worsened more than in almost any other region worldwide in the past thirty years.

Yet do Kenya's politicians ever worry about the pollution, or the experience of people walking in the city? If so, I never saw any evidence of it. They have one solution to the traffic: Build more bypasses. All over Nairobi new roads are being cut through the red hillside. A new overpass now runs alongside Uhuru Highway. The city rings out with the din of trucks and roads blocked as Chinese construction crews widen old roads and cut through new ones. And for a little while, they help.

But as the motorists trapped on the Eisenhower Expressway in Chicago could tell them, the freedom of the new open road never lasts. What happens is that when a new road opens, property developers realize that people can get into the city quicker and they buy up all of the land around it to build houses. In Kenya that is probably why building bypasses is so popular with politicians. Kenyan politicians rarely stick to just their day jobs; they tend to have large lucrative side businesses in things like property construction. But the trouble is that once those houses are built, the people buying them need to get cars and drive to work. Within a few years the traffic is just as bad as it used to be, and the pollution is even worse. And so the politicians realize that they need to build another bypass, and the whole process restarts.

The reason cars make our lives worse is not because there is something inherently evil about motorized travel. I too have enjoyed the thrill of loading up and driving out of a city to somewhere new, exciting, and far away. My favorite moments from my time in Kenya were those weekends when I took my knackered old Mitsubishi Pajero iO out of the city into the countryside and forced it wheezing up some mud track in the middle of nowhere to go camping. I have also driven coast-to-coast across the United States, zooming along straight roads through deserts and curvy roads through forests, and it was joyous. I still rent cars occasionally, mostly for work, and I have a soft spot for small, sporty vehicles that give you a buzz when you push the accelerator. I rented a Tesla to drive across Michigan once and it was far too tempting to push the accelerator to see how fast it could go.

The problem is that cars impose costs on everybody else. They are among the world's leading causes of what economists call "externalities"—costs imposed on others by your decisions. As I learned in Nairobi, your freedom to get around in your personal steel bubble is another person's freedom to have their lungs poisoned. Probably a much poorer person than you too. When you are sitting in traffic, you are not just being slowed down by everyone else, you are slowing them down too. When everyone drives to work, the car parking space uses land that could be used to build houses. When you burn gasoline or diesel to get around, the CO_2 emitted helps to heat up the entire planet. And of course, if you crash, you are far safer inside your metal box than the pedestrian you hit on the road. According to a study by the city of Copenhagen, every kilometer driven there costs society fifteen euro cents in higher pollution, congestion, and accident costs. Cycling a kilometer, by contrast, generates sixteen cents of benefits, almost all from the benefits of exercise, which reduces the amount of money the government has to spend on healthcare.

Worldwide, more than a million people die a year in car crashes. In America, the annual figure is more than 40,000, or about twice as many as the number murdered. Air pollution kills an order of magnitude more. Not all of that is due to cars of course, but a lot of it is. In London, around 9,500 people per year suffer early deaths thanks to the city's air pollution, according to one study by the Greater London Authority. That is almost all caused by cars. In India, more than a million people die each year of diseases caused by air pollution, much of it emitted by fleets of aging taxis and auto-rickshaws. Road transport also makes up about a quarter of CO_2 emissions worldwide, and much more in rich countries where we have relatively efficient electricity grids. In recent years, that figure has risen; cars have stopped getting more fuel-efficient, largely because they are getting bigger. In America, SUVs and trucks outsell sedans and hatchbacks by three to one. Such monstrous cars not only consume more fuel—because they are taller, they are also more dangerous to pedestrians.

And yet the world is not designed to take into account those costs. In fact, in most places, it is the opposite. We have designed our cities so that having a car is not a luxury but a necessity. Car drivers are given privileges such as free parking and free road space. While housing costs more and more, people still expect to be able to leave their car anywhere for a pittance. To live a "normal life" in many of the world's cities, you do not want to own a car, you need to own one. To create enough space for all of the cars, our cities are spread out so much that the distances you have to travel are simply too far to be practical by any means other than in your own personal vehicle.

People visit old cities—places like Venice and Amsterdam—and marvel at the fact that you can walk everywhere. They think it's magical. But then they go home and get back in their cars. It is not just in Kenya that building new roads leads ultimately to more traffic. A study of American cities from 1980 to 2000 found that a 10 percent increase in the amount of road space led to a 10 percent increase in the amount people drive. You cannot solve congestion by giving away valuable land to cars. You will just end up with more cars.

We have gotten so used to the domination of cars that we have forgotten how unpleasant the consequences are. We talk about traffic like we talk about the weather, as though it is something natural, outside of our control, to complain about but not to fix. We call car crashes "accidents" as though they are not preventable. We shrug at pollution, even when it leaves our children coughing their guts up after PE. One 2019 study showed that living next to a main road stunts lung growth in children by up to 14 percent.

Whenever we hear about how bad cars are, we feel a little angry, because by now, we do not know how to live without them. And after all, do car drivers not pay huge amounts in taxes and insurance, on the fuel they need, and indeed, on the damned things themselves? Do governments not make fortunes from egregiously expensive parking, and from issuing millions of parking tickets to those who fail to understand ever more complex rules? Do police forces not put up speed traps wherever they can to fine motorists who are merely going about their business? After all, how else are you expected to get the children to school, go to the shops, and get to work on time?

Yet in living memory, streets in even the world's biggest cities were free and safe for children to play in. In Britain as recently as the 1950s, and China as recently as the 1990s, the vast majority of people got around by bicycle, bus, or train, not in their own private car. Cities like Coventry, once the home of the British bicycle industry before it became a center of car manufacturing, used to have hundreds of miles of cycle paths. In America, the most violent, impoverished neighborhoods in cities like Detroit or St. Louis were once thriving, vibrant places that were cut apart by new motorways in the 1960s. Of course there were still plenty of other problems, from ill health caused by industrial pollution to diseases like tuberculosis and polio. But when people had to exercise to get around, they were considerably less likely to be obese or to suffer from diabetes or depression.

And it is not just to the past that we can look for inspiration. There are cities that are pushing back against the car—you may even live in one. In Tokyo, Amsterdam, and Copenhagen people live pretty good lives without needing anywhere near as many gasoline engines. They raise kids, they go shopping, they get to work, and for the most part, they are happier and healthier than people stuck in traffic jams. In Amsterdam just 27 percent of people drive to work, less than the proportion who cycle, and by getting rid of parking spaces and emptying roads of cars, the city has been able to give more space to restaurants, bars, and parks. In Tokyo, just 12 percent drive to work. (In London it is 37 percent, and in New York about 30 percent.) Japan's commuter trains are infamous for crowding, of course. But they are reliable, fast, and safe. Given a choice between Tokyo and Dallas, where 90 percent of people drive to work, I know where I would rather live.

The evidence that cars make us miserable is clear. One survey of Americans shows that after housework, the car commute is the daily chore that Americans hate most. Getting rid of an hour-long daily commute raises people's happiness by the equivalent of a $40,000 increase in income. Longer car commutes are linked to stress, fatigue, anxiety, social isolation, and higher blood pressure, according to another study published in 2019 in the *Journal of Transport & Health*. A Swedish study found that people who commute for more than forty-five minutes by car are 40 percent more likely to divorce. Of course, plenty of people have long commutes by train too, but multiple studies show that driving is the most stressful form of transport. A Canadian study published in 2014 found that walkers, train commuters, and cyclists are all dramatically happier than drivers, and even bus riders are about as happy.

That cars make us miserable ought to be obvious. The daily traffic news on the radio I listen to each morning in Chicago invariably reports unpredictable delays caused by crashes, bad weather, or damage to roads. A quarter of British drivers admit to chasing another road user to hurl abuse at them. More than 500 Americans a year are murdered in gun road-rage incidents. The need to have a car also drains people's finances. Rising gas prices, which are an inevitable part of the business cycle, even setting aside climate change, squeeze people's living standards suddenly. Car loans raise people's monthly bills too: It now takes seven years to pay back the typical one. Americans owe $1.3 trillion on car loans. Subprime car lending is one of the main reasons people go bankrupt in America now.

But drivers do not only make themselves miserable. They also make life harder for other people. Taking a long train ride to work every day does not force anyone else to. But when a city is designed for drivers, and most people drive to work, the amount of land needed for roads and parking means cities have to be more spread out. With businesses and homes farther apart, public transport works less well, and so everyone's commute is longer, even if they travel by train, bike, or bus.

The takeover of our streets by the car was not in fact inevitable. It was done deliberately, thanks to the greater political power of motorists over pedestrians, and thanks to planners who thought that the car was the future. We tore up our cities to create expressways and parking lots because we thought it would make life easier. Even today we subsidize car ownership by providing roads for free and insisting that businesses provide parking spaces for free with land that could be used for something useful, like housing. Government policy across the Western world seems to consider it a fundamental right to be able to drive from anywhere to anywhere, conveniently and inexpensively.

The number of cars being bought and being driven on the roads is going up everywhere, all over the world. The average American now drives 13,500 miles a year, or thirty-six miles every day. Transport emissions are up by 10 percent over the past decade. The fastest-growing cities worldwide are all sprawling places without much public transport. The outskirts of Delhi, India's capital, are now a sprawl of motorways. There is almost no African capital without a new bypass or expressway either being built or already clogged up by ancient secondhand Japanese cars. In countries where owning a car is at best a dream for most of the population, those making the decisions about how to plan cities seem to think that the small minority who can afford wheels should have priority.

The car industry, like the tobacco industry, wants you to think that we need them. And it is true that millions of people rely on the car industry for their livelihoods. But within living memory, millions of people worked in coal mines in Britain, America, and Europe. It is tough when industries disappear, but it need not be disastrous. To tackle climate change we need to change our economies to produce more wealth with fewer natural resources. And it goes beyond climate change. We live in a world where the biggest cities are where the best jobs are. But the biggest, most successful cities are also expensive, crowded, and unequal places to live. To tackle the housing crisis we need to make those cities more livable. That means we need more space for humans, and less for cars.

The car industry also wants you to think it has the solution to some of these problems. Electric cars will supposedly solve the problem of climate change emissions. Self-driving cars will solve the problem of traffic and make trains redundant. Ride-sharing services like Uber or Lyft will mean we do not need to own a car to always hail a ride. A few techno-lunatics even suggest that "flying cars" will shuttle people around cities quicker than ever before without even needing roads. All of these ideas are wrong. Producing enough batteries to replace every gasoline-driven vehicle will require untold amounts of cobalt, a large majority of which currently has to be mined in one of the poorest and most miserable countries on Earth, the Democratic Republic of Congo in central Africa, the source of more than half of the world's supply. Its revenues support a corrupt government that is among the worst human rights abusers on the planet. Powering electric cars will also require investment in a green electric grid on a scale that dwarfs what we are doing now.

The idea that self-driving cars will save our cities is also absurd. Even if they ever work, and can be made safe, they will only make things worse. A car uses up as much road space and parking space whether it is driven or not. It still requires gasoline (or electricity). And having to sit behind the wheel and concentrate is one of the few things that deters people from driving more even now. If we take away the requirement to focus on driving, people will only use their cars more. Every journey will take place in a car. Unless we all want to live in cities that look like Tucson, Arizona—a sprawl of roads and identikit suburban houses—self-driving cars will not save us either. Indeed, unchecked, they risk doing the opposite: destroying our cities once and for all.

And Uber and their ilk are perhaps the worst of them all. Investors have spent colossal sums of money—billions and billions of dollars—trying to persuade us that we can have a vehicle and a driver ready at any moment. To do so they have broken laws and flouted regulations intended to control traffic and pollution, while burdening millions of working-class people with loans that they can barely service. But their promise, that car-sharing would somehow alleviate traffic, has proven hollow. Uber's investors haven't even made a profit. All they have done is generate traffic. A 2018 study by Schallar Consulting found that Uber and Lyft increased the number of cars on some American city streets by 180 percent. Another study of San Francisco found that ride-sharing companies accounted for more than half of the city's growth in traffic. Lyft drivers spend a fifth of their time driving around empty, waiting for passengers. In Britain, Ubers are not carrying a passenger for 58 percent of the time they are driving.

Cars are not just about how you get around. They are about what the city you live in looks like and what your daily life feels like. The car goes to the core of almost everything, dominating almost all public spaces to the detriment of pedestrians and cyclists. From the backstreets of Mumbai, where the din of constant hooting is such a problem that the police occasionally go around with decibel meters to try to stop it, to the foothills of Los Angeles, where parking is free but there is nowhere affordable to live, the car affects almost every aspect of our lives.

But it can change. And when you cut back on the car, you discover that, in fact, you never needed it as much as you had thought. This book will explain how that is possible.

1

WHEN CARS WIN

To get a glimpse of what the car will do to our cities, if we allow it to, visit Houston. The Texas oil hub is America's fastest-growing big city. Since 1950 the population has grown from around 700,000 to 6.3 million. But Houston is not a city that has so much shot up as sprawled out. Though it has a "downtown" with lots of impressive skyscrapers, in fact it has no real center, in the way that an older city like London or New York does. If you try to navigate it on foot, prepare to be confused. Because this is a city defined by its roads.

There are four ring roads, known there as the *loops*. If you overlay the inner one on a map of Paris, you will discover that just the area bounded by the innermost one, Loop 610, covers an area twice as large as the city of Paris, about ninety-two square miles (24,000 hectares) to Paris's forty-one square miles (10,500 hectares). The whole metropolitan area of Houston covers an area roughly 260 times larger than the city of Paris.

Houston features perhaps the most insane stretch of motorway in all of America (and indeed the world), the Katy Freeway. At its widest point it has twenty-six lanes. A single one of its road junctions, the interchange between Loop 610 and the Interstate 10, covers roughly the same area as the entire Italian city of Siena, which manages to be home to a population of 30,000 people, as well as the world's oldest bank and one of its oldest universities. Across the whole metropolitan area of Houston there are roughly thirty parking spaces for every resident, or almost 200 million of them in total. That covers about 1,100 square miles, or more than ten Parises. Houston is—unsurprisingly given its core industry, oil—given over to the personal automobile more than perhaps anywhere else on Earth. Public transport is almost nonexistent. The city's single light rail line and buses together serve about as many people each year as the monorails at Disney World in Florida. About nine in ten people in Houston drive alone to work.

Is Houston a terrible place? No. In some ways it is one of America's most exciting cities. It has a thriving medical industry, a wonderful art museum, and a fantastic restaurant scene. It draws immigrants from all over the world with affordable housing and reasonably well-paid jobs. You can eat at a Nigerian restaurant, hop to a Mexican bar, and finish in a Korean karaoke club. But few tourists realize it, because to experience it all, you have to be willing to drive everywhere, on endless confusing motorways, and sit in traffic for hours. Lots of things in Houston are brilliant. But even its most enthusiastic residents generally agree it is not a pretty city. Its defining view is of endless billboards along the highways, imploring bored drivers to stop for fast food, or to buy new health insurance, or to hire a divorce lawyer. Its best qualities are hidden by the roads.

But there is a more fundamental problem than mere ugliness. The lifestyle that Houston represents is completely unsustainable, and yet it is among the fastest growing cities in America. It is, much more than New York or Chicago or London, a vision of how the cities of the future are developing. In large part because they drive everywhere, each person in Houston emits roughly fifteen tons of carbon dioxide per year. That is about three times what people emit in France or fifteen times what people emit in India. Incredibly, transport across the whole state of Texas accounts for 0.5 percent of the entire world's CO_2 emissions, or roughly twice as much as the entire country of Nigeria. All of those cars, driving between enormous air-conditioned houses, malls, and restaurants, are choking the planet. Actually, they are also choking Houston. The city's air is among the most polluted of any in America, mostly thanks to ozone emitted by cars.

There are more local problems too. Houston is flat and essentially built on a swamp that hurricanes periodically rip through, hurricanes that are almost certainly exacerbated by climate change. And with so much land covered in pavement there isn't much in the way of drainage. Uncovered green space absorbs water; roads and parking spaces do not. The Katy Freeway covers land that was once the Katy prairie, 600,000 acres of green space that used to absorb flood waters. Now the prairie is less than a quarter of its original size. As a result the city has flooded repeatedly, almost yearly. The road cuts across the city, east to west, while drainage goes from north to south, meaning that it acts as a gigantic barrier, trapping water in the city. In 2017 Hurricane Harvey flooded 96,000 homes. Across Texas it caused $125 billion of damage and killed sixty-eight people. There have been smaller floods every year since.

Sam Brody, an urban planning expert at Texas A&M University, reckons that each new square meter of tarmac built in the city adds about $4,000 in flooding costs. It also kills people. When Houston floods, "most people die in their car under an overpass," says Brody, because roads naturally direct water to the lowest point, where unlucky drivers can get trapped amid a rising flood. When Harvey hit, more than 800,000 cars were destroyed.

Since Harvey, the city has updated its building codes so that more homes are constructed on stilts, to stay above the water. But that does not help older homes. And the risk is rising, since the climate is warming, and more roads keep getting built. In October 2019 the Texas Department of Transportation announced it is planning to spend another $7 billion on road "improvements" in the city, intended to relieve the crushing congestion, though they will do no such thing. New suburbs, like the Woodlands, an enormous sprawl of "master planned luxury homes" continue to grow at the edges of the city. Thanks to the car, for large parts of the year, Houston is literally underwater. Yet the city cannot stop it. It is addicted to the personal automobile. And making space for the car means the entire design of the city is sinking it. "I think if Harvey hit Houston today, it would be worse," says Brody.

If you live somewhere like central London or Manhattan, what is happening in Houston may feel, well, thousands of miles away. In those cities car lanes are being taken away from roads to build cycle lanes, and congestion charges are spreading. It is easy to find stories about new urban advancements. The socialist mayor of Paris, Anne Hidalgo, has promised to wage war on the car, scrapping street parking to make space for bike lanes. Amsterdam has been pedestrianizing main roads since the 1970s. But in fact, such stories are interesting because they are rare. In most of the world the car is quietly becoming ever more dominant.

According to statistics from the US Department of Energy, between 2004 and 2014, globally the number of vehicles per capita rose in every region of the world except, perhaps surprisingly, America. (In America too, the number of vehicles is still rising, but about as fast as the population). In India, the figure jumped threefold. In China, fivefold. Even in western Europe, the land of new cycle lanes and traffic-free city centers, the number of cars per person climbed by about 4 percent in a decade. Every year the world's car industry manufactures around ninety million new cars—more than enough to make up for those destroyed in Hurricane Harvey. Far fewer old ones are taken off the roads, even in rich countries. Those that are often end up being shipped to poorer countries, where their aging engines can pollute the air there.

In Britain, almost everywhere outside of the inner London boroughs is becoming more, not less, car-dependent. Overall nationwide there are about 3 million new cars registered each year and only 2 million old ones taken off the road. There are now 38.7 million cars on the road, or three for every four adults. The total number has fallen in only one year since the end of the Second World War—1991. Traffic is increasing every year, while pavements become ever more crowded with parked cars. In 2019 Britons drove 256 billion miles in their cars, or about 4,000 miles for every person—adult and child— the highest figure ever recorded. For every district in London that has put in bollards to stop traffic, there is somewhere like Milton Keynes, where roads are frantically being widened to add more space for cars.

What is driving this automania? The answer is that we have done nothing to stop it. In fact, all over the world, governments encourage car ownership and do almost everything they can to make it easier. Whereas oil producers are often—rightly—pilloried for the pollution they cause, healthy car industries are seen as the bedrock of rich economies, from Japan to Germany to the American Midwest. This is despite the fact that it is actually a deeply troubled industry. Less than a decade ago, Volkswagen was shown to have systematically cheated on emissions tests so as to sell more polluting cars. The firm paid $33 billion in fines for taking measures that actually poison people, in order to sell more diesel cars. Yet what was the response of Angela Merkel, Germany's chancellor, to the scandal? She pointed out that VW employs huge numbers of people and threatened that "anyone who tries to pillory the entire automobile industry because of this misconduct in one area will have to deal with the CDU." That is, Germany's largest political party.

We encourage the car industry with policies that make it easier for them to sell more cars. For example, by making gasoline cheap. Pollution taxes have soared on fuels used in industry—rightly—putting coal miners and coal power plants out of business. But fuel for cars is taxed ever more lightly. Relative to GDP, taxes on gasoline have fallen by about 15 percent since 2002 in the European Union. In America the federal tax on gasoline has not been increased since 1993, even before adjusting for inflation. At four dollars a gallon, gasoline may seem pricey. But in fact, adjusted for inflation, it still costs less to fill up a car in America now than it did in the 1970s.

We also subsidize car producers directly—during recessions especially. In Britain in 2019, it emerged that Nissan was offered £80 million in government aid to continue manufacturing the X-Trail—a gasoline-guzzling, pollution-creating SUV—at its factory in Sunderland after Brexit. In the financial crisis of 2008–2009, car manufacturers were among the first firms bailed out. In America auto firms were given a $25 billion loan. In Germany the government introduced a car scrappage scheme whereby car buyers were paid to buy new cars. France has given away billions to keep Renault manufacturing. In 2020 a whole new raft of state support was introduced to help car firms through the coronavirus recession. The French government alone gave €8 billion to its car industry to keep it going.

Yet the problem is more fundamental than just cheap gasoline and direct subsidies for the car industry. If people did not need cars in their daily lives, it would not matter how cheap gasoline was or how many car factories were propped up with government subsidies. People buy cars because they need them. And they need them because we have let our cities be built like Houston, not like Amsterdam, Tokyo, or Manhattan. In cities where the roads dominate, you have to drive, whatever it costs. Even though a huge volume of research shows that depending on a car is stressful, dangerous, and expensive. Even though most people, if pushed, would prefer to live someplace where they can walk rather than where they can drive. The biggest subsidies we have given to the car industry are the hidden ones, in the way we have designed our cities around them.

Designed is perhaps the wrong word. Cities are not planned or designed for the most part. They grow organically from millions of decisions made by individuals. That is not an altogether bad thing—no government could perfectly decide how many restaurants or houses or shops any city must need. But the trouble with everyone acting in their own interests is that collectively we can all end up worse off. There is a prisoner's dilemma—a coordination problem. The classic prisoner's dilemma describes a situation where two prisoners are facing simultaneous interrogation for a crime. If they both can hold their nerve they will get off free. But if one rats on the other, he gets a shorter sentence. If you cannot coordinate with your partner, you will probably rat on him. You both end up worse off than if you could have coordinated.

This sort of dilemma explains why we do not invest enough in public transport. The cost of a mile of road in an urban area in America is generally around $5 million. A mile of underground railway costs $350 million and sometimes much more than that. But that cost does not reflect the true costs to society. Roads impose costs on other people that railways do not. For one thing, they cost the people using them more: Actually owning a car is much more expensive than buying a train ticket. But more than that, when everybody has to use a car, the city has to spread out more, like Houston, to accommodate people. And it is sprawl that is expensive. Over a large area, roads have to be much longer and wider than a subway would be. The more houses are spread out, the greater the cost of building sewers, putting in electricity connections, and of collecting trash. According to a 2010 study by Smart Growth America, a think tank, sprawl costs American cities $525 billion a year in extra infrastructure costs.

Public transport, by contrast, does the opposite. It costs more up front but it makes a whole host of other things cheaper. In a city like London or New York, with an underground railway system, the cost of renting or buying a house is higher the closer you are to a station. That is because railways are valuable—they increase the value of the land around them, far more than a monstrous great road does. It is not just that people want to live near railways. It is also that when people can get around without a car, so much land is not needed for parking, and more homes can fit on a given patch of land. The less land is needed for parking, the more useful the stuff that can be squeezed onto it. That is why the most valuable real estate in the world is all in cities with good public transport.

So why do more governments not invest in more walkable cities with public transport, given the returns? Well, here is the prisoner's dilemma. Public transport requires collective decision making. Building a new railway only works if there are already people there to use it. But if people have already moved to a city without public transport, they will probably already have bought cars and moved to homes they can only access with cars. If your city is already mostly sprawling suburbia, building trains is a bit useless—people will all live too far from the tracks to be able to use them without at least driving to the station. But if you do not have public transport, developers are unlikely to build anything other than sprawling suburbia. You cannot have public transport with sprawl, but without public transport, all you will get is sprawl. It is a catch-22. Many cities would like to become denser, but cannot find a way to start.

In the golden age of the railway, at the end of the nineteenth century, railway developers did not face that problem. Before starting construction, they bought up land on the outskirts of cities. Once the line was built, they sold the adjacent land to builders at a much higher price. That is really the only way to build a railway. Ticket sales alone will not cover the immense capital construction costs. But what railways do is raise the value of all of the land around them, because suddenly it is possible to build an office or a factory or an apartment building nearby that people will be able to get to.

That is what economists call a positive externality. And if railway developers can capture it in advance—by buying the land—then suddenly the economics of a new railway look pretty good. The increase in the value of the land more than covers the cost of building the railway. It is what built the Metropolitan Line in London in the 1930s, as well as dozens of other suburban railways and tram systems all over the world. Most British cities have railway suburbs. Moseley, where I grew up in Birmingham, is one. Didsbury in Manchester is another. Lots of neighborhoods in American cities were similarly built on streetcar lines, or on commuter lines. Chicago's northern suburbs rely heavily on commuter rail. Railway suburbs tend to be pleasant places with semi-detached homes or rows of townhouses, not exactly dense like a city center, but tightly packed enough that you can walk to the shops and kids can walk to school. They had to be, because the people who lived there had to be able to walk to the railway station to get to work.

The trouble is that the moment that the car arrived on the scene, that model of development no longer worked. Because long before developers would even think to build a railway, all of the land had already been bought and developed for suburban sprawl. So that is why there are almost no cities in the world built after 1945 that have decent public transport that a majority of people use. The car comes first, and once it is lodged into a city, it is extremely difficult to get rid of. It is not only the question of land. Once most of the public have been forced to invest in a car to get around, of course they will use it.

In fact, it is worse than that. Once most people use cars, what tends to happen is that a city starts adopting policies that actually entrench car ownership. The takeover of our streets by cars has always been driven by the rich. At the end of the nineteenth century it was rich drivers who lobbied for the lifting of speed limits and the scrapping of the laws that required cars to be preceded by a red flag–waving man. So it continues. In Britain, on average, the richest 20 percent of people drive 7,500 miles per year each, whereas the poorest 20 percent drive only about 2,800. Richer people also tend to have more political power. And they vote and lobby for policies that help cars.

The power of rich drivers is why, when Boris Johnson became mayor of London in 2008, the first thing he did was scrap the extension of the congestion charge to west London. It is also why in Westminster, the center of London, where space is at a premium, resident car owners can still get a car parking permit that entitles them to a patch of land to leave their vehicle on for the grand sum of £155. To rent 180 square feet of office space in the West End costs around £18,000 a year. Car owners get it for less than 1 percent of that.

In America it gets even more ludicrous. Let's look again at Houston. Fittingly for Texas's biggest metropolis, the city has no zoning code—that means that in theory you can build whatever you want on a patch of land you own. But in practice there are actually lots of restrictions. Some, like safety standards, are obviously reasonable. But then there are mandatory parking minimums. If you are planning to open a bar—not a business one would hope people would drive to—you are required to provide ten parking spaces for every 1,000 square foot of bar. A standard American parking space is about

180 square feet, which means you need almost twice as much space for cars as you have for people.

There are similar rules for almost any kind of business you can imagine. Hospitals require 2.2 car parking spaces per bed. A funeral home requires half a space for every seat. A church must have a spot for every pew. In the land of free-market economics, all over America, car parking is allocated by government dictate. Why on earth are such rules so common? Well, because cities have decided that since everybody drives, there needs to be enough parking. Most Americans consider free parking a fundamental right, even though free parking is far from free. It costs businesses a fortune, raising the cost of everything else. Supermarkets are more expensive when they need so much land covered by tarmac. Offices and homes too.

All of this means we end up with cities that look more like Houston than like Amsterdam. And once it is built, it is very difficult to unbuild. When everybody's homes are already so spread out, it is difficult to make public transport work. Cities end up with, at best, buses, used mostly only by those people unable to afford their own wheels. Buses can actually be an excellent form of public transport, and they are widely used in places like New York and London, but in car-dependent cities, they inevitably are slow and painful to use, because they have to share space with the cars on the roads. Since the bulk of people do drive and even those who do not aspire to, making any changes will prove unpopular.

It is not just the rich world where this is happening. In poor countries the rising middle class is discovering that the first thing they want to buy when they can afford to is a car. From Johannesburg to São Paulo, Bengaluru to Jakarta, the car is increasingly dominant. The fastest-growing cities all over the world look more like Houstons than like Amsterdams. And far more people live in them than in America or Europe. That is why unless we deal with the car, climate change is going to prove unstoppable.

2

HELLO, MR. TOAD

To find one of the earliest instances of the automobile in popular culture, a good place to go is *The Wind in the Willows*, Kenneth Grahame's classic children's book. The book, published in 1908, features one of the most memorable motorists of all time, Mr. Toad, of Toad Hall. Obsessed with speed, Toad is the "Terror of the Highway." Dressed in tweed, Mr. Toad encounters his first motor car when he, Mole, and the Water Rat are having a pleasant walk along the village's "high road" with a horse. "Glancing back, they saw a small cloud of dust, with a dark centre of energy, advancing on them at incredible speed, while from out the dust a faint 'Poop poop!' wailed like an uneasy animal in pain," goes the book. Before the trio realize what is happening, the vehicle is upon them, knocking them out of the way. "You villains!" shouts Rat, "You scoundrels, you highwaymen, you, you, road-hogs! I'll have the law on you! I'll report you!" But Toad is overcome with a different emotion. "His face wore a placid satisfied expression, and at intervals he faintly murmured 'Poop-poop!'"

Soon enough, of course, the aristocratic Toad gets his very own vehicle, a "new and exceptionally powerful motor-car." Fitted out in goggles, a giant overcoat, a cap, gaiters, and of course, driving gloves, he prepares to take it on the road—and is stopped by Mole, who laments the "hideous habiliments so dear to him, which transform him from a (comparatively) good-looking Toad into an Object which throws any decent-minded animal that comes across it into a violent fit." But soon enough, Toad finds another car and steals it, driving it furiously up the road. He becomes "Toad the terror, the traffic-queller, the Lord of the lone trail, before whom all must give way or be smitten into nothingness and everlasting night." He is thrown in jail for theft and dangerous driving and sentenced to twenty years. But then he escapes, and no more is heard of it. Mole imperiously tells Toad that he is "getting us animals a bad name in the district by your furious driving and your smashes and your rows with the police."

The character of Toad did not emerge miraculously from Grahame's mind. In fact, he reflected the common stereotype of car drivers in Edwardian England. Far from being the harbingers of progress, they were seen as loud, abrasive aristocrats barging their way down public highways at the expense of everybody else. Barely a decade earlier, Britain's first ever traffic "accident" death had killed Bridget Driscoll, a young mother who was hit by a newly imported Benz car at a motoring exhibition at Crystal Palace in London, driven by one Arthur Edsell. The death proved a scandal. At the inquest, a witness testified that the car had been driving at "a tremendous pace" that was "as fast as a good horse could gallop," perhaps 25 to 30 miles per hour. The coroner called the driver and witnesses to determine whether the car had been driven unsafely. Edsell claimed that he had in fact only been driving at 4 mph, and argued that he was not responsible, because he had shouted and rang a bell in order to warn her to get out of the way. After six hours of deliberations the jury ruled that the death was accidental: the first ruling in favor of a reckless driver.

To understand how the car became such a dominant part of our daily lives, we have to go back to that beginning. When Driscoll was mown down, there were perhaps 100 automobiles in Britain. Karl Benz's internal combustion engine was just eleven years old. Drivers did not need a license and there were not even any formal rules about which side of the road they should drive on. Cars were a novelty. Yet that was changing. Just weeks before Driscoll's death parliament had narrowly voted to lift the old Locomotive Acts, which had been designed to regulate steam-powered vehicles used for road construction and farming and the like. They had mandated that any vehicle traveling on public roads be limited to 4 mph and be preceded by a man waving a red flag. The new law allowed cars to travel up to 14 mph, without a red flag man. The repeal was celebrated as an "emancipation act" by rich drivers, who held the first ever London to Brighton rally, zooming in their vehicles from the Metropole Hotel on Whitehall to the seaside to celebrate with champagne. By the time Mr. Toad was written into existence, there were closer to 100,000 cars on Britain's roads, mostly driven by the rich or their chauffeurs.

It sometimes feels like the rise of new technologies is inevitable. Once the internal combustion engine made it possible to run a vehicle without horses, of course people would start to use them. And as the cost of any new technology falls, it becomes more popular. But in fact, the rise of the car was not inevitable. It took decades of lobbying by manufacturers, Mr. Toad-like car fanatics, and planners with auto-inspired dreams to change the car from being a toy for the superrich into something that a large majority of people consider a normal part of their lives. Participants in the Brighton rally were warned that they must drive safely, because "any rashness or carelessness might injure the industry in this country." The bill's passage had only happened thanks to an intense campaign of lobbying, supported by, among others, the Prince of Wales (later Edward VII).

It took from around the time that Bridget Driscoll died until the 1920s for cars to become a mass market product. In Europe it took longer, until the 1950s. That is not just because they were expensive. It was also because cities had to be completely rebuilt for them. Roads, previously open to anybody who wanted to use them, whether on a bicycle, on foot, or on a horse, had to be given over exclusively to the gasoline engine. And this process was slow and difficult. Even in the interwar years, many people did not actually welcome this new technology into their lives. They saw it as an invader, a dangerous killer of children and a creator of noise and smoke. Even the Ford Model T, which made up more than half of the cars on America's roads in the 1920s, was used mostly in rural areas. Urban Americans continued to use public transport.

When the 1896 act passed, it was controversial. The railway companies worried that it would take traffic away from them. Others feared that the noisy new vehicles would scare horses. But the biggest concern was that the roads were being taken away from the public in the interests of a few rich motorists. In 1903, by which time cars had become more than just a curiosity at exhibitions, parliament raised the speed limit to 20 mph. But it did not do so easily. One Liberal member of Parliament, Cathcart Wason, argued that cars were "slaughtering stinking engines of iniquity." "These cars," he argued, were "monopolizing the whole of their public roads." People who wanted to drive fast, he continued, should build themselves racetracks. In the same debate another MP, George Harwood, argued that "it was a question of the common right of citizens." Thanks to cars, he said, "a man could not take his family for a walk along the roads within a distance of thirty or forty miles of London with either comfort or safety."

Slowly, however, the motorists won. By the start of the First World War, ownership had spread among Britain's ruling classes. Among Britain's most enthusiastic motorists was William Joynson-Hicks, an MP who was also the chairman of the Automobile Association (the AA). In 1924, when Stanley Baldwin became prime minister, Joynson-Hicks became Home Secretary, and one of the first things he did was confirm that it was legal for the AA's patrols to warn motorists about police speed traps on the road ahead. When asked in parliament about crashes caused by speeding (at the furious rate of 30 mph), he said that he did "not want to limit the use of the road in any way to motorists."

By 1930 more than 7,000 people were being killed on Britain's roads each year—almost four times as many as happen in a typical year now. Among those injured was a young Roald Dahl, whose nose was sliced off when his 21-year-old sister, on her first day driving the family's new car, smashed it into a hedge. By then the law was being so widely flouted that that year parliament decided to lift it altogether. One lord noted in 1932 that the only reason that the 20 mph limit was abolished "was not that anybody thought the abolition would tend to the greater security of foot passengers, but that the existing speed limit was so universally disobeyed that its maintenance brought the law into contempt." A driving test was not introduced until 1935 and even then it only applied to new drivers—those who had purchased their driving licenses before then could carry on.

This happened not only in Britain but all over the world. In America the takeover of streets was particularly fraught. By the 1920s, traffic deaths in America reached 30,000 a year, a level that they have never fallen below in the century since. (Albeit the population has grown a lot more, as have the miles driven.) Back then, drivers who killed somebody were often tried for manslaughter. Cars were seen as dangerous "pleasure" machines that killed children, while taking the road away from ordinary folk.

The historian Peter Norton's book *Fighting Traffic* brilliantly uncovered much of this forgotten history. "One of the reasons I wrote the book, is if you look at any other historical book on that era, you never encounter anything like that," he told me. In most histories, cars are depicted as having been quickly accepted as technological progress. But in fact, they were powerfully resisted. Norton says, "there was just amazing opposition." As he writes, "To many city people in the 1920s, the car and its driver were tyrants that deprive others of their freedom."

In 1924 the *New York Times* reported that the country was "roused against motor killings." It illustrated the story with a cartoon of the grim reaper driving an evil-looking sports car. One newspaper letter writer suggested an incredibly American way to deter reckless drivers who wanted to dominate the road. "When you get to the crossing, look to your left, pull out your automatic from the holster, step into the street and level the gun at the chauffeur coming. When in the middle of the street level it at the nearest chauffeur coming the other way." The car was an infringement of liberty, and Americans knew how to guard against that.

Huge "safety" demonstrations were organized in opposition to the spread of cars, taking on a level of grief comparable to that about the deaths in the First World War in Britain. In New York in 1922, a "memorial division" of 1,054 children marched, one for each of the children killed in accidents in the city the previous year. In St. Louis, Missouri, a monument was erected "in memory of child life sacrificed on the altar of haste and recklessness." Hundreds of people gathered for its unveiling, and a band played a dirge as an airship dropped flowers. In Memphis, Tennessee, the city's Safety Council displayed a black flag at sites where children were knocked over.

The backlash could have stopped the rise of the car. Judges all over the country began to take a harsh view of drivers speeding, treating the deaths that resulted as homicide, rather than as "accidental." In Cincinnati, Ohio, more than 10 percent of the public signed a petition calling for cars to have speed limiters fitted that would stop them from going above 25 mph. In New York City, the traffic magistrate proposed banning cars south of Fourteenth Street. In 1923 sales slumped, and car dealers blamed it partly on a panic about traffic accidents, says Norton. The car's takeover of our streets could have been stopped in its tracks (or perhaps in the driveway) before it even started. But unfortunately, the car industry was beginning to see the problem and respond to it.

The industry came up with a simple solution—to stop cars from hitting people in the street, take away the street from pedestrians. Motorists were encouraged to join automobile clubs, and to lobby their local and state governments. Dealers began setting up "citizens' committees" that ostensibly lobbied for safety improvements, but in fact pushed back against speed limits and other rules intended to control traffic. They bought advertisements in newspapers arguing that cars represented progress and that the deaths caused by cars were a problem of management of traffic. Amazingly, they organized under the sort of name that sounds almost like a comic parody now: Motordom. Motordom included car manufacturers, but also dealerships, automobile clubs, and influential car-driving rich people.

Motordom was extraordinarily effective, combining public relations genius with effective political lobbying. "They worked very hard and—they were extremely clever about it," says Norton. "The cleverest thing at all was to launch a new free news wire service, where newspapers got free news about the traffic problem, and it looked very scientific, and it had a lot of data, so the newspapers were glad to have it." In these reports, of course, it was invariably pedestrians who were blamed for their own deaths. After all, how could motorists be blamed for children running into the road?

What happened then in America is remarkable. In a country that considers itself the land of the free, city governments began to legislate to make it illegal to cross roads without permission. The crime of "jaywalking" was invented in Los Angeles, which passed an ordinance in 1925 to stop people from walking across streets where they might be hit by cars. It came from an older term, "jay driving," which referred to drivers using the wrong side of the road. But the idea behind jaywalking was a radical one: that the street was not for people, but for vehicles, and that only crossing at marked stops at intersections ought to be legal. And somehow, people accepted it. California decriminalized jaywalking only in January 2023. Before then, the Los Angeles Police Department issued around 3,000 tickets a year, each one with a fine of $196.

In New York City, the "safety parades" previously organized in opposition to the car started to be organized by the car industry themselves. Boy Scouts were enlisted to hand out flyers warning others not to jaywalk "for safety's sake." These campaigns continued for decades. A jingle playing on the radio in New York in the late 1960s warned pedestrians, "Don't cross the street in the middle, in the middle, in the middle . . . And wait . . . Until you see the light turn green." Indeed, they continue now. In Montreal, Canada, an advertisement agency in 2021 came up with the idea of putting interactive billboards on pavements to show pedestrians how their bones stood no chance against the steel of cars. There were no similar billboards telling people to drive more slowly.

The aim of the 1920s campaigns against jaywalking was not to reduce the risk to pedestrians. It was to speed up cars, by persuading people that it was pedestrians themselves who were to blame for car accidents, because of their terrible habit of wanting to walk in the road as they always had. Traveling at 15 to 20 miles per hour, a car can stop pretty easily before it hits a pedestrian unexpectedly crossing the road. Modern research shows that when traveling at 20 mph, 75 percent of drivers will yield to pedestrians. Just 5 percent of collisions at 20 mph result in death. At 30 mph, the pedestrian has a much worse chance: 45 percent result in death. At 40 mph, there is a 90 percent chance of death. This was straightforwardly a campaign to give motorists what they wanted: the freedom to drive through cities fast, without worrying about any pesky pedestrians.

Many cities felt that they could not resist the rise of the car, even if they wanted to. By 1929 there were already twenty-nine million cars in America, almost all of them owned by individuals for their own personal transport. Controlling them was swallowing up police time. In Detroit, where in the 1920s Henry Ford's factories were already mass producing millions of Model Ts per year, fully one quarter of the city's police force was occupied trying to control traffic by the middle of the decade. And so like other cities, it quickly followed Los Angeles, adopting a municipal traffic ordinance drawn up with the help of the auto industry. It said that pedestrians should only be allowed to cross the street at right angles at marked crossings.

And, like a car rolling down a hill, the momentum of the motor industry only grew. In the brand-new cities of America, it became hard to resist. Take

Los Angeles—for all that we think of it as an automotive paradise, as Norton was at pains to remind me, it was not in fact built like that. The broad boulevards that stretch from the city center to the beach at Santa Monica were built for trams (or streetcars, in American parlance). The Pacific Electric railway, with its distinctive red trams, first started operating at the end of the Victorian era. By the early 1920s it was the biggest electric railway system in the world. The Pacific Electric company funded their construction by developing suburbs, where people could buy houses within a short walk of the tram that would take them to work.

But by the 1930s Pacific Electric trams had to share space with cars. Cars slowed down the trams, as they could no longer zoom through intersections between stops. Instead of the efficient service it had been, the Pacific Electric became a slow, painful one to use. So what happened? Frustrated commuters began to buy cars. And the trams got even slower and had to stop more often as the traffic at the intersections grew.

There is a theory that the disappearance of the trams was engineered by car companies. It was actually rather wonderfully adopted into the plot of *Who Framed Roger Rabbit,* the 1980s live action/cartoon mashup, in which the villain, Judge Doom, wants to cheat Toontown and its residents out of their land to close down the "Red Car" and build a freeway. And the theory has some basis in reality. In the late 1930s and '40s, two companies owned in turn by, among others, General Motors and Standard Oil, bought tram companies in dozens of American cities, including Los Angeles. One of the two, National City Lines, was later indicted by the government for corrupt competition practices.

But in fact, the conspiracy theory that the car industry deliberately killed the streetcars is not completely true, as Norton is keen to point out. By the time General Motors and Standard Oil bought out the tram companies, they were practically bankrupt already. For years, city governments had banned fare rises, while insisting that tram companies pay excessive rates to subsidize electricity companies. In the end the trams were actually killed by the rising traffic congestion, which made them slow and frustrating to use. With just 10 percent of people driving, the streetcars were reduced to speeds that made them essentially unviable. Without bailouts—which were not forthcoming from pinched local governments during the Great

Depression—they were doomed. The car companies did not need to buy them up to wipe them out. Cars ruined the trams without the auto executives having to spend a penny.

Almost as soon as cars were allowed to take over the roads, cities began changing. In London, the Metropolitan Line was built essentially as a speculative property investment. Metroland, the sprawl of semidetached houses that spread out along the railway into Middlesex and Buckinghamshire, promised green space, big gardens, golf courses, and clean air. But unlike the suburban railway developments of the past, it also promised a new motorized future, free of the city. People would drive to their railway stations and then get into the city that way. The houses sold were larger, with bigger gardens, and they were farther apart, meaning that if you didn't want to drive, you did not have that much choice.

Cities then were unpopular, for good reason. They were polluted by industry and by millions of coal fires. The Victorian terraces we now value were overcrowded, with families packing into single rooms. Diseases such as polio and tuberculosis were still rife. And it was that urban misery that motivated the planners of the day—people like Ebenezer Howard, the father of the Garden City movement in England.

Howard's most influential writing predated the motorway age. But his ideas ended up informing it. In his utopian manifesto, *Garden Cities of To-Morrow*, he argued that cities should be replaced by modest towns with populations of no more than 32,000 people. They would be split between industrial, commercial, and residential areas, with "magnificent boulevards" 120 feet wide cutting between them. Greenbelts, on which construction would be banned, would stop them from growing too big; when the population expanded, the residents would simply build another town. New technology would solve the problems of today. "The smoke fiend is kept well within bounds in Garden City; for all machinery is driven by electric energy."

Howard got his way—Letchworth, a small town north of London, was his idea. But by the 1920s his ideas were already being adapted to the automobile. George Orwell wrote in his essay "The Lion and The Unicorn," "the place to look for the germs of the future England is in the light-industry areas and along the arterial roads." New towns like Slough, Dagenham, and even, indeed, Letchworth promised what Orwell considered "a rather restless, cultureless life, centering round tinned food, *Picture Post*, the radio and the internal combustion engine."

Drive out to Heathrow from central London on the old Great West Road and you get glimpses of what was the future a century ago. The old Hoover Building, an art deco masterpiece, was one of several factories, most now demolished, that promised a sort of urban living where people would drive. More new houses were built in the 1920s and '30s than in any other period in British history. It was a great and perhaps surprising improvement in living. But it came at a cost: They were built in new suburbs, embedding the automobile.

In America too, suburbia was growing. When writing about the emergence of suburbia, many historians focus on William J. Levitt, and his Levittowns—seven different suburbs of identical tract housing built from the 1940s onward. But in fact, America's automotive sprawl began before then. Even by 1925, when F. Scott Fitzgerald wrote *The Great Gatsby*, the rich were already retreating from their havens around the parks in Manhattan and out to new neighborhoods with much more space on Long Island, in New Jersey and Connecticut, and in New York's Hudson Valley. Radburn, New Jersey, was founded in 1929 as a "garden city for the motor age," on explicitly Howard-esque lines. The developers deliberately planned it with separated road and pedestrian areas. In theory it was meant to be a place where people could walk anywhere if they wanted to—but also drive. The houses are accessed from the front by cul-de-sacs, while pedestrian pathways led from the back gardens so that people could walk into town without ever having to cross a road.

It was such a popular idea that Walt Disney, who later in his life became a tireless campaigner against the takeover of cities by cars, tried to copy it for his Experimental Prototype Community of Tomorrow (EPCOT) at Disneyland in California. Disney imagined that with separate paths for people, children walking to school would be "completely safe and separated from the automobile." In practice, though, this was the sort of safety from cars that the industry liked—one that did not mean ever limiting their access. Radburn's chief innovation ended up not being the segregated walkways; it was the large, spread out "superblocks" and houses built around cul-de-sacs that were copied everywhere. The average car ownership in Radburn is still two per household.

And these early suburbs were just the start of the transformation of the West's cities that was to come. The idea of segregating traffic—so as to have more of it—was also inspiring more visionary thinkers than the planners of Radburn, New Jersey. It was also in the 1920s that Le Corbusier, the French Brutalist architect, first began to develop his ideas of how the city should be rebuilt. A painter as well as an architect, Le Corbusier was a true modernist. He was not interested in bit-part estates built by private developers. He wanted to reshape the city in a way that would only be possible with the hand of the state, a state far more powerful than the ones that existed in the 1920s and '30s. He thought that the old Victorian world had to be swept away, and that scientific ideas could build a new one in its place. His ideas would prove catastrophic.

In Le Corbusier's first plan for how to rebuild Paris, the Plan Voisin, displayed at the 1925 Paris exposition, a diorama showing the idea was labeled "If Paris Americanized itself." The idea was breathtaking. Paris's beautiful boulevards, which now feel timeless, but were then only half a century old, were to be replaced with blocks of skyscrapers, situated in parkland. Three million people would live in towers, separated from new wide roads. You will, predicted Le Corbusier, "find yourselves walking among spacious parks remote from the busy hum of the autostrada." His plan was not explicitly driven by the car—he wanted underground railways and an airport too, to be the first thing visitors saw. But the idea was, of course, sponsored by an automobile manufacturer—Le Corbusier's friend, Gabriel Voisin, the owner of Avions Voisin, a plane-turned-car producer that sold glamorous vehicles with modernist lines of the sort that looked good in Le Corbusier's plans.

Le Corbusier would only get bolder. In 1935 he visited New York, then the home of the world's tallest buildings, and declared that the skyscrapers were not big enough. American cities were wonderfully modern, he thought, but "utterly devoid of harmony." He admired the parkways then being built by Robert Moses, New York City's transport supremo. But he worried (not wrongly) that they would simply empty the city into the suburbs. What he wanted to do was to bring the advantage of the suburbs into the city—expressways and tunnels would move cars around, but tower blocks and parks would preserve the population density. In New York, he thought, the blocks were too small, the roads not wide enough, and the homes crammed in too close to businesses. Everything would have to be transformed, from scratch.

The bow-tied, bespectacled French architect inspired a note of disbelief in New York, on his tour. The *New York Herald Tribune* mocked him up in a cartoon looking through Coke bottle glasses, overly inspired by the possibilities of rebuilding America. But his tour was a success. "This is architecture's hour," he said on a radio broadcast, which was widely reported. Four years later, General Motors hosted an exhibit at New York City's World's Fair entitled Futurama, designed by Norman Bel Geddes. Its "vision of the future" looked like something Le Corbusier could have designed. A scale model spread across an acre depicted a city of towers and parks—and highways, eighteen lanes wide. It featured more than 50,000 model cars and 500,000 individual buildings.

People queued for a day to see it. And it was not just the model cars that moved. Fully sixteen years before Disneyland opened its doors, this was an idea delivered in true theme park style. Visitors were transported around this model city on a sort of people-mover conveyor belt, in comfortable seats with speakers affixed that narrated what was going on. "Come tour the future with General Motors! A transcontinental flight over America in 1960. What will we see?" went the voiceover. As the viewers zoomed over the mock-up motorway they were promised a future of "safety, safety with increased speed." A huge bridge was described as a "gateway to the city," with the feature of "the elimination of congestion." The city itself was a mass of spiraling towers, "much larger, rebuilt and revamped."

In an accompanying book, Geddes said that almost all of the most enthusiastic visitors were motorists, "harassed by the daily task of getting from one place to another, by the nuisances of intersectional jams, narrow, congested bottlenecks, dangerous night driving, annoying policeman's whistles, honking horns, blinking traffic lights, confusing traffic signs and irritating traffic regulations." He promised that his vision gave people a "dramatic and graphic solution to the problems they all face." Motorways would be designed to "make automobile collisions impossible" and "to eliminate completely traffic congestion."

It was an alluring vision, one that occupied planners for much of the next century. Of course it was; it would be incredible if engineering could solve traffic problems, allowing everybody to get around in a car, with no downsides. And this idea coincided with the biggest growth in the ambition and size of states in world history. For the next six years, it would be put on hold, as America's prodigious industrial might was redirected from building the new tomorrow to fighting Nazism. But after World War II, governments across the world, in rich countries and newly independent poor ones, wanted not just to restore the pre-war world but to restart it completely. They wanted to modernize. And as the Futurama exhibit had shown, what was more modern, at the end of the war, than the car and the motorway?

3

MOTORWAY CITIES OF THE FUTURE

When J. B. Priestley, an English writer, visited Coventry in 1934, for his book *English Journey*, he claimed that it was "one of those towns that have often changed their trades and had many vicissitudes, but unlike nearly all of the rest, it has managed to come out on top." The city, he wrote, was so pleasant on the eyes "that it might have been transported to Italy." "Genuinely old and picturesque," he went on, "you peep around a corner and see half-timbered and gabled houses that would do for the second act of the *Meistersinger*" (a Wagner opera).

Yet Priestley, with his shrewd eye for change, also noted that the city was "besieged by an army of nuts, bolts, hammers, spanners, gauges, drills and machine lathes, for in a thick ring around this ancient center are the motor-car and cycle factories." The city, he wrote, "made bicycles when everyone was cycling, cars when everybody wanted a motor, and now it is also busy with aeroplanes, wireless sets and various electrical contrivances." His own car, a Daimler, was built there, and while he was sure that the children of Coventry were well cared for, "nobody has attended to them as their fathers are attending to the proud young Double-Six Daimlers."

The automobile industry had grown out of the bicycle industry. One of the first modern-style safety bicycles, invented by Henry John Lawson in 1876, was produced in Coventry. On the back of its success, Lawson went on to try to monopolize the British car industry. At the end of the nineteenth century, he bought up patents for gasoline-powered cars from all over the world, which he hoped to use to extract money from potential car manufacturers. Somewhat ironically, given what has come since, it was roads often built by enthusiastic wealthy cyclists that his cars first traveled on.

Lawson's hope that cars would make him even richer failed. In 1904 he was convicted of defrauding his shareholders and sentenced to a year of hard labor in prison. But it did not end Coventry's association with cars. The First World War accelerated the growth of the city's industry. The first tanks, invented to try to break the deadlock on the trenches of the Western Front, were powered with engines designed and built in Coventry. As Priestley noted, the city was one of the few places in Britain to survive the Great Depression without enormous decline, largely thanks to the insatiable demand of the affluent for automobiles.

In the Second World War, it was this manufacturing industry—then focused on airplane engines—that made Coventry a target for the Luftwaffe. The Coventry Blitz, which peaked on the night of November 14, 1940, destroyed 4,300 homes and the city's fourteenth-century cathedral. It damaged two-thirds of the city's buildings. It was devastating. What it also did, though, was create space for the replanning of the city, to create a new city out of the ashes. And inevitably, for this car-centric city, the automobile would be at the forefront of it. Coventry would become a symbol for how cities would be transformed by the car.

The architect behind this was a man called Donald Gibson. Appointed to be the city's architect at the age of just twenty-nine, in 1939, Gibson was inspired by Lewis Mumford, an American sociologist who wrote a book arguing for radical changes to cities. Gibson handed out copies of Mumford's book, *The Culture of Cities*, to councilors to impress upon them the importance of its ideas. Mumford believed that the industrial revolution had wrecked cities by making them too dense. Like Ebenezer Howard, he believed that cities were ugly, dirty places, "megalopolises" that had developed to make a few people rich. The next stage, he believed, was "nekropolis"—a city dying. "The owners of the instruments of production and distribution subordinate every other fact in life to the achievement of riches and the display of wealth." So cities had to be replanned.

Gibson started on his ideas right away; his first plan for Coventry was developed before war broke out. But it was the bombing that gave him the opportunity to put it into action. Indeed, just a few weeks after Coventry was blitzed, he gave a speech in London arguing that it could, perversely, be an opportunity. "Many citizens had despaired of the possibility of having a dignified and fitting city center," he claimed. "High land values, the delays involved by town planning legislation, together with a lack of plan for the central area made it seem impossible. Now, in a night, all this is changed."

Under Gibson's tutelage, the industrial slums could be cleared and replaced with new, more spacious council homes. New roads would facilitate traffic. Despite his love of Lewis Mumford, who was always critical of the takeover of public space by automobiles, Gibson embraced it. Much more traffic had to be accommodated, he argued. And "it would be fitting for the center of the motor car industry to give a lead" to the rest of the country.

Under the postwar governments, bombed Coventry thus became a place to experiment with new ideas. With the full support of the government in Westminster, a new ring road was constructed around the city center, which was designed to allow car traffic to flow around it, rather than having to drive through it. Around the shell of the cathedral, a wholly new central business district was built where previously there had been a warren of narrow streets. Visit Coventry now and you will not find a medieval city besieged by the automobile, as Priestley did. You will find that the automobile has conquered and overrun it entirely.

Central Coventry is not a miserable place. The "precinct" that Gibson planned is, as he envisaged, pleasant and even a little grand. There are still a few older buildings around; bombing and demolition did not destroy everything. And some of the new buildings are rather good. The modernist cathedral built alongside the ruins of the ancient one is stunning and rather moving. The Belgrade Theatre is a masterpiece of postwar architecture. There is plenty of space for shoppers to sit and chat, with coffee shops and bars, away from the hum of traffic, exactly as Gibson hoped. Though the car factories in the city have now closed, its two universities have kept it afloat economically.

Students from all over the world fill the bars and cafés around the University of Coventry campus, which is right in the city center.

But nobody would compare visiting Coventry to being transported to Italy now. It is a fine enough little city, but no longer a medieval beauty. The mix of architecture can often be quite jarring, and a few of the postwar buildings, particularly the car parks, are hideous. The bigger problem with the city center as it was replanned, however, is not that bits of it are ugly. It is that it is choked by the ring road. In fifteen minutes, you can walk from one side to another, but then you hit the "concrete collar." If you want to walk or cycle beyond the city center into any of the surrounding neighborhoods, you have to cross swathes of tarmac, on which drivers zoom along at 40 miles per hour, or brave stinking, damp underpasses.

On the other side of the ring road, instead of shops, restaurants, and cafes, space is taken up by enormous warehouses selling carpets or car parts or kitchen tiles, surrounded by acres of car parking. With the exception of the students, who pay extortionate rents to live in new flats or a few older houses inside the ring road, almost nobody walks anywhere in Coventry. In the city that invented the modern bicycle not many people even cycle. They drive, and park at a number of multistory garages, and then walk from their cars. The city center has, in effect, been turned into a mall.

And this model of development was adopted all over Britain, by planners who saw the rise of the automobile as inevitable and desirable. The postwar city would become what Sir Colin Buchanan, a civil servant in Britain's department of planning, called, "one of the most interesting reconstructions in Europe." He was the author of "Traffic in Towns," a government paper published in 1963 that generated so much buzz that it was reprinted by Penguin and sold tens of thousands of copies. Buchanan's report makes for fascinating reading, precisely because it perfectly anticipated the rise of the automobile and what damage it would do to British cities—and then argued exactly why it could at best only be mitigated, rather than stopped. The moment that the car could have been contained was then, in the 1960s. Instead, everything was changed to accommodate it.

"Traffic in Towns" begins with a brilliantly ominous explanation of the coming calamity. When Buchanan did his research, there were around ten million cars in Britain. Within a decade, he predicted—accurately—this number would double. "The population appears as intent upon owning cars as the manufacturers are upon meeting the demand," he wrote. And yet the problems were already evident. Congestion was a drain on "the economic efficiency of the country." Traffic violence was terrifyingly common, and not falling. Cars were depriving children of the chance to play in the street. Noise and pollution were growing. Looking across at America—by then already much more automotive than Britain—he noted that the car was not beautifying cities but rather "producing unrelieved ugliness on a great scale."

Yet Buchanan argued that it would be difficult to stop. "Perhaps because we have all grown up with the motor vehicle, and it has grown up with us, we tend to take it and its less desirable effects very much for granted." The car had become a status symbol, and it was no good to tell people that their desire had downsides too. Indeed, Buchanan himself sang the praises of owning a personal vehicle. "Why cannot we be less hypocritical and admit that a motor car is just about the most convenient device that we ever invented?" he wrote, singing the praises of "marvellous holidays," camping and caravanning around continental Europe. "Possession of it and usage in moderation is a perfectly legitimate ambition for all classes of people."

The problem with this assessment was that the public's idea of "usage in moderation" apparently involved using it all the time, for almost any journey. Since having a car had become a status symbol, and nobody would dare to challenge its growth, Buchanan concluded that instead our urban fabric had to be transformed. Motorways—what Americans tend to call expressways, or freeways—were essential, he argued, to get cars into and out of cities en masse, and to separate pedestrians from cars. Ordinary roads had to be widened. Older buildings had to be demolished and replaced with newer ones that could accommodate car users. Other transport systems would have to make way. Everywhere had to do what Coventry was doing.

According to Otto Saumarez Smith, an architectural historian at the University of Warwick (which, despite its name, is actually in Coventry), "the rebuilding of British city centers during the 1960s is arguably among the single most dramatic moments in British urban history." It was a time of great optimism: The "white heat of technology" and the new "affluent society" would transform everything. Harold Macmillan, the prime minister from 1957 to 1963, promised 300,000 new homes a year, and infamously told voters they had "never had it so good." And mass car ownership was part of this aspirational culture. The minister of transport, Ernest Marples, embraced Buchanan's report, arguing that "we have to face the fact, whether we like it or not, that we have built our towns in entirely the wrong way for motor traffic. We want an entirely different type of town."

The need to bring in the car went hand in hand with the idea that "slums" (typically overcrowded, but not necessarily bad, Victorian houses) needed to be cleared, and their residents decanted to more salubrious homes (typically out in new suburban estates built on green fields in the countryside, where they could use their new cars). Government made available huge subsidies for redevelopment. In London, redevelopment was based on Patrick Abercrombie's Plan, which proposed building a series of ring roads around London. In 1965, the newly formed Greater London Council proposed to add to this the "London Motorway Box," a square of multilane highways cutting through central London.

Entire streets were slated for demolition and boarded up, in anticipation of the new road. Near where I used to live, on Coldharbour Lane in Brixton, South London, there is a social housing estate, Southwyck House, which was built in the 1970s in anticipation of the motorway that was planned to run by it. From the outside it looks like a fortress (some locals nickname it "barrier rock"), because instead of proper-size windows, it has slits that look like they should be used in a gunfight. The design was intended to keep out the sound of the intended motorway. In the end, however, it was never built. The only part of central London to get a motorway was Hammersmith, in West London, which got the Westway. There are still campaigns to get rid of it.

Other city councils, then far more powerful and richer than today's local governments, joined in more enthusiastically even than London. Birmingham, under the tutelage of Herbert Manzoni, its chief architect, surrounded its city center with a tight ring road, and demolished much of what was inside. "There is little of real worth in our architecture," he claimed. Leeds enthusiastically became the first city to allow a motorway to be built through its center, and branded itself the "motorway city of the world." Croydon embarked on building a "mini-Manhattan." "Traffic architecture" was a particular vogue. Architects such as Alison and Peter Smithson proposed building entire neighborhoods on top of cars, hidden in underground tunnels and car parks.

A lot can be learned from the local government plans of the time. Leicester's "Traffic Plan" envisioned pedestrians alighting from buses and cars and going up escalators to elevated overpasses with "travelators" to get around. The ground level would be given entirely to the automobile, with roads buried. Buchanan himself planned a rebuilding of London's Fitzrovia, a neighborhood of Georgian and Victorian houses, on such principles. The architectural drawings from above depicted a bright new modernist "deck," pedestrianized with smart new buildings around Fitzroy Square, the Georgian heart of the district. But another drawing showed what would come underneath. Multiple layers of car traffic, with car parking and escalators taking people up to the pedestrianized area.

These were bold modernist plans, intended to transform war-battered Victorian cities into something a bit more like California. Oddly enough in the architectural drawings it was never raining, the concrete was shiny and white, and the cars seem to be moving at a decent pace, never stuck in traffic. Yet as Saumarez Smith, an enthusiast for the period's optimism, wrote in his book, *Boom Cities*, when constructed, the actual result was largely schemes "made up of a gimcrack modernism of tacky pedestrian precincts, grim underpasses, budget megastructures and gargantuan car parks." The need for developers to make money meant that architects did not always get their visionary way. Instead, car parking did.

And Britain was scarcely alone in this. All of Europe was doing it. Italy began building an orbital motorway around Rome, the Grande Raccordo Anulare, in 1952. Paris started construction on its "peripherique" motorway, which runs where the old city walls were, in 1958. Brussels got its ring road in the 1960s; so did Amsterdam. All came with a panoply of architecture intended for cars.

The new designs certainly helped cars get around. But the trouble is, they also made it more difficult to get around by any other way. Britain's cities, like most in industrialized Europe, were built on public transport. Before mass car ownership, trams had generated big profits for local government, which allowed them to subsidize other services—particularly road building, since under the 1870 Tramways Act, tram operators subsidized the maintenance of roads. But when car ownership took off, this model did not work so well. With their fixed routes, rails, and overhead infrastructure, trams blocked car traffic. And as car ownership grew, profits also dropped off, just as they had in America a couple of decades before.

By 1950, London Transport was losing £1 million a year running the trams; a far larger sum then than now. Many thought buses could do the job better. The trams themselves and their tracks were dilapidated and, consequently, incredibly noisy. Nobody wanted to pay to upgrade them. The officers of London Transport also felt that the system was impeding traffic. Because they operated on fixed rails, trams were difficult for cars to overtake. And as traffic lights proliferated to control car traffic, trams got slower.

The very last tram was driven on July 6, 1952, by John Cliff, the deputy chairman of London Transport, who had been a tram driver fifty years earlier. Crowds of people slowed its journey down to a crawl, and when it reached New Cross, its final destination, they sang "Old Lang Syne," while a Pathé News crew filmed it. In the words of Lord Latham, the chairman of London Transport, "in twenty-one months the face of London has been changed." Other cities soon followed. Birmingham closed its trams, which had been instrumental in the development of the city's suburbs, in 1953. Leeds closed its trams in 1959. Glasgow in 1962. Instead, buses, which were cheaper to run, were introduced. Today there is only one original tramway left in Britain—in Blackpool, which is mostly used by a trickle of nostalgic day-trippers. And there are several new ones, built at great expense decades later, when government realized its mistake.

Worse was what happened to Britain's railways, which had been nationalized in 1948, but were also losing money for the government. In 1963 Richard Beeching, another hugely influential civil servant, proposed shutting down more than half of Britain's railway stations and removing around a third of the track. Almost all of the cuts he proposed were implemented. Entire lines, such as the Varsity Line, which connected Oxford to Cambridge, were abandoned. Most of what was cut was branch lines, which connected villages and smaller towns to mainline rail links, meaning that suddenly entire communities found themselves isolated from the railways again for the first time in a century. Inevitably, they turned to cars.

Of course, it is easy to wax nostalgic about older forms of transportation. The trams were noisy and not always fast; branch railways were often inconvenient, running infrequently, and costing ever more in subsidies. Cycling can be pretty unpleasant in winter, and it is hard to carry much with you. But when these old forms of transport were replaced, they were not replaced with anything better. London Transport had promised that the buses of the future would surely be more comfortable, smoother, and quicker. They did not really get so. A few cities did do visionary things. Newcastle built its own miniature version of the Tube, the Tyne and Wear Metro, which opened in 1980. But most plans, such as one to build a new subway under Manchester, faltered before they even began. Instead, the rise of the car replaced them; and in doing so, it sucked up all of the space that there was in cities, and made it considerably more difficult for any other type of mass transport to work.

From 1960 to 1975, the annual number of passenger journeys on Britain's railways declined from 1.1 million to around 650,000. Cycling collapsed even faster, from 18 billion kilometers a year in 1950 to less than a quarter of that in 1970. Light rail journeys (the trams) reduced to literally nothing. But even though buses were meant to replace all of these journeys, the number of passengers on buses also declined, by a quarter from 1960 to 1970. All of the growth in transport came from private cars. From 1952 to 1971, cars went from accounting for 27 percent of journeys to 75 percent. The number of miles driven grew from 58 billion to 300 billion.

Transport policy explicitly followed a model of "predict and provide": Planners would try to predict how many people would want to drive, based on past trends, and extrapolate out to decide how many roads to build. What the planners of the 1950s and '60s had not understood, or refused to understand, was the principle of induced demand (more on this later). In economic terms, they had not understood that the number of drivers was "endogenous"— not "exogenous." That is, the policy of "predict and provide" actually helped accelerate the rise of the car in the first place. If you build more roads, and do all you can to speed the flow of traffic, then the main result is that car ownership becomes more attractive. And so more people buy cars, right up until the point that there is as much traffic as there was before.

In 1981, John Adams, a geographer at University College London, wrote a fierce critique of this model, and how it was transforming cities all over the world. Working from the Department of Transport's own forecasts, he pointed out that the more that growth was predicted and provided for, the more growth there would be, until eventually all possible resources were used on motor vehicles. Casting a slightly absurdist eye over the Department of Transport's forecasts, by 2205, he imagined, every single family in Britain would have its own lorry (what we Brits call a semi-truck). Roads would no longer be roads, but rather, the entire country would simply be one enormous expanse of asphalt. "People will spend most of their time driving around in the family juggernaut picking up piles of machine-made stuff from automatic warehouses or wandering about the tarmac plain searching in vain for someone to carry out repairs when it goes wrong." Like a suburban version of *Mad Max*. Or less kindly, the reality of modern Houston.

Adams's argument was that the endless growth of car mobility was not in fact obviously progress. Rather, it was driven by the desires of the wealthy for convenience, and would come at the expense of the poor. "Consider the example of a rural bus that regularly carries fifty passengers. If one of the fifty passengers were to acquire a car, the remaining forty-nine passengers could take up the car owner's share of the bus overhead costs without too much strain. But when the forty-ninth passenger leaves, the remaining passenger immediately has his (or more likely her) share of the overhead costs doubled."

Inevitably the fiftieth passenger would probably be the poorest member of society, who is left with no means of getting around. (And Adams was right, that statistically, that last person was more likely to be a woman.) The government was profoundly hypocritical about this. It might subsidize buses, but because it also encouraged car ownership, it undermined them as well; politicians were "simultaneously supporters of public transport and promoters of the main cause of its decline," Adams noted.

All of this reconstruction of cities would only serve to marginalize poor people even further. The disabled, elderly people, and anyone else who cannot drive were finding that their mobility was in fact diminishing as everyone else got cars. Simultaneously, the rich sucked up ever more natural resources in their demand for instantly available, comfortable, and convenient travel. The growth of the oil industry, to feed demands for transport, Adams noted, had already created a "concentration of incredible wealth in very few hands, and a situation that is economically, politically and militarily extremely unstable."

That was in the 1980s. It has only continued since. From 2009 to the start of 2020, just before the pandemic knocked much of what life was left out of public transport, the number of bus journeys taken annually in Britain declined by 17 percent. Since 1982, the figure is down 12 percent. The discrepancy is slightly caused by the fact that in London and London alone, the buses boomed during the early part of the 2000s, probably due to the creation of the congestion charge. That, together with rising gasoline prices, helped briefly send the cost of driving back up, and in turn reduced some of the congestion that made using the buses so painful. Since around 2012, however, even that progress has been undone, and the number of journeys by bus in London has been falling as fast as in the rest of the country. Cars are simply too cheap and easy to use.

To drivers, this might sound unlikely. Isn't the cost of insurance going up every year? And parking harder than ever? Is there not a war on the motorist, encouraged at every level of government, with councils busy sticking bollards in and closing roads to all but bicycles? Well yes, that is because there are so many more drivers. The decision to transform our countries into car owning ones was made long ago. The incentives are set. We are now just trying to restrain the growth toward a completely automotive society. We have to, though, because the alternative is gridlock, pollution, and poverty. Indeed, what happened in America was even worse.

4

DETROIT BREAKDOWN

If you want to get a sense of what the automobile did to American cities, a good place to start is from the air. Compare satellite photos of almost any city today, whether it is Chicago or Atlanta, New York or Los Angeles, to aerial photos taken in the 1950s (and there are plenty) and immediately what stands out are the freeways. It is easy to do online—the school of architecture at the University of Oklahoma has a tool on its website that lets you pick any number of neighborhoods in cities all over the country.

Take one example they offer, of Pittsburgh, Pennsylvania, comparing 1952 to 2014. On the right, in black and white, is a neighborhood dense with homes and factories. Slide across sixty-two years into the future and suddenly half of the buildings are gone. Instead, an enormous highway, with an interchange, cuts through the neighborhood like a ribbon. Around it, most of the buildings are gone. Huge patches of gray suggest they have been replaced with parking lots. A caption helpfully explains the context. "The Hill District was a prosperous African American neighborhood that descended into crime and poverty during the urban renewal period and was further destroyed by riots following the assassination of Martin Luther King."

If what happened in Europe in the 1950s and '60s was dramatic, what was happening in the United States was revolutionary. In America, already the richest country in the world by the mid-1920s, car ownership climbed far earlier than it did in Europe. With its adoption of the car, America set in motion a project that would only deepen its preexisting racial and class hierarchies, in ways that almost nobody predicted.

America's cities were not always the car-centric sprawls that they are today. At the start of the twentieth century most American cities somewhat resembled European ones. They had grid layouts, but they were densely populated. Most people got around by bus, train, streetcar, or simply by walking. In most cities, the working classes still lived in tenement blocks in the center of the city; the middle classes lived in inner suburbs—typically row houses modeled on British terraced designs—close to public transport. Only the rich lived in the enormous sorts of homes with big gardens you see in old Hollywood movies.

Because this was the industrial era, of course, it was often miserable. Cities still contained huge factory complexes and coal power stations that pumped dust into the air. The tenements were overcrowded and unhealthy. But you did not need a car to get around. The pedestrian was king. Footage of New York City from the early twentieth century shows people walking in the streets—not stuck to sidewalks but right in the middle—with a level of ownership unimaginable today.

By the mid-1930s there were already more than 30 million cars on American roads—at a time when the population of the United States was only a little more than a third of what it is today, at around 120 million. Henry Ford's Model T, constructed on a revolutionary assembly line at Highland Park in Detroit, had brought cheap motoring to a mass market; more than 15 million of the cars were manufactured between 1918 and 1927. At a time when the average salary in America was around $3,000 a year, the Model T sold for just $850, well within the range of affordability for even working-class families.

It was after the Second World War, however, when the automobile really began to transform America. Indeed, America was where many of the cars made in Coventry in the 1950s were exported to, because after the end of World War II, such was the pent-up demand that even America's prodigious factories could not keep up. In 1948, William Faulkner, the novelist, wrote that the automobile had become "our national sex symbol." The American man, he wrote, "really loves nothing but his automobile: not his wife his child nor his country nor even his bank account." While he might "live in a rented rathole," he will still replace his car "in pristine virginity" as often as he can. Mobility was the watchword of the day. Motels; drive-thru restaurants; freeways. They all emerged in the 1950s, promising a new sort of life, on the road, as Jack Kerouac had it, forever moving freely.

But while America had the cars, what it did not have yet, at least in 1945, was cities that were easy to navigate in them. Traffic jams were increasingly common; there was not enough space to park. Driving was a frustrating experience, and often a dangerous one. Americans were acquiring automobiles fast, but they increasingly were not able to use them in the way that they thought they should be able to—at speed, on open roads, without a lot of other drivers, or worse, pedestrians, getting in the way.

So to make way for this new love, America had to be transformed completely. In 1956 President Dwight Eisenhower signed the Federal-Aid Highway Act, which authorized the spending of $25 billion with which to construct 60,000 miles of roads. That was equivalent to 5 percent of the country's entire GDP, the largest construction project ever undertaken in the United States. The investment was justified on defense grounds—at the height of the Cold War, America needed to be able to move troops around quickly in case of invasion. But the more compelling logic was the same optimism, and the rising sense of a new, hypermobile society, that wanted to be able to get anywhere by car.

Eisenhower, somewhat ironically, was inspired by his time in Europe as Supreme Commander of the Allied Forces. Germany's Nazi-era autobahns, which in fact were rather limited, "had made me see the wisdom of broader ribbons across the land," he said. Those too had been built primarily to transport troops, but ended up having a much bigger effect on civilian life.

America's Coventry in the 1950s was Detroit. The city was then the richest in the world, per capita, with a population of almost two million people. Almost all of its wealth was built on the car industry. In 1927, flush with the success of the Model T, Henry Ford opened a new plant in Dearborn, just outside the city limits, the River Rouge plant. When it opened, it was a transformational step forward in American industry. In Highland Park, Ford had perfected the assembly line, making it possible to produce cars far more quickly than had been possible in the artisan workshops that preceded it. In

Dearborn, he went one step further. The facility covered the best part of six square miles; it had its own deep-water port, its own steel mills and furnaces, and its own metal shops. The idea was that every part of a Ford car could be produced there, from raw materials shipped in down the river. It grew to employ 90,000 people, and it was the biggest manufacturing facility in the entire world.

I visited Detroit toward the end of 2021. The Dearborn plant is one of its major tourist attractions. There are still a number of Ford factories there, including the assembly line that puts together the Ford F-150 pickup truck, America's best-selling vehicle. From the Ford Museum of Innovation you can take a bus and tour the factory itself. A short film takes you through a rather rosy history of Henry Ford (his virulent anti-Semitism unsurprisingly does not get a mention, though his union bashing does). It notes Ford's most famous innovation—paying high enough wages that his workers could afford to buy the cars that they manufactured, allowing them to join the great American middle class. There is a display of half a dozen wonderful old cars, all produced in Dearborn over the preceding half century.

After the film, you are allowed to walk around a gangway looking down on the workers as they bolt together the massive trucks. For sure, Ford makes a lot about its innovation—the genius aluminum engineering of the truck's body, or the brand-new electric versions that are to replace the enormous gasoline-driven engines. There is an entire viewing platform, from which factory buildings stretch for miles. And yet visiting feels more like visiting a monument of a forgotten past. Around 6,000 people are employed across the facility—a fifteenth of the number in its heyday.

Sadly, these days, the name Detroit does not summon up ideas of a glorious motoring future. Rather, the city has become a byword for decline. In 2013, after decades of struggling to pay its bills, it went bankrupt, the biggest municipal collapse in American history, defaulting on some $20 billion of debt. The poverty rate is 30 percent, making it the second poorest city in America, after Cleveland, Ohio. Its population has declined in every census since the 1950s, and it is now down by around two-thirds on its 1950s peak. There are typically more than 300 murders a year, or as many as in the whole of New York City, with more than ten times the population. There are more than 70,000 empty buildings and 90,000 empty lots.

It is an eerie place to visit. Entire neighborhoods have been simply abandoned. Less than a couple of miles away from the city center you can walk through neighborhoods such as Core City, which in the 1950s had the same population density as London does now, and not see a single other person, or even anybody driving a car. I stayed in one of these neighborhoods, in a beautiful little house constructed in the early part of the twentieth century. The owner, who rents it out to visitors, had renovated it into a perfect little home, with wooden floorboards and an original roll-top cast-iron bathtub. But the house stood almost alone, surrounded by empty lots where others had been demolished, and a few that were derelict. The main buildings remaining in the neighborhood, evidently having escaped demolition, were churches—the sheer numbers of them a reminder of how many people once lived here.

Ironically, Detroit is no longer even much of a motor city, at least for a substantial proportion of its population. While 98 percent of residents with a household income of more than $60,000 own at least one car or motorcycle, fewer than half with incomes lower than $30,000 do. One-third of Detroiters cannot afford a car. The carless are far more likely to be Black and female. According to a survey conducted by the University of Michigan, four in ten have missed important appointments or work because they were unable to get there. In 2015 the *Detroit Free Press* ran a story about James Robertson, a fifty-six-year-old resident who walked twenty-one miles each day to his factory job in Rochester, an outer suburb, after his aging car broke down and he could not afford another one. The $10.15 an hour he earned was not enough to cover the payments. Revealingly, when readers clubbed together to give him a huge sum of money—around $360,000—he not only bought a car, he immediately moved out of the city.

The decline of Detroit has many causes. Dysfunctional local government is one, racism another, corruption a third. But all of them are linked to the automobile. From the 1950s onward, Detroit entered into a slow-motion death spiral, which culminated in the 2013 bankruptcy. The invention of the automobile built Detroit into a glittering town, nicknamed the "Arsenal of Democracy" in World War II for its contribution to the Allied war effort. But it also helped to set in motion the collapse that followed. From the 1960s onward, white flight hollowed out American cities. It was enabled by the car. Nowhere did it happen more dramatically than in Detroit.

Like Coventry, Detroit did not just produce cars—it also used them. Even as early as 1930, 34 percent of the city's workers drove into the city. By the late 1940s, traffic jams snarled it up and sapped at the commercial viability of the city center. When it was so difficult to get downtown, many Detroiters started shopping in new suburban shopping malls, dozens of which opened in the 1940s and '50s. The city's leaders decided that the problem was that their old city was simply not easy enough to get around by car. The roads were too congested, the parking too difficult to find, and the homes too densely crowded. In 1944, the city produced a report arguing that of all the improvements needed, "none is of greater importance to Detroiters" than wider roads and a system of highways.

Detroit arguably built the first American freeway, the Davison, which opened in 1942, six lanes wide and segregated from other traffic so that drivers could always move at 60 miles per hour or more. It went across the city, from east to west, and decreased the time it took to drive into the city center from the edge of the city to a matter of minutes. It was the first of many. The Walter P. Chrysler, the Edsel Ford, and others followed in the 1950s. As June Manning Thomas, an academic at the University of Michigan's planning school, wrote in her history, *Redevelopment and Race: Planning a Finer City in Postwar Detroit*, this was difficult to resist. Thanks to Eisenhower's transport bill, most of the cost of roads was funded by the federal government, whereas there was no federal money for public transport.

But the freeways did not help keep the city alive. Instead, they almost killed it. As it became easier to drive into the city, more people moved out to the suburbs. Suddenly developers could build new homes in the countryside, with gardens and plenty of parking and white picket fences, and the promise that the buyers could speed back into the city to their jobs, bypassing the neighborhoods they left behind entirely. The developers were subsidized directly by the Federal government, which offered people cheap mortgages to buy new homes being constructed in the countryside.

Suddenly the city began losing residents, and with them, tax revenue. As people left, services became harder to maintain, and taxes had to rise further, which only encouraged more people to move out. And so the city responded by building more freeways. As Manning Thomas recounts, "at the same time that the city worked to attract people to the central business district ... it helped them leave by constructing expressways. One of the causes of decline was dependence on automobiles, but a solution was to accommodate more automobiles."

As people left, Downtown Detroit began to decline. Why drive into the city center, where parking was scarce and you might hit traffic, when you could go to a new suburban mall much closer to your home? So to compete, the city only leaned further on accommodating more cars. Buildings were demolished to make space for parking. "Many city staff seemed to believe that building highways and parking ramps would resolve central city congestion and make downtown competitive with suburban malls," she wrote. New buildings, such as the Renaissance Center, were designed to be accessible by cars, with huge garages and ramps to reach them. But that meant that the people coming to work in them no longer needed to leave their offices. They arrived by car and left by car, not stopping for a drink or to go shopping. The streets lost their charm. They became dangerous.

Overlaid on this was, sadly, America's deep history of racism. The Interstate system did not just cut through land to connect cities. It also cut through the cities themselves, often brutally, and with deep consequences for Americans, especially Black Americans. The 1950s were part of the "great migration," when millions of African Americans moved from the South to the industrial cities of the north in search of better lives, away from the cruelty of Jim Crow and backbreaking, poorly paid labor on sharecropped cotton farms. They moved mostly to the inner cities of places like Baltimore, Chicago, Philadelphia, and, of course, Detroit—cities of smokestacks and steel mills and pounding factories. But while factories in need of labor for America's postwar boom welcomed them, many of their new neighbors did not. In the North, Jim Crow did not exist, and Black people could use public transport and sit in restaurants like anybody else. But that did not mean that white Americans in the North were without prejudice. In fact, rather than share space with Black people, many chose simply to leave.

As documented brilliantly by Richard Rothstein, an economic historian, in his book *The Color of Law*, Federal government policy in practice excluded Black people from the subsidized mortgages that were allowing white people to flee to the suburbs. They did so not by excluding individual Black people, but by in effect writing off any district in which Black people lived as "declining" and, therefore, too risky for a loan. In districts that were so "redlined," getting a mortgage was essentially impossible, while federal subsidies flowed almost exclusively to brand-new suburbs built exclusively for white people. Even if developers wanted to, they could not sell houses to Black people, because they would risk the Federal finance that underpinned their entire projects being withdrawn. Partly as a result, in new suburbs, houses were often built with racist covenants, decreeing that properties should be occupied "exclusively by members of the Caucasian race," meaning that Black people could not move there even if they somehow got mortgages or didn't need them.

As Rothstein recounts, this redlining was explicitly tied to roadbuilding. The new subsidized suburbs were typically at the edges of cities, and only really accessible by automobile. But roads had to be built through existing neighborhoods—often precisely the ones that were redlined. Highway officials saw roadbuilding as an opportunity—not only to improve transportation but also to demolish what they called "slums"—in reality, generally the ghettoized neighborhoods where Black people were forced to live. Alfred Johnson, of the American Association of State Highway Officials, recalled that "some city officials expressed the view in the mid-1950s that the urban Interstates would give them a good opportunity to get rid of the local 'niggertown.'" Detroit was a particular victim. When the tiny independent city of Hamtramck, for example, which is completely surrounded by Detroit, cleared out 4,000 families to build the Chrysler Freeway (now I-75), almost all of those families were Black.

Planners probably thought that in doing this, they were saving their cities, "clearing" out slum neighborhoods defined by poverty and beset by crime. But in fact they were destroying their own cities, essentially out of spite and fear. Segregation built decline into the very structure of their cities, creating the abandoned neighborhoods that today remain blighted. Poor Black people were decanted to new public housing projects, which were meant to be an improvement but in reality were often far from where the jobs were, and had no good transport, unless the inhabitants could buy cars. Instead of becoming good neighborhoods, they became reservoirs of poverty, trapping their inhabitants without access to work. As unemployment climbed, tax revenues fell further, meaning that the city was even less able to help its residents than it had been.

In the summer of 1967, Detroit was devastated by riots, which were among the most destructive in American history. Virginia Park, a neighborhood of grand houses built in the late nineteenth and early twentieth centuries, had become a slum. Absentee landlords had subdivided the houses into tiny apartments, in which tens of thousands of Black Americans had been concentrated by racist housing policies. White people had left, to the suburbs, and with them, so too had many of the jobs, but Black people still struggled to leave. The Detroit Police Department, which had just fifty Black officers, essentially policed it like an occupying army. On a sweltering night on July 23, a police raid on an illegal nightclub turned into a riot. As the police and National Guard tried to contain it, they shot sixteen people. The Federal government in Washington, D.C., sent in the army. Within a few days, about 1,400 buildings had been burned, and 1,700 looted. Some forty-three people were dead, thirty-three of them Black.

The riots were provoked by deep racism. But they only helped to accelerate the city's decline, as more businesses, especially those owned by white people, began to move out to the suburbs. "Our nation is moving toward two societies, one black, one white—separate and unequal," declared the Kerner Commission, created by President Lyndon Johnson to look into the disturbances. It was reversible, the panel declared, but the commission was ignored. By the 1970s, once proud white Detroiters increasingly found that the only time they came back into the city was at Christmas, when families packed into Hudson's Department Store with its spectacular lights and ornaments. The rest of the year, however, its business struggled. Black Detroiters, trapped in the city, found opportunities for work increasingly rare. Crime spiraled. Hudson's closed in 1983, by which time, Detroit had already lost a third of its residents.

By then, even the car industry, which had lobbied for and taken a preeminent role in the construction of the city's highways, was struggling. In the late 1970s and '80s, as gasoline prices soared, the big, yacht-like cars that the Detroit automakers produced were suddenly no longer as popular. Instead, Japanese cars—smaller, cheaper, and more efficient—began flooding the market. The Detroit carmakers, by then reduced to three big firms, General Motors, Ford, and Chrysler, were sluggish and uncompetitive. They began to lay off workers. Factories even in the suburbs closed. The American car industry began to move elsewhere, to where union labor was not so expensive, in places like Atlanta and Texas. The whole state of Michigan, not just the city of Detroit, began to feel the pinch. People were no longer just moving to the suburbs, they were moving to new states entirely, particularly those in the South and West.

Funnily, in the eight years since the bankruptcy, Detroit has begun to make a bit of a recovery. But it is doing so precisely because finally, it has abandoned the car-centric sprawl model that so defined it. In a few square miles in the city center, a new city is being reborn. The 1920s and '30s skyscrapers that survived the worst years are being resurrected as smart hotels, restaurants, and office blocks. A local billionaire, Dan Gilbert, who runs Rocket Mortgage, a huge mortgage provider, helped to start it by buying up dozens of downtown buildings and investing in private security. He moved thousands of his employees to the city, offering them rent subsidies if they lived downtown.

These days you can live in a prime apartment in downtown Detroit, shop in Whole Foods, and patronize any number of fine small plates restaurants and bougie cocktail bars. Young people are moving in. They may even be drawn by the fact that, unlike in many big American cities, you do not actually need to drive everywhere. In 2017, a new light rail system opened, the QLINE, running from the Art Institute, with its priceless Diego Rivera murals, down to the waterfront, funded entirely by private money. There are now bike lanes and bikes and electric scooters for rent on many corners. The mayor, Mike Duggan, talks about the need for effective public transit. Private security has made the city center safe, if occasionally rather sterile feeling. It is walkable—something that Gilbert understands the appeal of well. He likes to show journalists photos of Detroit streets from before the car took over, with tram cars and thousands of men and women in hats and coats walking the streets.

But it is an unequal sort of improvement. Most of the people moving into the city center apartments now are young white college graduates. Many Black people continue to leave. If the city does begin to thrive, some might benefit, as the value of their properties rise. But most Detroiters rent, so they will have to compete with new, richer residents. A new, dense city will benefit landowners near the center—people such as Mr. Gilbert. That is not a bad thing. The tax they pay is certainly helping Detroit get back on its feet. It is creating jobs that benefit poorer people too. Businesses are hiring. But for many Black Detroiters, left in neighborhoods farther away from the growth that continue to rot, that may be scant consolation. As long as the rest of Detroit's enormous sprawl continues to struggle, which seems almost inevitable, its residents will continue to leave.

Lest you think Detroit is unique, there are similar places all over America, albeit few where the decline was anywhere near as dramatic, or where the car industry itself played quite such a directly critical role. The combination of "urban renewal"—which generally meant road building—and mass suburban development hollowed out any number of neighborhoods. Weequahic, a neighborhood in Newark, New Jersey, is one I think of. It is where Philip Roth, the novelist, grew up and where his book *American Pastoral* is set.

Architecturally, it is a lovely place. The houses are wonderful old-fashioned American homes; the high school, which Roth attended, is an art deco masterpiece built in the 1930s, with a mural by Michael Lenson called "The Enlightenment of Man." But the neighborhood has one big problem. It is cut off from the rest of Newark by a highway, I-78, which goes from Manhattan to Harristown, Pennsylvania, and from there into the Midwest. By the time the road was built, in the late 1950s and early '60s, the white and Jewish populations of Weequahic had mostly fled to newer suburbs. Those who had not did so after the race riots of 1967.

The population now is overwhelmingly Black, and struggling. Having lost most of its tax base, the city went into a spiral of decline. Policing remained violent and abusive for decades. The poverty rate in census tracts in the area reaches as high as 45 percent. The median household income is roughly half what it is elsewhere in New Jersey. Violent crime is sadly far too common. When I visited Weequahic several years ago, one of the high school's history teachers took me on a short walking tour of the neighborhood. He pointed out the places where his students had been shot in gang violence. Weequahic is a place that ought to be thriving. It is just ten miles from the wealth of Manhattan. But you can only easily get there by car, and it feels a world away. The road is literally a wall, cutting off the neighborhood from the New York metropolitan area.

Not all of this can be pinned on the car, of course. America's awful history of slavery and segregation would have been just as dreadful had Karl Benz never invented his engine. Racism was the fundamental reason cities hollowed out so easily, not cars. But it was mass automobile ownership, and the construction of highways, that made white flight possible. Without it, the new suburbs that white people fled to would never have been viable. And the fact that white people could afford cars, and most Black people could not, made it possible for the car to be used to enforce segregation indirectly, at a time when the Civil Rights Act was making it harder for it to be enforced directly, as it had been for decades before.

Even cities that we do not typically think of as having declined were still damaged by the toxic combination of racism and the obsession with cars. Take Atlanta, the capital of Georgia. Atlanta is now one of America's boom cities—a fast-growing, diverse metropolis, with, ironically, a thriving car industry. But it is also among the most segregated cities in America, perhaps unsurprisingly given the state's history—the birthplace of the Ku Klux Klan and home to Stone Mountain, an enormous carved stone effigy to Confederate leaders. It is also deeply dependent on the car, which is beginning to affect its ability to grow further. According to INRIX, a firm that does global surveys of traffic, Atlanta, in 2017, was the eighth most congested city on earth, with drivers spending around seventy hours stuck in gridlock each year. And it has been shaped by the same combination of racism and car ownership that helped to wreck Detroit.

In the 1950s, Atlanta suffered many of the same racialized roadbuilding projects that happened everywhere. Most egregious was the Downtown Connector, which was designed to run straight through the headquarters of the Atlanta Life Insurance Company, one of the city's biggest Black-owned businesses. Highway engineers had the idea that the roads could provide actual segregation, and so perhaps prevent white flight from the city proper; essentially the idea was that roads would create multilane barriers that would split apart white and Black neighborhoods. But while they certainly wrecked the Black neighborhoods, they did not "protect" the white ones—white flight to the suburbs only intensified, and with it, so did the city's traffic problems.

By the 1960s and '70s, congestion had got so bad on the Connector that Atlanta was actually ready to invest in public transport. But this was also the era of the Civil Rights Act and its related various Supreme Court rulings, which outlawed the segregated areas on buses, in cinemas, and the like. And many white Atlantans certainly did not want to have to share buses or trains with Black people. In 1965 the state of Georgia created the Metropolitan Atlanta Rapid Transit Authority, or MARTA, to serve the city of Atlanta and its core suburban counties, but it did not fund it. Over the next six years, though traffic jams were snarling up the city even then, racism essentially crippled the attempt to create a functional public transit system.

The basic problem was that the residents of predominantly white counties that border Atlanta—Cobb, Clayton, and Gwinnett—did not want to pay for public transport that they thought would mostly benefit Black people in the city. They also did not want it to bring those Black people into their suburbs, or their children into mostly white school systems. Quickly, MARTA was joked to stand for "Moving Africans Rapidly Through Atlanta." And so when they were asked in referendums, in 1965 and then again in 1971, whether they would pay an extra sales tax to fund the new system, they said no. Again and again, the system was starved of the money that might have made it functional to most Atlantans because of essentially racialized reasons.

Instead, what happened was the city kept widening the roads. After all, in your car, you do not have to share space with somebody of another color. Billions of dollars were pumped into road-widening schemes. In the late 1970s the Downtown Connector was widened from three lanes in each direction to seven each way. But the extra capacity only encouraged housing developers, taking advantage of the flow of white migrants leaving the deindustrialization of places like Detroit, to build ever more sprawling suburbs farther and farther along the road, funneling them onto the highway. The result, argued Kevin Kruse, the author of *White Flight: Atlanta and the Making of Modern Conservatism*, was that "Atlanta's transportation infrastructure was designed as much to keep people apart as to bring people together."

The legacy is deep even in cities that have mostly recovered from the worst. In New York, the leader of the campaign to bring cars into the city was Robert Moses, an unelected bureaucrat who managed to become one of the most powerful men in American history. Moses, a wealthy scion of German Jewish background, accumulated a dozen posts in New York's government simultaneously. Through his control of various state commissions and public authorities, he amassed an astonishing amount of power, which he used to rebuild New York, again, for the car. "You can draw any kind of picture you want on a clean slate and indulge your every whim in the wilderness in laying out a New Delhi, Canberra, or Brasilia, but when you operate in an overbuilt metropolis, you have to hack your way with a meat ax," he said of the city.

So New York got hacked up, by new bridges, parkways, and highways—all of which sped cars into Manhattan. They included the Cross Bronx Expressway, a six-lane highway that was the first major expressway to be built through a preexisting city neighborhood anywhere in the United States. More than 60,000 residents had to be relocated, mostly to enormous new public housing projects, to make way for it. It took ten years longer than planned and cost at least three times its original budget, but Moses was determined to get it done.

In total Moses was responsible for the construction of 700 miles of road across the city. According to Robert Caro's masterful biography, *The Power Broker*, he expressly worked against those New Yorkers who could not afford to buy cars. He himself went everywhere in a fleet of chauffeured limousines, paid for by taxpayers. Some of the roads he built, such as the Southern State Parkway, purposely had bridges over them that were too low for buses to be able to pass through. Ostensibly that was to stop trucks from using them, but the reality, at least according to Sid Shapiro, the chief engineer of the Long Island State Parks Commission, was that is also kept out the masses (and particularly Black people) from the beaches that Moses had opened.

Public transport, meanwhile, was allowed to decline. The tram that crossed the Brooklyn Bridge had its tracks torn up, immediately reducing the number of daily passengers crossing the East River by public transport from 400,000 to less than half of that. The subway network, which had grown dramatically from almost nothing in 1904 to be the biggest underground rail network in the world by 1940, suddenly ceased to be invested in. No new lines opened; the existing ones were neglected and became unreliable. It saw its ridership drop dramatically, from a peak of two billion riders annually in 1946 to under half that by the 1970s, and as fares declined, so too did the money available to invest, creating a downward spiral. Instead, cars were the future.

But they had the same effect as elsewhere: Existing neighborhoods were wrecked. Even as the light industries, which had defined entire city neighborhoods—like the garment industry—disappeared to cheaper places, Manhattan became ever more traffic clogged and polluted, only accelerating the rush of people out of the city. Crime climbed and more well-heeled residents left. Between 1970 and 1980 the population declined by more than

10 percent—nowhere near as bad as the decline in places like Detroit, but a sizable hit for the financial and cultural capital of the United States. In 1975 the city came close to bankruptcy. In 1977, a blackout led to widespread looting. Crime rose precipitously, through to the early 1990s.

It was in New York, however, that the backlash against this car-centric tearing up of American cities also began. There is a reason the city remains the only place in America where a majority of people do not drive alone to work, and where public transport continues to carry millions of people every day. Looking back, it can seem inevitable that the city bounced back from its worst period, when the murder rate hit more than 2,000 per year and anyone who could afford to moved out. But it was not inevitable. Rather, people made it happen. And one woman in particular had a leading role.

5

JANE JACOBS AND THE FIGHT BACK

Not everywhere in America was destroyed by the onslaught of the automobile. If you want to get a good sense of which places survived, you can just pull up a list of the most densely populated neighborhoods in America. Of the top one hundred most crowded zip codes, eighty are in New York City. The rest are in the New York suburbs, or else in San Francisco; Washington, D.C.; and Chicago. One of the places to have survived is Greenwich Village, a neighborhood in Lower Manhattan that is now one of the most bourgeois places on Earth, but in the 1950s was considered, much like other parts of the city's deindustrializing areas, to be a bit of a slum.

By the beginning of the 1960s Robert Moses had transformed huge swathes of New York. He had built expressways, bridges, tunnels, and, through his New York City Committee on Slum Clearance Plans, demolished dozens of neighborhoods across the city. But not everything was finished. One of his last plans was to finish the motorway connection from New Jersey across Manhattan to Brooklyn. The idea was the Lower Manhattan Expressway, also known as LOMEX, or the Canal Street Expressway. The idea was for a ten-lane elevated highway running right across the neighborhoods now known as Little Italy and SoHo, to link the I-78 expressway then being built in New Jersey to other parts of New York City.

Moses had originally conceived the idea of an expressway running across Lower Manhattan in 1941. It took until 1960 for it to be first approved by the New York City Planning Commission. The plan involved the eviction of roughly 2,000 families from 500 or so buildings that would be demolished, as well as hundreds of businesses. Much like the other freeways being built across America, the cost was to be almost entirely covered by the federal government. Of a budget of $100 million, just $200,000 was to come from city funds. The same basic logic of it was clear: A fast road would let people in the new, fast-growing suburbs of New Jersey and Connecticut get into, out of, and indeed across Manhattan without ever really having to stop to pause. Workers on Wall Street (New York's financial district) or in the skyscrapers of Midtown would be able to drive right from their new detached houses into the city each morning without getting stuck in traffic. The people who lived along the path of the proposed expressway would be given new, more salubrious, less overcrowded homes elsewhere.

But unlike previous efforts to build expressways through the middle of American cities, this one was not going to be easy. In fact, it would prove the beginning of the end, at least temporarily, for the whole postwar moment of car-focused "urban renewal." Moses had changed plenty of neighborhoods, but by the early 1960s, the power of his machine was waning. He had been through half a dozen different mayors, but each one had to be bent to his priorities. And in Lower Manhattan, he was about to encounter a surprising new nemesis, a middle-aged journalist and housewife originally from Scranton, Pennsylvania, named Jane Jacobs.

Jacobs had moved to New York City in 1934 at the age of eighteen, initially to Brooklyn Heights, a neighborhood just across the water from Manhattan. Within a few years she had decamped to Greenwich Village, right underneath where Moses planned his expressways. As Anthony Flint, an American journalist, wrote in his book *Wrestling with Moses*, her career took off quickly. Having started out as a secretary, in the late 1930s, she began selling articles to *Vogue* about her neighborhood's various businesses: the flower markets, the jewelers cutting diamonds, the intricacies of manholes and subterranean pipes that provided steam, water, and electricity. Jacobs developed a deep love of the city, eventually, with her architect husband, buying and restoring an 1842 townhouse in the neighborhood in 1947. In 1952 she persuaded the editor of *Architectural Forum*, Douglas Haskell, to take her on as a writer.

The *Forum* was a relatively obscure magazine, part of Henry Luce's Time Inc. empire, which ran spreads celebrating architects such as Frank Lloyd Wright. And at the start of her career, Jacobs had written fairly straight sorts of articles. Her beat was hospitals and schools. She later said that she was "utterly baffled at first" by architecture and had to be taught the details by her husband. At first, she generally accepted the planning dogma of the day. But as she visited more places, she began to question it. A trip to Philadelphia in 1954 was a turning point. Ed Bacon, the power broker there, gave her a tour of a "slum"—a neighborhood in which people were evidently working, interacting, and shopping on bustling streets. And then he took her to one of the new planned neighborhoods that was meant to replace the slums and it was desolate. "He showed me the 'after' street, all fixed up, and there was just one person on it, a bored little boy kicking a tire in the gutter," she told a panel in San Francisco much later, in 2004. That motivated her despair.

In 1961, Jacobs published a book, *The Death and Life of Great American Cities*, which remains probably the best book about urban planning ever written. In the introduction she talks about the visionaries who believed, if they just had enough money, that could "wipe out all our slums in ten years, reverse decay in the great, dull gray belts that were yesterday's and day-before-yesterday's suburbs, anchor the wandering middle class and its wandering tax money, and perhaps even solve the traffic problem." The reality, however, was that with all of the money that expressway advocates had already spent, they had created only "cultural centers that are avoided by everyone but bums," "commercial centers that are lackluster imitations of standardized suburban chain-store shopping," and chief of all, "expressways that eviscerate great cities." This, she wrote, was not rebuilding; it was "the sacking of cities."

The Death and Life is a magnificent piece of work. I read it at the age of about twenty-four, newly hired at *The Economist*, while on a reporting trip to Estonia. Tallinn, the capital, with its mix of Soviet-era modernism and medieval architecture, is pretty far from New York City. But Jacobs's insights applied there too. You could see perfectly well how the ancient public squares, free of cars, and narrow streets lined with small shops, were vibrant, safe, pleasant places to be. It was equally apparent how the grandiose Soviet-era blocks, with their wide-open spaces and roads, probably looked beautiful on the architects' drawings, but in fact were rather soulless and empty. They might have seemed impressive to officials driving through in their ZIL limousines, but would actually turn out to be fairly grim to live in.

When Jacobs mentioned expressways, she almost certainly had one in particular in mind: the LOMEX. As early as 1955 she had written to the mayor of the time, Robert Wagner, to express her dismay at the plans to run the highway through Washington Square Park, one of the few pockets of green space in southern Manhattan. "It is very discouraging to do our best to make the city more habitable, and then to learn that the city itself is thinking up schemes to make it uninhabitable," she wrote. By 1958, her letter had evolved into a full-blown campaign, one that would last a decade, bringing in voices as powerful as Eleanor Roosevelt in support. They held balls, rallies, and all manner of other events to raise funds and gather attention. It was a campaign straightforwardly against the domination of the city by the automobile.

Moses reacted with bemused anger, writing that it was "preposterous" to "choke off all traffic in Washington Square." As the years went on, and the fight continued, he would inveigh against the neighborhood, summoning up statistics about the number of building code violations, the number of vacant buildings, and the transience of the population. He pointed out the value to the rest of the city of being able to reduce traffic congestion. Where Jacobs had Eleanor Roosevelt, Moses had David Rockefeller, the tycoon in charge of Chase Manhattan Bank, who argued that the neighborhood was clearly in decline. This, rebutted Jacobs, was entirely predictable. Why would anyone invest in a neighborhood where an expressway was planned to knock through?

Not everyone loved Jacobs's views. Despite agreeing with her about the need to keep cars out of Washington Square Park, Lewis Mumford—who inspired Donald Gibson in Coventry—called her a "confident but sloppy youngster." Jacobs, he thought, was a naive woman who could not understand cities in the scientific way that he did. Others noted acidly that it was easy for rich women like Jacobs to sing the praises of "slums," because they were not the ones actually crowded into aging houses—they had the money to occupy whole buildings that poorer people had to share with other families. Before the term "gentrification" was even termed, they noted she was a gentrifier.

But what Jacobs realized was that this system of "planning" would inevitably fail, because what made cities successful was the people living in them, using the streets, not the people who drive in from far-off suburbs each day. The way planners tried to rebuild cities, and their obsession with solving "the traffic problem," was like bloodletting to cure disease: It in fact worsened the situation, but people persisted with it out of lack of imagination. "What if we fail to stop the erosion of cities by automobiles?" she asked. "There is a silver lining to everything. In that case we Americans will hardly need to ponder a mystery that has troubled men for millennia. What is the purpose of life? For us, the answer will be clear, established and for all practical purposes indisputable: The purpose of life is to produce and consume automobiles."

Long before planners realized it, Jacobs had realized the problem of "induced demand" that roads create. This is also known in effect as Jevons paradox. That is, if you make something more abundant, the price of it will fall, and people will use it much more than they previously did. William Stanley Jevons was an English economist in the nineteenth century who looked at coal. Jevons noticed that when James Watt improved the efficiency of the steam engine, so that it did not need anywhere near as much coal to use, the result was not that demand for coal fell. Rather, it meant that running steam engines was much cheaper, so people did it much more. In a similar way, increasing the amount of road space does not lead to less congestion. Rather, it increases the number of cars.

The problem, Jacobs recognized, was not the cars themselves. "We blame automobiles for too much," she wrote. The problem was in fact the planning that designers, obsessed with the car, insisted on. "Highwaymen, traffic engineers and city rebuilders, again, face a blank when they try to think what they can realistically do, day by day, except try to overcome traffic kinks." She pointed out that before the car was even invented, traffic jams of horses and carts sometimes snarled up the streets of London and left the streets encrusted with manure. Replacing that traffic with cars was actually a good way to improve the city.

The problem was that, because running cars would inevitably become so much cheaper than feeding a horse and owning a cart, there would be far too many of them. Instead of replacing each horse with one vehicle, cities replaced each one with six—or more. Le Corbusier, in his "Radiant City" plans, had imagined wondrous elevated freeways, but he had done no actual calculations to work out how many would be needed. "His vision of skyscrapers in the park degenerates in real life into skyscrapers in parking lots," Jacobs wrote.

Jacobs recognized, in a way that Lewis Mumford, Le Corbusier, and the other visionary planners of the time did not, that segregating traffic and people would in fact just create barriers, chopping up a city into smaller parts. And as that encouraged more people to drive, it would only worsen it. "Because of vehicular congestion, a street is widened here, another is straightened there, a wide avenue is converted to one-way flow, staggered-signal systems are installed for faster movement, a bridge is double-decked as its capacity is reached, an expressway is cut through yonder, and finally whole webs of expressways. More and more land goes into parking, to accommodate the ever increasing numbers of vehicles while they are idle." It all adds up, she wrote, to a positive feedback loop. The more the city was changed to accommodate cars, the more people would want cars, and the more the city would have to change further still.

In 1968, the campaign against the Lower Manhattan Expressway culminated in a public meeting organized by the New York State Transportation Department. The crowd chanted "We want Jane." Jacobs stormed in and delivered an address, denouncing the road. "This city is like an insane asylum run by the most far-out inmates," she declared. As the meeting wore on, it turned into a sort of riot. Protesters tore up the stenographer's record, meaning that the meeting could not be counted as having been done, and the project might be delayed further. "There is no record, there is no hearing, we're through with this phony, fink hearing!" she shouted. And then she led the crowd to the exit, where she was promptly arrested. "I couldn't be arrested in a better cause," she told a *New York Post* reporter waiting at the doors.

That was the beginning of the end of the project. In 1969, Mayor John Lindsay canceled the project entirely, citing a lack of community support. In 1970 Congress passed the Clean Air Act and New York City, it quickly emerged, was not in compliance. Even without a new raised expressway crossing Lower Manhattan, the existing traffic had turned the island into a gas chamber. In one city at least, the turn against the car was finally beginning.

And the backlash was not only in New York. Jacobs's model was adopted elsewhere. The highway revolts, as they became known, managed to do something remarkable. They united white liberals with Black working-class communities against an overly powerful government that seemingly cared nothing at all about the neighborhoods they were wrecking. In Washington, D.C., protesters argued against "White Roads through Black Men's Homes." They succeeded in stopping the construction of a ten-lane highway that would have cut the epicenter of the city's Black life, along U Street and Shaw, off from the rest of the city. In Boston in 1969, 2,000 people gathered at the State House with posters reading "Ban the Belt," and by 1970, the governor of Massachusetts, Francis Sargent, promised to cancel the road.

Even in Chicago, a city that certainly did not escape much of the redlining and car-driven destruction of the period, one highway revolt succeeded. Charlie Roche, a fifty-year-old Irish immigrant, managed to rally a coalition that included the Catholic Church, Black Protestant ministers, activists inspired by Saul Alinsky, and others to stop the city's imperious mayor, Richard J. Daley, from building the Crosstown Expressway, which would have run north to south through the city's western neighborhoods. The money was instead used on the Chicago Transit Authority, which had been created in 1947 to take over the city's ailing elevated railway system.

Highway revolts spread worldwide. In the 1970s protesters stopped the construction of highways through Amsterdam, Utrecht, London, and Melbourne. In the Netherlands, activists led protests against the ever encroachment of the car onto city streets under the banner "Stop the Child Murder." Hundreds of children cycling together blocked roads to car traffic. Amsterdam now feels like a city that never had much traffic to begin with—with its beautiful pedestrian boulevards and elegant cyclists on heavy upright bikes. But look at pictures of it from the late 1960s and you will see roads choked with cars. The activists managed to turn it around completely. In London the "Homes Before Roads" movement put up eighty candidates in the Greater London Council elections of 1970. Though they did not win, the Labour Party, which was in government, adopted their views—and killed the London Motorway Box.

New York had the chance to do more than just avoid the worst damage of car dependency. It could have become a world leader, not just an American one. In the 1970s, Sam Schwartz—he who invented the term "gridlock"—was one of the first city officials worldwide to propose congestion pricing. In his book *Street Smart*, which is part memoir, part polemic, Schwartz recounts that when he started in New York's department of transportation, he felt like a traitor. He was a Brooklyn native who grew up without needing a car and preferred cities in which people could get around by public transport or just by walking. Most of his colleagues were "car guys," graduates of highway engineering programs, and they felt "secure in the knowledge that their only job was moving cars faster."

When I interviewed Schwartz, he told me, in his thick Brooklyn accent, how the passage of the Clean Air Act created the ideal conditions for change. The city had to, by law, improve its air quality, and the only way to do that was by reducing the traffic coming into the city. "We had an incredibly enlightened mayor, John Lindsay, who was a Republican, and we had a Republican governor, Nelson Rockefeller. Both were moderate, but Lindsay, he was pretty far to the left when it came to city planning issues," Schwartz recalls. Lindsay gave him a surprisingly wide remit to try out new ideas. "We felt we had a green light from the mayor to develop strategies that would meet the demand for the Clean Air Act," he says. These strategies included closing Prospect and Central Parks to cars, and opening the roads through them up to bikers and pedestrians. Some streets in Brooklyn and in the financial district were pedestrianized. Parking rules were tightened.

But that was nothing compared to what they wanted to do. By the mid-1970s, Schwartz had managed to persuade Lindsay of a bigger idea. That was to introduce tolling on the bridges into Manhattan. Most of those bridges had not been tolled since 1911. "At that time, I hadn't heard the term congestion pricing," recalls Schwartz. But he had heard of an economist, a man called William Vickrey, who had argued that drivers ought to pay for the land they use. "He schooled me on congestion pricing." And Schwartz in turn schooled the city government. The city government and the State of New York passed a law imposing the new tolls. "I was as happy as could be, my city would be saved," he says. "The city had no money. This would be a revenue source that came from the wealthier people in the city. And nothing could stop it but an act of Congress."

Sadly, that was exactly what happened. Encouraged by protests from suburban New Yorkers, two Congressmen wrote a bill that killed the tolling. One of them was Daniel Patrick Moynihan, a senator who, a decade before, had adeptly argued that it was family breakdown causing problems in African American society, rather than the ghettos created by the combination of racism and automobiles. Mayor Lindsay was succeeded by Abraham Beame, who had no interest in rolling back the rise of cars. Schwarz had to content himself with engaging in what he says was "the role of Deep Throat within the city," leaking documents to environmental groups to help push his plans. Quietly, he widened sidewalks and eliminated parking where he could. He even let a road through Prospect Park in Brooklyn grow over. But congestion charging was put on ice.

Highway revolts stopped more motorways being built, especially through city centers. But they did nothing to dismantle the ones that had already been constructed. Once people had cars and had moved to suburbs, they wanted to use them. And by the 1970s, suburbs were emerging as the most important political territory in America. Whereas urban party machines could reliably turn out Democrats, suburbs were where the swing voters lived (and still live). So Congress bent to their desires. Only now, fifty years later, is New York finally coming around to implementing what was proposed then. And it is still being held up, mostly by concerned suburbanites.

In the end, Jacobs's legacy is mixed, because while she stopped the Lower Manhattan expressway, and contributed to the stopping of many other destructive motorways, she also was one of the first NIMBYs—Not In My Backyard. Her critique of city planning at the time is hard to fault. But it is fair to say that she was not exactly clear on how to adapt cities either. The Greenwich Village she idolized—with its disparate industries—was going to change with or without the expressways, because of the growing economies of scale and new technology. Some passages of *The Death and Life* read a little like paeans to a world in which people made their livelihoods in fairly back-breaking ways.

And the accusation that she was a gentrifier is the most biting—because it was true. She arrived in Greenwich Village when it was a working class, semi-industrial neighborhood and began the process of converting it into a rich one. Not everyone can live in a lovely nineteenth-century townhouse in a city center while it still retains the density necessary to support all of the street life she so admired. Then, it relied on people sharing homes and having very little space. If you are going to have density while still ensuring that people have a reasonable amount of living space, occasionally you need to demolish some old buildings and build bigger ones. Jacobs's home, at 555 Hudson Street, last sold in 2009 (at the bottom of the financial crisis) for $3.5 million. Now it would likely sell for a few million dollars more. Her protest depended on the interests of the relatively rich and engaged, so it contributed to an ideology which opposed change of any kind.

In America especially, but even in Europe, the city neighborhoods that were saved by the highway revolts were relatively few in number. Jacobs did an incredibly good job of arguing for the defense of cities, but she did not offer much of a solution for how to produce new ones. And as populations grew—which they did all over the world, rapidly, throughout the postwar era—and people got more prosperous, they needed more space to live. The result, inevitably, was that the neighborhoods saved by Jacobs and her ilk became more exclusive. In cities such as New York; Washington, D.C.; London; and Amsterdam, the neighborhoods that were seen as overcrowded slums in the 1950s are often now incredibly popular, precisely because they are not wrecked by cars as everywhere else has been.

And since the car has already penetrated cities around the world, Jacobs's tactics now end up being flipped upside down. Now, protesters against new housing that would reduce car parking space in places like Los Angeles, or give priority access to buses over cars, do so using Jacobs's rhetoric. The same NIMBY tactics that stopped highway construction are increasingly used against railways even, such as HS2, a new high-speed train line being built across England to relieve the congestion on Britain's overcrowded Victorian railways, and so allow more people to take the train between cities instead of driving. Just as Jacobs did in Lower Manhattan, activists are flooding meetings, bombarding politicians with letters, and even camping out in woodlands trying to protect them.

At least the HS2 objectors do seem to genuinely care about the impact on ancient woodlands. In Lower Manhattan, less than two miles from where Jacobs once defended Washington Square Park from destruction, people are now defending a parking garage from developers who want to build housing there. Suddenly parking is a "community asset" too, which cannot be built over without the consent of existing residents—or in reality, those residents who can be bothered to turn up to public meetings or hire lawyers, who tend to be the ones who have cars. Acres of asphalt are being defended with the same tactics used previously to defend actual neighborhoods.

And yet, when it comes down to it, Jacobs recognized—at a time when almost nobody else in power did—that planners in big city offices cannot distill what a city ought to look like into architect's drawings and models. Cities are fundamentally not composed of buildings, roads, or railways, but of people, and people react to the environment around them. The planners of the day had one aim: to accommodate the automobile. But they failed to realize that if you make space for cars, people will fill that space with cars.

In 2014's *Dark Age Ahead,* Jacobs's last book, she offered a bleak critique of America's development over the previous half century. She argued that it was "not TV or illegal drugs but the automobile has been the chief destroyer of American communities." Unfortunately, it was not just American communities. Or indeed just those of the rich world. We have never in fact completely unlearned the habit of trying to solve the problems of "traffic" rather than those of people. Indeed, the worst mistakes of the 1960s are already being made again, in the fast-growing cities of the developing world.

6

THE NEXT FRONTIER

Jane Jacobs was writing in the 1960s, at a time when mass car ownership—anywhere—was a new thing. But there are parts of the world today that are only now going through what cities like New York, Chicago, and London began going through a century ago. If you look at the most densely populated places on Earth, most of them are big cities in the developing world. Places like Manila, the capital of the Philippines; Dhaka, the capital of Bangladesh; and Mumbai, the financial capital of India. If you want to get a sense of where the car is coming for next, it is worth visiting one of them. Mumbai (formerly known as Bombay) is a good place to start. The city has a population of roughly twelve million people packed into an area of 233 square miles. That gives it about the same population density as Manhattan, but over the entire city, including the suburbs. The area covered by the islands—the original city—is more crowded still. It is a city where you never find yourself on an empty street. Everywhere you go, there are people occupying space.

Mumbai, I strongly suspect, is probably one of the most stressful places to drive on Earth. I do not say this from personal experience, or not exactly. I never once sat behind the wheel of a car in my time living and working in the city. That is because, as most Western firms do for their expatriate workers in India, *The Economist* employed a driver for me. His name was Govind, and he was one of the loveliest men I have ever worked with anywhere. Each day he would come to my apartment in Bandra, a neighborhood just north of the island proper that was originally built as a pleasant suburb in colonial times, to pick me up in his car, a Toyota minivan. In this vehicle, originally bought for a predecessor who had a rather larger family than me, he would ferry me to meetings about the city, as well as run errands for me.

But I can speak about what it looked like from the passenger seat. Driving in Mumbai means navigating almost constant traffic, which consists not only of cars and buses, but also rickshaws, men pulling carts, motorcyclists, cyclists, pedestrians, and even the occasional herd of emaciated cows being gently led through the heart of the city. At all times in most of the city, there is the sound of car horns as drivers try to negotiate their way through, with varying degrees of aggression. Traffic lights are unreliable, and instead police officers man most intersections, blasting on whistles as vehicles weave around them. The roads are full of potholes, and during the monsoon season, which lasts typically from June until late August, the streets can often flood several feet deep, making them invisible to the motorists. Stranded vehicles with flooded engines are a relatively common sight.

Ordinary people do not wait for walk signals, because there aren't any, or at least, there aren't any that anybody in a vehicle pays any attention to. They simply walk out in the streets in front of vehicles, and frankly, I did not blame them, because otherwise nobody would ever be able to cross. Every now and again, in my neighborhood at least, I would see somebody—a Bollywood star or a tycoon, I liked to imagine—in some extraordinarily expensive sports car trying to navigate through this and wonder why on earth they would bother. What do you get out of driving a Ferrari at 10 miles per hour, hooting at people ahead of you pulling handcarts? When I was walking, knowing that I had the privilege to do so without getting run over, I would often make a point of not getting out of the way of a particularly entitled car owner. Poorer Mumbaikars have less choice.

Never before or since have I wrestled with so many conflicting feelings about my daily transport. On the one hand, I did not really want to be ferried around quite as much. Where I lived was a fifteen-minute walk from a train station, where I could hop onto reliable (if crowded and sweaty) trains that would take me up and down the city rather effectively. I was acutely aware of the fact that by sitting in my air-conditioned car, with Govind hooting away at traffic, I was adding to the unlivability of Mumbai. And if I did not need to arrive somewhere looking fresh, I rather liked taking public transport. It made me feel a little less of a cosseted foreigner, and it even shocked a few wealthy Indian friends. On the other hand, we employed Govind, and I did not want him to feel like his work was not valuable, or that his job might be at risk. So I let him take me most places.

Yet the reality is that almost anybody earning a similar salary to me in India has not only a car, but also a driver. The tricky relationship wealthier Indians have with their drivers, in fact, is almost a cliche. Aravind Adiga's 2008 novel, *The White Tiger*, covers it well. It is about a teenage boy who escapes his miserable village by becoming a driver for a wealthy Indian American and (spoiler) ends up murdering him. I never thought that Govind was going to murder me, obviously. But I was acutely aware of the inequality in our relationship. All of it mediated through the car. Had he not worked as a driver, in his day-to-day life Govind would almost never have gotten into a car. As a member of India's rising lower middle class, he owned a motorcycle for his own travel, on which he rode into the city each morning to pick up the car, thereby avoiding traffic.

And the traffic in Mumbai is completely awful. Some studies reckon it is the most congested city on Earth. Yet this is a relatively new phenomenon. As we made our way across the city, Govind would frequently remark about how, when he started out as a driver in the early 1990s, it was never as it is now. When you travel down what is Mumbai's most iconic route, Marine Drive, a two-mile promenade that Salman Rushdie described as "a glittering art deco sweep" of which "not even Rome could boast," it is now invariably thick with cars of all sorts. Clips from the 1980s that you can find on YouTube show only a few stately Hindustan Ambassadors—the only cars available in India for most of the post-Independence era—moving at a far faster clip down it, against a sky that is remarkably bluer than the present haze visitors to Mumbai have to endure.

The cause of this is an astonishing explosion in car ownership. In 1981, Mumbai had only 320,000 registered cars on its roads. It took until 2000 to reach one million. By 2018, the figure had passed three million. And yet the city's road space has not grown. Indeed, it hardly could, so densely jammed in are people already. The one exception to this is near where I used to live, in Bandra: the Bandra-Worli Sea Link. The Sea Link is a toll road, built at a cost of $300 million, that runs on pillars over the Arabian Sea, connecting Bandra to the original islands of Mumbai. It is an engineering miracle, and Govind and I used to drive across it often. But the trouble with the Sea Link is that it funnels more cars into the city than otherwise could even enter. At either end, you immediately hit traffic again.

The costs of this congestion are clear. India is a country where only a third of the population live in cities. Most of the population continues to live in backbreaking poverty in villages. If more people could move to cities, living standards would increase enormously. One of the things I have learned, reporting from poor countries all over the world, is that while the countryside is where food is grown, perversely, people are generally much less hungry in cities than they are in the countryside. That is because people in cities earn more.

And so why do more people not simply move to cities to get jobs? One of the reasons is simply the sheer amount of congestion. What congestion does, in effect, is shrink cities. My rent in Mumbai, for a modest two-bedroom apartment in Bandra, cost more than the rent on my three-bedroom apartment in Chicago. It cost more in fact than the typical Mumbaikar family earns in total in four months. And yet that typical Mumbaikar family already earns more than four times more than what rural Indians make. If the rent were cheaper, more people could live in the city and earn such relatively high salaries. Or, since Mumbai is already so incredibly densely populated already, a better way to put it is, if more people could commute into the city in a realistic amount of time, then more people could earn those higher salaries.

To illustrate this, I asked a friend, the freelance journalist Abhishek Kumar, to speak to some Mumbaikars about their commute for me. One of the people he spoke to was a forty-year-old consultant named Akhilesh Mattoo, who lives in Thane, a suburb to the northeast of Mumbai proper. Akhilesh is practically an elite, in Indian terms. He is wealthy enough to own a car, something that 90 percent of Mumbaikars cannot afford. But he does not use it to get to his job in Navi Mumbai, another new suburb being built to the east of the city proper. Instead, he takes a rickshaw. "I will go crazy if I take my car," he says. "Ghodbunder Road is so unpredictable that I can't say what time will I reach." The advantage of the rickshaw is that its driver can weave around traffic and take occasional shortcuts across unpaved roads. Even so, the commute can still take two hours per day.

Most Mumbaikars cannot afford a rickshaw to take them to work. They rely on the trains, which have not been updated much since the colonial era, or on buses, which get stuck in the ever more punishing traffic, and which are almost as old as the trains. That means that fewer people can realistically get to work from the places that they can afford to live. Instead of taking relatively highly paid jobs in the city, they are forced to work nearer to their homes, at much lower wages.

The proliferation of cars makes it harder, not easier. Akhilesh keeps his car mostly for local errands, but even he sees the problem with the numbers of them. "Look I am not blaming anyone for owning a car," he says. "Everyone wants a luxurious life . . . But the point here is about sustainability. We have reached the tipping point." The trouble with a lot of luxury, unfortunately, is what makes something luxurious is exclusivity. And in India, car ownership is less exclusive than it was.

Decades ago, when my driver Govind was first starting out, the only cars you could get in India were the Hindustan Ambassadors, which were based on a British design from the 1950s, the Morris Oxford Series III, and manufactured in a plant near Kolkata (formerly Calcutta). Foreign imports were mostly banned. Car ownership was tiny—there was one vehicle on average for every 200 people. By the early 1990s, however, India began to open up its economy. And in the 2000s, it went into overdrive. Now, even Indians on relatively modest incomes can get loans to buy vehicles. From 2009 to 2019, the number of vehicles in India as a whole tripled. The biggest sellers have been motorbikes. But cars are following closely behind.

According to the International Energy Agency, the number of cars in India could grow from its current level of around 22 per 1,000 people to almost 8 times that by 2040. That would give India 175 cars per 1,000 people—still a fifth of the level in the United States. And yet even at that still relatively modest level, without similar investment in roads, the country would grind to a halt. All of India would have to transform, perhaps even more radically than America or European countries did in the 1950s and '60s. For people to be able to use them would require a vast investment in suburbs and roads, which most Indians simply cannot afford. And the country might simply not have the space. With 1.4 billion people, India is already incredibly crowded, without adding hundreds of millions of cars. And an enormous amount more CO_2 would be emitted, adding to the climate change that is already making large parts of the country literally too hot to live in without air conditioning.

Indeed, even with its current low level of car ownership, India is already suffering enormously from the pollution. As India has industrialized, the sheer amount of particulate matter has grown such that living in Delhi is said to be like smoking fifty cigarettes a day. Not all of the pollution comes from vehicles. Much comes from India's coal power stations and from things like farmers burning crop stubble to clear fields, as well as from woodburning fires used for cooking and staying warm. But vehicles are the primary cause. "The primary source of anthropogenic NMHCs [non-methane hydrocarbons, or particulate matter] in Delhi was from traffic emissions," according to one extensive study published in *Faraday Discussions*, the journal of the Royal Society of Chemists, in 2020.

What India needs to invest in is making its cities livable without requiring so many cars. And in fairness, it is, rather more than a lot of places. Mumbai is building an enormous new Metro system to augment its colonial trains. The Delhi Metro has grown from literally nothing in 1998 into a network 216 miles long that today carries 1.9 billion passengers per year, or more than the London Underground. Even some relatively smaller Indian cities such as Bhopal and Jaipur have metro projects. But the trouble is, for the Indian middle classes, traveling by car remains a status symbol. And so road building is also a huge priority. Indeed, many of the newest suburbs being constructed are essentially built for cars. Go to somewhere like Noida, on the outskirts of Delhi, and along the new highways you will find enormous new apartment complexes, with huge underground garages and car parks. By the time they fill up, and their owners manage to fill their parking spaces, the roads will be too crowded for the cars to be much use.

To get a sense of the problem, I spoke to Reuben Abraham, a native Mumbaikar who runs the IDFC Institute, a think tank with bases in Mumbai and London. He told me that one of the problems that his country faces is essentially political. If you look at a city like Mumbai, he says, "the most widely used form of transportation, are actually your legs. Most people walk. In some form or fashion. And yet if you look at how the city is being built out, it is as though the primary form of transportation is actually cars." The reason, he says, is "the classic Mancur Olsen problem." Mancur Olsen was an American political scientist who wrote about how exploitative governments arise. That is, in short, "a powerful organized minority will always trump the interests of the majority." And the powerful minority wants cars.

That is why some of the biggest projects in Mumbai, such as the Sea Link, are for cars. In fact, the leaders of the state of Maharashtra, home to Mumbai, are so proud of the Sea Link that they are building another, farther north from the original, from Andheri, a suburb north of Bandra. The idea is that they will connect to form part of a new "Coastal Road," an eight-lane motorway proposed to travel along much of Mumbai's western seafront. Computer renderings show a plan that looks not unlike the Katy Freeway in Houston. That is, enormous elevated roads with thousands of cars zooming along it, and enormous curving interchanges, running for twenty-three kilometers. If it looks a little like an American project from the 1960s, that is no coincidence. The original idea was proposed by an American transport consultancy, Wilbur Smith Associates, in 1962.

Nikhil Anand, an anthropologist based at the University of Pennsylvania, described the coastal road project to me as not a real proposal, but rather "a dream." He notes how in the mockup videos, and unlike in real life, the traffic is always moving at high speed. "All of these dreams are related to ideas of progress and modernity," he told me. "But they're also related to the special interests of construction companies and industries that expect to make huge amounts." That combination of construction industry interests and the windscreen dreams of a car-owning elite is what produces motorways everywhere.

To be clear, investing in roads in India is not an inherently bad idea. India could benefit enormously from a more extensive road network, says Abraham. Projects like the Sea Link, and even the Coastal Road, could be incredibly useful in helping more Indians travel to their work. The trouble is what they are used for—that is, transporting a privileged minority in their own individual cars. A much better solution, he says, would be for the roads to be used for transport that benefits most people—in particular, buses. Indeed, instead of investing in big, expensive Metro projects, many Indian cities would do better investing in their bus networks and giving them priority on the roads.

"Buses are way cheaper!" he says. But officials do not like them, for precisely that reason: Unlike other big construction projects, they do not generate big contracts with the possibilities for kickbacks.

At the moment, bus travel in most Indian cities is pretty miserable. I used to catch them occasionally myself, in Mumbai, and the typical bus was an ancient double decker, of the sort used in England half a century ago. The paint was peeling; bits of metal were falling off; and fares were collected by conductors, who had to squeeze themselves through passengers who crowded not just into the seats but also the aisles. There was never air conditioning. You got off sweaty and stinking. The buses are, in fairness, cheap, at around five rupees (or about seven cents) per ride. But nobody who can afford otherwise ever uses them by choice. (I was a strange aberration.) Hence why the emerging middle classes buy motorbikes as soon as they can afford them, and then cars when they get even richer.

In Mumbai, car owners act with almost total impunity. Parking is incredibly scarce, but people with cars simply leave them wherever they can, often just on the streets used by ordinary people. When poor people occupy land without paying for it, Abraham jokes, "it's called squatting, when the rich do the same thing, it's called parking." And just as they can avoid having to park their cars properly, the rich and powerful can also avoid being punished for driving dangerously.

Unfortunately, it is not only India that is suffering from this elite motorhead syndrome. In Nairobi, an enormous new bypass has been constructed with funding from China's EXIM Bank, as part of a project to create a new ring road to the city and motorways into its center. The city has in fact repeatedly tried to ban not cars, which are used only by the rich, from its city center, but rather, the *matatu* minibuses which transport most Kenyans. The plans are invariably withdrawn after protests. You can find similar stories all over the world.

The trouble is, the number of cars on the streets of developing world cities is only going to keep growing. You might imagine that traffic congestion would eventually force the leaders to stop it. Indeed, that is what has belatedly happened in parts of China, where in a few of the biggest cities, strict rules now govern who is allowed to buy a car. A few much poorer countries, such as Ethiopia, impose hefty import taxes on vehicles, which also usefully limits congestion. But most poorer countries seem unable to stop the growth in cars. Indeed, they do not want to stop the growth. What is bad for society as a whole can still be good for individuals. If you are a young professional in a city such as Lagos or Jakarta or Delhi, it still makes sense to buy your own vehicle if you can afford it, because the alternatives are so utterly awful and local leadership has no interest in investing in them. So the number of vehicles on the road proliferates.

And governments, seeing the roads jam up with cars, decide much as European and American ones did in the 1950s and '60s that they have to accommodate them. Hence, ever more road-building projects. These are in turn supported by international organizations, such as the World Bank and the European Union as well as European and Asian aid and development agencies, which give or lend money to poor countries to build more roads, inevitably hiring contractors from the donor countries. In Kenya, for example, America has lobbied hard to fund a new motorway connecting Nairobi to Mombasa. For sure, outside of city centers, more roads are mostly a good thing in countries that lack them. They mean that more farmers can get their crops to market, and more people can migrate to cities for work. But the benefits are quickly lost when they also just enable more of the relatively wealthy to buy cars.

If you look at middle-income countries—places like Brazil, South Africa, or Indonesia—they all have cities that are as congested as Mumbai. And their economies are stagnant. In São Paulo, the financial capital of Brazil, the traffic is so bad that many of the richest get around by helicopter. The city has 500 helipads and a fleet of around 700 helicopters, the biggest in the world. Ordinary people, who now own almost half as many cars as Americans, spend their days stuck in traffic. São Paulo has the world's second longest commuting times, with drivers spending an average of forty-three minutes each way getting to work and public transport users well over an hour. A huge amount of economic growth has been squandered, with the extra income that people are earning being spent on sitting in traffic on ever-more polluted roads, instead of on actually living better lives.

And those people who cannot afford cars are worse off still. They often have to walk on the roads to get to work, because there are no sidewalks. Street lighting is often nonexistent. The result is that even with relatively low levels of car ownership, traffic collisions kill more than one million people globally, almost all in poor countries. Air pollution worldwide now kills around seven million people per year, according to the World Health Organization, of which 4.2 million are killed by pollution outdoors. Most die as "a result of increased mortality from stroke, heart disease, chronic obstructive pulmonary disease, lung cancer and acute respiratory infections."

Big numbers can be difficult to process, but for comparison, according to my employer, *The Economist*, which developed a tracker of "excess deaths," roughly eighteen million people were probably killed worldwide in total by the coronavirus pandemic in 2020 and 2021. So outdoor air pollution kills half as many people each year as coronavirus did—year in and year out—and yet we shut down our economies to prevent COVID-19 from spreading, but with air pollution we often carry on as though it is normal—an acceptable risk. The reason is partly that the vast majority of deaths happen in the poorest countries. A map of PMI 2.5 levels worldwide—that is, the tiniest sort of soot particles that can penetrate deeply into a human being's lungs—shows that they are highest almost entirely in the poorest countries. But even in rich countries, because air pollution kills slowly, not quickly, it is easy to ignore.

The cars that ply the streets of cities such as Kinshasa or Yangon are not the relatively clean, efficient, modern vehicles you get in Paris or New York. They are generally cars abandoned by western consumers years or even decades ago, and exported to poorer countries where things like safety inspections and pollution rules are less onerous. In Kenya, for example, the law says that vehicles that are older than eight years cannot be imported. But since the car industry in the country is essentially nonexistent, and few Kenyans can afford new cars, that just means that the cars that are imported are exactly eight years old (or, if the right palms are greased, older still). Every December importers rush to bring in cars built eight years previously to beat the deadline, which updates every January. And because they are expensive to import, old cars are never taken off the road, even after decades.

If countries like Kenya and India were richer, they would probably enforce stricter regulations on vehicles and vehicle pollution. But as we will see, even rich European countries often struggle to do that. Car manufacturers do not exactly make it easy. Sadly, it seems as if poor countries are simply repeating what happened in rich ones. Indeed, the American Department of Energy publishes on its website data about car ownership worldwide that tracks it relative to the historical figures in the United States. Almost everywhere in the world is climbing toward American levels of car ownership.

And is that surprising? America is the world's cultural leader. These days it does not export many vehicles itself, but it exports its ideals. Anywhere you go in the world, people watch American movies and see Americans living idealized suburban lives, driving from their grass-fronted homes to their downtown offices along beautiful freeways. The idea that car ownership offers independence, freedom, and prosperity is taking off in the poor world even as it looks increasingly hackneyed in the rich world. The lessons of the 1950s and '60s are simply being ignored; the modernism of that period, the assumption that if you just build enough road space, it will all work out, is incredibly popular. The wealthy elites of the world's poorest countries inevitably spend time in America. They send their children to school there. Worldwide, fifty-eight serving monarchs, prime ministers, and presidents were educated in the United States, and fifty-seven in Britain. What do they take away, but the idea of what cities ought to look like?

There is still a hell of a long way to go. According to the International Energy Agency, in 2019, there were 1.4 billion cars on the roads worldwide. If the world matched American levels of car ownership, that would grow to more than eight billion. If you assume that most of them would be powered by gasoline or diesel, CO_2 emissions just from transport would increase by at least three times the deeply unsustainable levels the entire global economy produces already. Even if you imagine that they will be powered by electricity, where will it be generated? Solar and wind are growing, of course. But the biggest fuel for electricity in most of the developing world is still coal. And those countries have enough energy needs already without adding millions of electric vehicles to their grids.

Sadly, we in the rich world have set a poor example. But we can perhaps set a better one. There are places that are beginning to find ways of living with cars less, and reversing the trend of the past.

7

ELECTRIC DELUSIONS

The city of Kolwezi, in Lualaba province in the south of the Democratic Republic of Congo, is not a place you will expect to find many electric cars. The population is around half a million, but it feels much smaller. At the center is a grid of wide avenues, sided by handsome but crumbling bungalows. The tallest building is the cathedral, leftover from the 1950s, when this was the industrial heart of the Belgian Congo. The roads are mostly rutted, and some are little more than mud tracks. You want a big four-wheel-drive car to get around—something like a Land Cruiser. A Tesla Roadster, all low slung, would get stuck quickly. That is if you could find a place to charge it. The electricity goes out often, and most businesses run diesel generators to keep the lights on.

And yet any electric car you buy in America or Europe will likely have a piece of Kolwezi in its battery. Barely a mile out of Kolwezi's city center, the mining starts. The entire landscape has been transformed. Huge earth banks rise out of the ground, like the motte of a Norman castle, except in fact they have been excavated, not built up. On every road, you see young men on bicycles and small motorbikes carrying improbably large sacks full of minerals. In the Luilu River that runs through the city, women wash off the earth. And along the main highway, for a distance of perhaps a mile, depots where Chinese buyers purchase the product line the sides of the road. Farther outside the city, the landscape is dominated by huge industrial mines, run by Glencore, an Anglo-Swiss firm; Eurasian Resources Group, a firm from Kazakhstan with a headquarters in Luxembourg; and several Chinese firms, where trucks and giant diggers cut the ore out of pits miles wide.

Kolwezi is the biggest site in Congo for the production of copper and cobalt—key ingredients in the lithium batteries that power everything from your mobile phone to your electric car. Cobalt makes up between 3 percent and 20 percent of a battery by weight. Since car batteries are much bigger than phone batteries, these days, it is electric cars driving most of the demand for cobalt. There's probably sixty-six pounds (thirty kilograms) of cobalt in one car. And Congo is the world's biggest supplier of the metal. Roughly three-quarters of the world's supply comes from the country, which is one of the poorest in the world. Its reserves are genuinely incredible. Cobalt ore, a dull light blue rock, can often be found sticking out of the ground. There are neighborhoods in Kolwezi where the residents have dug it out literally from underneath their houses.

I went to Kolwezi because the car industry's promise is that it can fix the problems gasoline cars generate. In their telling, we simply need to replace most of our gasoline engines with electric motors. European law requires that by 2026, all new vehicles purchased by European governments should be electric cars, which it calls "zero-emission vehicles." By 2030 they want thirty million electric cars to be on European roads—still just 10 percent of the total, but a vast increase on the current figure of around 1.5 million. The motor industry has made promises that are just as ambitious. Ford has announced that all new cars sold by 2030 in Europe will be electric. General Motors has promised to make all of its new cars worldwide electric by 2035. So too have a host of other car manufacturers, from Jaguar Land Rover to Volvo.

And it is obviously not just the old car companies. There have been few hotter stocks in recent years than Tesla, the electric car company founded by Elon Musk, the world's richest man. In recent years the share price of Tesla has traded at roughly one hundred times its profits. The company, which as of 2021 makes just 930,000 vehicles a year, is valued more than the world's nine biggest car companies put together. That means that investors are expecting the firm to grow exponentially. By 2025, it will supposedly make ten times as many cars per year as it does now. By 2030, who knows? "We will not stop until every car on the road is electric," says Mr. Musk. Whatever the future is, it apparently involves electric cars.

I wanted to see what this would mean in Congo, where the materials for these cars will come from, at least unless mines elsewhere can be developed. Because it illustrates some of the problems with replacing literally every car on our roads with an electric one. Congo raises the question of whether it is at all realistic to make this change. And even if we can, what will it mean for places like Kolwezi? What happens in rich countries has ripples in poor ones. And already, even in the incredibly early stages, when electric cars account for just 2.5 percent of all new cars sold, there is a huge cobalt boom already underway that will have deeply meaningful consequences for Congo. Though manufacturers such as Tesla have promised to engineer out cobalt from batteries, so far, they have had only limited success. So as the electric car boom grows, Congo's importance will almost certainly grow too—more than half of the world's known reserves are in Congo, and the ore there is far richer than in the other places it has been found, such as Canada and Chile.

And it is far from clear that the consequences will be positive. Indeed, all of Congo's history, going back to the rubber and ivory booms of the late nineteenth century, suggest that environmentally, socially, and even economically, when people in rich countries need what is beneath Congo's red earth, it does not go well for the Congolese.

Copper and cobalt products make up roughly 90 percent of Congo's exports. In the past decade, as the sales of electric cars has begun to take off, the price of cobalt has roughly tripled. That in turn is spurring a new boom of investment in the mines around Kolwezi. Yet very little of this money gets to ordinary Congolese people. Across the country GDP per capita is about $600 per year; roughly four-fifths of the population lives on less than $1.25 a day. In Kolwezi, even as billions of dollars are pulled out of the ground, people live mostly in crudely constructed shacks with corrugated steel roofs, no electricity, and no running water. To understand why the wealth does not flow to the people, you have to understand how the mining industry works in Congo.

First there is industrial mining, done by large firms such as Glencore, which supplies Tesla, and China Molybdenum, which supplies many other firms. Those firms raise money in London or Beijing, and they acquire licenses from the Congolese government to mine. They bring expensive equipment, expertise, and management from all over the world, and set up camps for their workers, with catering, healthcare, and even schooling. The upper echelons, the engineers and the mining experts, are invariably mostly expatriates—in the case of Glencore, South Africans, Americans, and Brits; with the Chinese firms, Chinese workers. The Congolese are drivers, machine operators, and the like. Industrial mining employs at most a few tens of thousands of Congolese people, but it accounts for at least 80 percent of the output.

The second type is what academics call "artisanal" mining—artisanal meaning crude, rather than fancy and handmade like the "artisanal sourdough" you might buy in Brooklyn or Santa Monica and carry home in your Tesla. The artisanal type of mining accounts for 15 to 20 percent of production of cobalt (and more of other minerals, such as gold) in Congo. But it employs perhaps as many as two million people, or one in twenty Congolese adults. They work chopping minerals out of the ground by hand, in the sort of mining that would be familiar to the Victorians. Or the Romans even. In Kolwezi you can see these mines from the road. Deep holes are cut into the side of hills with shovels. The ore is broken up by hand, and then carried down on people's heads, to be loaded onto motorcycles or bicycles.

There are problems with both types of mining. While industrial mining is extremely efficient, in Congo, the allocation of mining permits is riddled with corruption. In theory, Gecamines, a state company, is in charge of issuing permits and licenses to explore and mine for cobalt, and it should sell to the highest bidder. The royalties generated should flow to the Congolese state, to invest in infrastructure, and spend on education, healthcare, and the like. But little of that happens. What actually happens is that politicians find ways to make sure that the money flows to them, personally. In Congo, the way that has worked has been through a middleman, Dan Gertler, an Israeli billionaire who is a close friend of Joseph Kabila, Congo's president until 2019.

According to the United States Treasury, which put Mr. Gertler under Global Magnitsky Sanctions in 2017, Mr. Gertler used his friendship with Mr. Kabila to "act as a middleman for mining asset sales in the DRC." In doing so, he siphoned off billions of dollars of money meant for the Congolese state. The Treasury department reported that just between 2010 and 2012, Congo "lost over $1.36 billion in revenues from the underpricing of mining assets that were sold to offshore companies linked to Gertler." Mr. Gertler disputes that claim. But there is no doubt that he and his friend Joseph grew rich.

Congo suffers what economists call a resource curse. It is a bit like the old cliché of a man winning the lottery and ending up miserable, but on a nationwide level. Countries that stumble on rich natural resources often end up extremely poor. This is no coincidence. Rather, it is because natural resources support a political economy that couldn't exist any other way. The lottery winner might blow it on champagne. So too can whole countries. In Kinshasa, Congo's capital, supermarkets stock jeroboams of champagne priced in the thousands of dollars. There are plenty of fancy restaurants and half a dozen five-star hotels. They all cater to the political elite. Because that elite get their resources from the mining boom, rather than from taxes, they see little incentive to invest in things that might improve the lives of ordinary people, like schools or roads. And the problem with the electric car cobalt boom is that it only intensifies that dynamic.

For ordinary people in Congo, life is extremely expensive, because corruption pervades everything. Food, beer, even mobile phone credit: They all cost more than in other African countries like Kenya or Tanzania, and often more even than in rich countries. In a country with some of the most fertile land on Earth, where drought is close to unheard of, twenty-one million people are close to starving, according to the World Food Programme. More than three million children are "acutely malnourished," which means that they may die. Even products that are produced in Congo, like coffee, are expensive, because the cost of getting them to market is so high.

So what can ordinary Congolese people do to get something out of the electric car boom? Some workers get jobs at the smart hotels in Kinshasa; a few might drive trucks at the mines. But for most people, the industrial economy happens without them. It barely touches their lives. And this is where artisanal mining comes in. With no means of getting a share of Congo's mineral wealth through the big firms that dig it, many Congolese instead turn to digging it themselves. To get a sense of it, I met a lawyer called Donat Kambola Lenge, known as Master Donat. Donat is an activist who works to investigate the wrongdoings of industrial mining firms, and the poor conditions that artisanal miners face, and there are few better guides to Kolwezi than him.

He took me out to a neighborhood called Kapata, where many artisanal miners live. It is a scrubby place. Originally built by Glencore for its workers, there are some modest but decently built houses, and the streets are wide. But these days the population has grown enormously and lots of new shacks have been built, as more people flock to what Donat calls an "El Dorado." But of course the reality of El Dorado was that it was mythical. People flock to Kolwezi hoping to make a lot of money. In fact, they are barely surviving. Bernard Tshibangica, one of the miners Donat introduced me to, explained his situation, in the eloquent French of the Congolese. "Life, it's full of problems," he said. "Children go to school very little. There is no medicine. We are abandoned. There is nothing here at all." Some people who come to Kolwezi to make riches end up returning to the fields to farm crops. But for most, "there is nothing to do other than mining."

"The buyers are monopolists," said Claude Mwansa, another miner, sitting on the earthen stoop outside his home. "When the price falls, it falls here. But when it goes up, it does not go up for us." Almost all of the buyers of artisanal cobalt ore are Chinese middlemen, who sell it to smelters at home. Each one can typically operate as the sole buyer in an area because they are protected by local politicians and the police, who stop miners from transporting their ore to other areas.

And mining is dangerous. The pits sometimes collapse, killing everybody inside. Or the diesel pumps that refresh the air at the bottom fail, forcing the men at the bottom to scramble out as quickly as they can before they run out of oxygen. When there are accidents, there is almost nothing in the way of compensation. Mr. Tshibangica told me that if you are injured, your colleagues in the cooperative will usually put together enough cash to pay for your hospital treatment. "But after that, there is nothing. If someone is injured for life, there is little we can do."

It is also poisoning even for those not directly involved. A study in the *Lancet*, the British medical journal, published in 2020, found that children who grew up in a neighborhood with artisanal cobalt mining in Lubumbashi, another mining city in southern Congo, had incredibly high levels of arsenic, manganese, lead, copper, and even uranium in their urine and blood. Working in mining, for both fathers or mothers, was associated with a much higher risk of birth defects in their children.

If the "Democratic" Republic of Congo lived up to its name, and like Norway, or Australia, managed its natural resources for the benefit of the public, a cobalt boom might even be a good thing. But it doesn't and it won't, probably for a while. Toward the end of my trip to Kolwezi I met a politician, Theo Mafo, who had been in Kolwezi for decades. He is not one of the elite Kinshasa politicians making it rich from mining. "All of Kolwezi is copper," he told me. "Everywhere you put your shovel there are minerals. There is so much treasure." But "all the industrial miners have left the population in poverty." The big problem, for Mafo, is politics. "We need leaders who are genuinely responsible. There are people in this country who eat five times per day, and those who eat once every five days." Cobalt just fuels that.

All of this is not to say that we should not still manufacture electric cars. On a technological basis, there is a lot to like about electric cars. Internal combustion engines do not just dirty the air. They are also a really inefficient use of energy. The clue is in the word "combustion." Most of the energy they generate from gasoline comes in the form of heat, not motion. Electric motors by comparison convert a vastly higher proportion of their stored energy into momentum. Per kilojoule put in, they are roughly three times as efficient as traditional cars. And of course, that electricity can come from renewable sources. Without electric motors, it is hard to see how we will ever reduce the enormous and growing share of carbon emissions put out by transport. We also cannot clean our cities' polluted air without getting rid of diesel and gasoline engines, which put out more than just carbon dioxide. Electric cars by contrast offer the chance to convert renewable or nuclear power into motion.

But the problem with electric cars is that, for all of their technological advantages, they are not a panacea that will fix all of the problems with our cars. Cobalt mining in Congo is just the beginning of the problems. Electric cars are still cars. Each one will still fill up the same amount of road space as a gasoline car. They can still hit pedestrians, and thanks to those batteries, they will be all the heavier when they do, and so more likely to kill. Their faster acceleration if anything makes more them more dangerous. And they still generate pollution too. There may be no exhaust emissions, but when tires rub on tarmac, they release particles that are just as bad for the lungs as the ones that come out of the engines. According to the British government's Air Quality Expert Group, dust from tires and braking account for half of the dangerous particulates produced by vehicles. None of that will disappear when the engines are converted to electric motors.

More than that, for all of that energy efficiency, electric cars still use a lot of energy. According to data gathered by the European Union, an electric car with one passenger uses around four times as much energy per passenger mile as a high speed train (even though the train is going much faster). That creates one big problem: We will need a lot more power to charge all of those cars.

A 2018 study by the US Department of Energy estimated that American electricity consumption could increase by 38 percent by 2050 to account for the needs of electric vehicles. That is on top of the extra capacity that will be needed to replace the natural gas we use to heat our homes, cook our food, and so on. And the reality is, most countries in the world have been struggling to decarbonize electricity grids at a time when demand for electricity is actually falling. Wind farms are brilliant, but there are too few of them, and many people dislike the sight of them. Solar has similar problems. Germany, one of the world's great petrolhead countries, has managed to increase its renewable electricity supply to roughly 45 percent. But it still relies on coal for almost a third, which it does not plan to phase out until 2038. Worse, Germany is phasing out nuclear power, which is clean, but deeply unpopular. So those electric cars will surely be fueled at least in part by the emissions of coal power plants. For now, electric cars are powered overwhelmingly with the energy of fossil fuel plants.

This is no small thing. According to the Department of Energy's Alternative Fuels Data Center, running on the average for America's grid, where coal still provides 22 percent of electricity and natural gas a further 38 percent, an electric car driven a typical distance over a year produces roughly 4,000 pounds of CO_2, against 6,250 pounds for a hybrid car or 11,425 pounds for a traditional gasoline-powered car. That is not a huge gap, especially given the higher carbon costs of building those electric cars. Worse, the Department also produces figures state-by-state, and if you pick a state where coal is the primary source of power, electric cars actually produce more CO_2 than hybrids (pure gasoline cars remain worse), because as much as electric engines are more efficient than gasoline ones, coal is far worse a source of energy than oil. In Kentucky, for example, where more than 70 percent of electricity is still generated with coal, an electric car driven a typical distance produces nearly

8,000 pounds of CO_2, substantially more than the hybrid. In West Virginia, where coal provides 90 percent of power, the electric car produces 9,000 pounds of CO_2. That is not much less than the average resident of New York City produces in total, on everything, not just driving.

The use of coal to generate electricity has been declining, of course. But that has been helped by the growing energy efficiency of household electronics and the like, which has reduced demand. Electric cars threaten to reverse that. In the United States a typical home uses around twenty-eight kilowatt hours of electricity a day. Charging up a Tesla with a 100 kWh battery uses almost four times that. If a commuter drives eighty miles a day—which is not unusual in America—they will have to do one full recharge roughly every four days. Their car will double their domestic electricity usage. At the moment, with electric cars still rare, many grids across America and Europe are struggling. So for electric cars to successfully reduce transport emissions by a lot, we will need radically different electricity grids.

With clever management of grids, it could be mitigated. Turning on the charge when wind turbines are spinning fast in the middle of the night is a good way to use up excess clean electricity charging cars, for example. But motorists who are used to being able to fill up whenever they want may not easily switch to charging only when an app tells them they should. They will also resent the difficulty and cost of using superchargers when they run low, especially if these are charged appropriately with the pressure they put onto the grid.

We could confront these problems. But for politicians, it is easier not to. The problem is that electric cars are popular precisely because they provide an excuse to avoid doing harder things, like rebuilding our cities, or changing the habits of lifetimes. Persuading people to switch from their old gasoline car to a shiny Tesla is much easier than persuading them that they can live without a car. Hence governments are pushing electric cars, often with incentives that make no sense. For example, in London, electric cars get a 100 percent discount on the congestion charge, and in Westminster, the center of the city, they also get street parking at a discount of up to 96 percent on the normal price, even though they cause the same amount of congestion and take up the same parking space. These inducements might encourage some people to switch from driving gasoline cars to electric ones. But they are at least as likely, if not more likely, to encourage people to switch from public transport, or cycling, or walking, to driving.

Western governments are unwilling to fix the fundamental problem, which is that we have built our societies around automobiles, not people. Until we reimagine how we actually should live, the problems that having so many cars create will not be going away, however many of them are electrically powered.

And there is a bigger problem with electric cars. Or rather, with the idea more generally that technology will get us out of the environmental disaster that is mass car ownership without people driving any less. People like Elon Musk do not limit themselves to wanting to replace internal combustion engines with electric motors. If they did, that would be rather admirable. The trouble is, they go further. People like Musk argue that we can do away with things like public transport altogether. They posit a future where every human has not only an electric car but also a self-driving one, complete with its own home-entertainment system, a sort of perfect robot taxi, ready to take you anywhere automatically at the touch of a smartphone. And frankly, it is nonsense. Indeed, it is worse than nonsense. It is actively an enemy of real progress. Let me introduce you to the concept of bionic duckweed.

8

BIONIC DUCKWEED

Imagine, if you will, that scientists came up with a miracle pill. Something a little like an antibiotic, perhaps, but for almost any illness. Genetic therapy, let's say. Cancer, heart disease, depression, dementia, you name it. Imagine if everything could be cured with a simple, mass-produced pill. Everyone would live full, happy, healthy lives until they clocked out quietly in their sleep at the age of 105. What would it mean for society? Well, the obvious one is that we need not worry any more about running hospitals, or nursing homes, or research centers for cancer treatments or whatever. Pretty quickly we could simply almost get back the entire chunk of GDP devoted to healthcare. We would be a lot richer.

Now imagine that we knew the invention of the pill was just around the corner. For the next ten years, for sure, disease will carry on, but pretty soon, it will be abolished. So what would we do then? Well, we probably wouldn't close our hospitals. But would we carry on training new doctors, knowing that they would be redundant in a decade? Would we keep on building new facilities for elderly people to live in, if they would simply empty out? Investment in the entire healthcare industry would stagnate, as people waited for it to be replaced with the miracle pill.

Finally, imagine that you are a politician, or a journalist, or a billionaire—somebody of influence, anyway, who would rather not pay taxes for the maintenance of all of that healthcare infrastructure. Somebody, let's say, who thought it was all a bit of a waste even before the miracle pill. If you heard about this impending bit of technology that would render everything redundant, that would suddenly make your preexisting opinions seem more arguable, you would scream about it from the rooftops. But then what happens if the pill does not work? By the time we realize, well, it's too late then. The doctors have already gone untrained. The hospitals gone unbuilt. Everyone is in trouble.

The "miracle pill" I am suggesting is a fairly outlandish example of what Stian Westlake, a fellow at Nesta, a British innovation charity, calls "bionic duckweed." He borrowed it from a railway engineer named Roger Ford, who in 2007 gave evidence to a committee in parliament about railway electrification. Britain's government, he said, had failed to invest in electrification on the argument that "because we might have ... trains using hydrogen developed from bionic duckweed in fifteen years' time," there would be no point. Bionic duckweed is, essentially, a technology that may never materialize, because it is not a real technology at all. Rather, it is an excuse to avoid doing something expensive now, like converting trains from traveling on diesel to using electricity.

There are occasionally real technologies that do emerge that render previous investments redundant. In fact, the internal combustion engine itself was one. By the beginning of the twentieth century, you would have been unwise to have invested in a business breeding horses, manufacturing carts, or cleaning up manure from roadsides. In Victorian Britain, there were more than three million working horses. Today the figure is a tenth of that, and of course, most are essentially posh pets. Similarly, at the turn of the twentieth century, you did not want to be in the business of manufacturing or selling pagers or landline telephones. Occasionally new technologies do come along that transform entire industries, and if you do not anticipate them, you may end up wasting a lot of time and energy.

But the thing about technology is that it tends to build on preceding technology. In fact, the makers of horse carts did not always go bust—many of them got into the business of producing motor vehicles. Similarly, pager manufacturers quickly became mobile phone manufacturers. Bionic duckweed is usually different to that, in that it promises something transformationally different, then when you examine it, does not hold water. The idea that we could extract hydrogen cheaply from biomass—literal "bionic duckweed"—is unrealistic when you think about the difficulty of extracting hydrogen from anything. It is typically an incredibly energy-intensive process that creates a gas that is then extremely difficult to store or transport. It would be brilliant if we could use hydrogen—which when burned, generates only water—to power more stuff. But it is very far away from being practical.

In the transportation sector, unfortunately, there is an awful lot of bionic duckweed. Electric cars, for all their faults, are not bionic duckweed. They are very real bits of technology that do, on the important measure of carbon emissions at least, starkly improve the damage done by cars to the environment. But much else is. Chief among them is the idea of autonomous, "self-driving" cars. According to their boosters, self-driving cars are about to change the planet. In December 2021, Elon Musk told a conference hosted by the *Wall Street Journal* that they are "absolutely coming," and "will be one of the biggest transformations ever in human civilization."

The idea is that when all cars are self-driving, they will be able to far more efficiently use the road space available, hugging each other like train cars. People will also be able to work as they get around, meaning that society will become even more hypermobile. Roads will supposedly become safer and more efficient. Because the computer in each car will communicate with the other cars around it, if one brakes suddenly, all of the others around it will know automatically that they have to brake too. The result will, supposedly, be a big increase is the capacity of motorways, as people no longer have to travel several car lengths apart for safety reasons. Already, this is used as an argument for why investment in new public transport, such as trains, is redundant. In Britain Matt Ridley, a Conservative member of the House of Lords who was chairman of Northern Rock, the only British bank to suffer a bank run in more than a century, is among those who reckon that HS2, Britain's new high-speed railway, will quickly be made redundant by autonomous vehicles. So too do the Taxpayers' Alliance, a group that opposes any government spending on anything.

In the immediate term, the problem with this is that despite decades of development, autonomous driving technology has scarcely improved enough to navigate normal suburban streets at 30 miles per hour. The thing about driving is that it is actually a rather taxing intellectual endeavor. You can program a vehicle pretty easily to follow a track, to make turns after a certain distance, or whatever. It is also easy to fit out cars with computers, radar, cameras, sensors, and the rest of it. But driving is far more complicated than that. Vehicles need to be able to assess the speed of other vehicles, and adjust for it. They need to be able to tell whether a mark on the road is a pedestrian or a shadow. They need, essentially, intelligence.

Creating a self-driving car is a question of programming a computer to be able to make decisions independently, accounting for hundreds of thousands of variables. And since these are potentially life and death decisions, involving vehicles carrying humans moving as fast as 70 mph, they have to be right, every single time. To achieve this, the developers have to rely on what computer scientists call "machine learning." Until relatively recently, most computer programs were essentially about pre-programmed logical decision trees. If A happens, do B. When I was learning to code as a teenager, the programs I wrote looked like that—a series of constant forks. Ultimately, that is how almost all computer programs work, even the most complicated video games. But it would be impossible to program a computer to be able to anticipate every possible event when driving. So they have to rely on the computer training itself, by making mistakes and being corrected. Trial and error.

Trial and error is not a great model for development when the errors involve vehicles weighing several tons traveling at high speed. Even in American cities like Phoenix, Arizona, where Google has experimented with its Waymo self-driving car project, they are yet to be proven to be safe. Tesla's self-driving features—its so-called autopilot—have led to so many crashes that the National Transportation Safety Board encouraged the firm to turn it off. "It's time to stop enabling drivers in any partially automated vehicle to pretend that they have driverless cars," said its chairman, Robert Sumwalt, in 2020. (In January 2021 Tesla responded by releasing a car with a video game console built in, which drivers can use while their car is moving—essentially two middle fingers stuck up at the regulators.)

That is why most of the attempts to develop truly self-driving cars have proven so difficult. Uber and Lyft, the taxi companies, had invested heavily in trying to develop the technology, on the basis that getting rid of the drivers was probably their best hope of becoming seriously profitable. But Uber abandoned its project in 2020 after spending $1 billion on it, selling its unit to a firm called Aurora. Lyft sold its own unit in 2021. An accident that killed a pedestrian probably pushed Uber to give up. Elaine Herzberg, a forty-nine-year-old, was wheeling a bicycle laden with shopping bags across the road when Uber's adapted-Volvo plowed into her. Investigators allege that the driver, Rafaela Vasquez, who was meant to be monitoring the vehicle, had been streaming an episode of *The Voice*, the reality TV show, at the moment of the crash. Uber settled a lawsuit; Vasquez has been charged with negligent homicide, though she pleaded not guilty, and the trial is still pending.

Some projects are still ongoing. You can take a Waymo taxi around a relatively smaller suburban part of Phoenix, Arizona, and unlike self-driving cars elsewhere, it does not have to have a driver. Phoenix is probably as perfect a city as you can develop for self-driving cars. It has 291 sunny days per year, which are less confusing to cameras than rainy or overcast days. It is also sprawling, with wide, fairly easy to navigate roads, with not many pedestrians or cyclists to have to navigate around. But the cars still struggle occasionally, getting confused by things like traffic cones. That is despite Google developing an enormously complicated map of the area, recording essentially every street sign, every traffic light, and anything else needed to guide the cars.

In a real city, rather than a perfect suburb, getting autonomous cars to work is far harder. The streetscapes of places like Manhattan are too complicated, and the number of pedestrians, other vehicles, and strange objects in the road is simply too high. For sure, Google does not think those problems are insurmountable. In November 2021, a few Waymo cars started driving around Manhattan, beginning the process of mapping the city. They were not automated, however; each car had two staff, one driver, and one person to manage the mapping technology. It will be years, if not longer, before they can deploy autonomously. Nonetheless, Eric Adams, New York's mayor, described the process as "holding the promise to dramatically improve traffic flow."

And that is kind of the problem with self-driving cars. They are perhaps not pure bionic duckweed. Eventually, Google or Tesla or some other competitor may be able to map enough of the world, and improve the technology enough that you really will be able to hop into a car with nobody at the wheel in quite a few cities. That, however, is many years away. And in any case, when self-driving car advocates argue that their rise will mean that technologies such as trains will be made redundant, or that traffic will be solved, they are almost certainly wrong. Self-driving cars still take up space. And however brilliant the engineers designing them are, they will simply never work well in the congested, complicated big cities of the world. Just think of a common situation where lots of individual cars come to pick people up—a taxi rank at an airport perhaps, or a school run. It is simply impossible to load that many people into vehicles especially fast, without using up lots of space, however efficient the cars are.

Funnily, at least one person has realized this—Elon Musk himself. In that *Wall Street Journal* interview, in which he described automated cars as one of the most transformational technologies human civilization is likely to invent, he went on to argue that they will also force America to come up with "something to deal with extreme traffic, he said. "As autonomous vehicles come to the fore, and it's easier to drive without going through the pain of having to drive yourself . . . there will be more cars on the road and the traffic will get much worse." He was quite right. And not even alone among car executives in realizing it. Bill Ford, the executive chairman of the Ford Motor Company, of all people, has also warned that autonomous vehicles could create "global gridlock" by 2050. "Our infrastructure cannot support such a large volume of vehicles without creating massive congestion," he wrote in a newspaper opinion piece in 2014.

If they ever do work, autonomous cars will prove so popular that they will quickly overwhelm our road capacity. Imagine, for example, if you did not need a parking space in your downtown office to be able to drive to work—if you could simply have the car drop you off and then drive out of the city to park, before coming back in later to fetch you? Suddenly you have doubled the amount of driving. People will start using them as delivery vehicles to run errands. Sam Schwartz imagines businessmen taking meetings in Manhattan sending their cars to drive around in circles rather than find a parking space. As the technology gets cheaper, more and more people will buy them, and use them for ever more outlandish things. It will be chaos. Jevons paradox will win again.

And yet, inevitably perhaps, given he is a car executive, Musk does not think that this means we should not all buy autonomous vehicles. Rather, the solution, apparently, is "some combination of tunnels and double-deckering freeways." He did admit that "flying cars" are not the answer, because people do "not want the skies to be swarming with helicopters." On that he is right, despite the vast sums of money being poured into the development of "flying cars" using the sort of quadcopter technology now used for smaller drones. "Flying cars," if they ever work, will at best provide service only for the superrich, allowing them to skip traffic jams while the rest of us struggle in them, like the superrich already do in São Paulo. The less said about them the better. But if Musk thinks the skies being taken over by helicopter is bad, apparently he still thinks entire cities being taken over by car infrastructure is fine. We would end up with the world imagined by John Adams in the 1980s, in which every patch of land is covered in tarmac.

Musk, however, thinks that he has the solution. Apparently, he thinks that traffic can be "abolished" by creating a network of underground tunnels and elevators to carry people's Teslas up and down into them from street level. The idea is essentially that we can make up for the limited amount of land available aboveground by building what he calls a "3D" infrastructure below. The Tesla boss introduced this idea at a TED Talk in 2017. He began with a remarkable insight, at least for a car-industry executive, that most driving sucks. "One of the most soul-destroying things is traffic," he said. "It affects people in every part of the world. It takes away so much of your life. It's horrible. It's particularly horrible in LA." Against a video of cars being lowered onto essentially giant Scalextric tracks—Musk called them "skates"—he described a world in which you would be zoomed along at 125 mph underground below the city. "There is no real limit to how many levels of tunnel you can have," he argued, preempting the rebuttal that the tunnels would quickly fill up just as fast as the roads overground.

Despite how much I disagree with him, I think Musk genuinely is a visionary. And he has put more than just his voice behind this tunneling idea. In 2016 he launched the rather well-named firm, The Boring Company. Initially a subsidiary of SpaceX, Mr. Musk's space firm, the idea is that it might do for drilling underground tunnels what SpaceX has done for putting satellites into space. SpaceX has, it is fair to say, proven to be anything but bionic duckweed.

Its reusable rocket, the Falcon 9, which, unlike previous rockets, can actually land, has helped it to cut the cost of launching something into space dramatically. The Falcon 9 and its successor, the Falcon Heavy, accounted for twenty-six out of fifty orbital launches in 2020. It has helped contribute to a fall in the cost of putting one kilogram into orbit from around $18,000 twenty years ago to just $2,000 now. I would not put it past Musk to achieve some way of reducing the cost of tunnelling too.

And if he did, it would be an incredible achievement. Digging underground tunnels is one of the things that makes creating new public transport systems in densely-populated cities such as London and New York so expensive. The cost of Crossrail, for example, the new underground train line that recently opened in London, was £18.7 billion (about $25 billion), or about £2,000 for every man, woman, and child in the city. The Second Avenue Subway in New York, which will initially add just three more stations, is costing $6 billion. The vast majority of the cost in both cases was accounted by the difficulty of tunneling through the ground. Similarly, HS2, the new high-speed railway being built in Britain, requires an enormous amount of tunneling to avoid various villages and natural beauty spots. If Musk could somehow bring to tunneling the efficiency gains his space rockets brought to launching satellites, it would make transformative public transport investments look a lot more realistic.

The trouble with Musk's idea is not the tunneling itself (though I doubt it will be easy to reduce the cost of tunneling by anything like the amount you can reduce the cost of rockets), but rather the idea that you could funnel people in individual cars through them. It is simply a question of space. Take, for example, a single train on the Victoria Line in London. With a length of 133 meters, a single Victoria line train can hold around 1,000 passengers. A single Tesla Model S is just shy of five meters long, meaning that, bumper-to-bumper, you could fit twenty-six of them in the space occupied by one train. Even if each one held five passengers, that still gives you eight times fewer passengers than the single train. And obviously the cars could not actually drive exactly bumper-to-bumper, even on skates, nor would they be occupied by five passengers each. (The median car in Los Angeles has a driver and no passengers.) If you fill them with cars, as Musk imagines, for his tunnels to provide the same capacity for moving people per dollar, they will need to be at least ten times cheaper to dig. Even as you dig ever deeper.

Musk has in fact built a functional version of this transport system. It is in Las Vegas, and it runs for 1.7 miles, connecting various parts of the enormous Las Vegas Convention Center. The tunnel itself is rather fine—it is about the same size as the ones that make up the London Underground. But instead of rails, or even the electric skates that Musk's TED Talk depicted, it is lined with a road, and passengers are transported around it in individual Tesla cars. On its site, the Boring Company admits that the model is essentially "Teslas in tunnels." Each one, with a capacity of four tightly squeezed passengers, has to have its own driver.

The cars have to stop as they arrive, so that passengers can climb out and new ones can get in, which obviously generally takes longer than it does to get in and out of a train. The cars are limited to traveling at 35 miles an hour, a pace that sounds rather fast when you look at the narrowness of the tunnels. They have to be removed occasionally to charge, since, unlike with trains, the electricity cannot be supplied to them as they move. Hilariously, sometimes the cars even get backed up in the tunnel, causing a traffic jam. If you don't believe me, search on YouTube for Tesla tunnel traffic jam.

And the trouble with this is that it means that the tunnel is simply not very efficiently used. The Boring Company says that the capacity of the original first tunnel, to the Convention Center, is about 4,500 passengers per hour. By comparison, a single New York City subway station can handle 50,000 passengers per hour in each direction. Musk is sacrificing perhaps 95 percent of the potential capacity of his tunnels. And that figure of 4,500 is actually an optimistic estimate, since it assumes that every passenger is not traveling in a normal Tesla. According to Steve Hill, the president of the Las Vegas Convention and Visitors Authority, which runs the convention center, the plan is to replace the individual cars with "trams" able to hold up to sixteen passengers. In essence, Elon Musk has reinvented the subway train. Visionary, as I said.

The Boring Company is already planning a bigger network In Las Vegas. In October 2021 Clark County, which covers most of Las Vegas, agreed to a fifty-year concession with the firm to build it over the next fifteen years.

Supposedly the system will eventually grow to cover twenty-nine miles of tunnels with fifty-one stations. It will carry 57,000 passengers per hour and supposedly cost the Nevada taxpayer nothing. It will link the convention center to the city's airport, as well as to various casino hotels on the Las Vegas Strip and to a new football stadium.

And it is not just Las Vegas where the Boring Company intends to build these tunnels. Musk has apparently also talked to the mayor of Miami, Francis Suarez, about building one there. Suarez released a video in February 2021 promising a "project that will have the maximum utility for our residents for the least amount of money." Another is apparently planned for Fort Lauderdale, connecting the beach to downtown with a length of about 2.5 miles across. The prices being proposed by The Boring Company are remarkable. The Fort Lauderdale tunnel will apparently cost around $15 million per mile. Most tunnels cost at least ten times that (and even the Las Vegas tunnel cost at least five times that, by The Boring Company's own admission). Many people think it is unrealistic.

All of these are cities that currently have limited public transport. In Las Vegas, there is a monorail that runs the length of the Strip, used almost exclusively by tourists, and that is about it. In Fort Lauderdale, there is a bus network, as well as a train, that goes to Miami. In Miami, there are a couple of light-rail lines. Cars dominate all of these places, however. If Elon Musk could genuinely build a public transport system for cities like those, then he would deserve a lot of credit. But let's imagine that he does construct these tunnels. Having spent however many hundreds of millions of dollars building them, what makes more sense? Using them as efficiently as possible, by filling them with higher capacity vehicles (perhaps those "trams" could be linked together, to reduce the number of drivers)? Or filling them with individual cars? Similarly, as a passenger, which are you more likely to use? A single ticket, at perhaps the cost of a few dollars, to get into a "tram," or one perhaps ten times as expensive, but for your own vehicle?

I struggle to believe that even if Musk really does build out his tunnels, that he will keep building new ones, ever deeper into the ground, adding endlessly to the complexity, so as to simply buy people the comfort of avoiding other passengers. Musk has said that he hates using public transport because he worries about other passengers being "serial killers." But he is a billionaire. Other people have to assess costs. I genuinely think he may achieve a modest reduction in the cost of tunneling, but even if he does, it will be so incredibly obvious that using tunnels to transport private cars will quickly wipe out the gains. At best what he is offering is more traffic jams in tunnels.

9

WHY YOU CAN'T BEAT TRAFFIC

The morning of December 15, 1973, was not an especially eventful date. John Paul Getty III, the grandson of the oil tycoon, was released from his kidnapping. Idi Amin, the dictator of Uganda, launched a mocking "Save Britain Fund" with £600 of his own money. And in New York City, a road collapsed, proving, remarkably, that the amount of traffic congestion in a city is only tangentially linked to the amount of road space.

The road was the West Side elevated highway, one of the world's first "freeways"—that is, a road segregated from pedestrians and the street to allow vehicles to move faster, with grade separated crossings and entrance and exit ramps to connect it to other streets. It was built between 1929 and 1951, long before President Dwight Eisenhower set aside the money to build them all over America, and when it finally opened, stretching from the southern tip of Manhattan all of the way up to Seventy-Second Street on the Upper West Side, it became a symbol of New York's postwar vitality. Simeon Strunsky, a *New York Times* editorialist, described it as Robert Moses's best work. "The traveler comes and goes in a setting of beauty which [it] is not too much to call intoxicating," he wrote. It meant that tens of thousands of workers on Wall

Street and in the skyscrapers on the southern tip of Manhattan could travel down into the city in their cars.

Unfortunately (or perhaps fortunately), however beautiful it was, it was not especially well built, and it was worse maintained. That day in December 1973, as a heavy dump truck overloaded with nine tons of asphalt went over it, several of the supports failed, and the truck plunged onto the street below, followed by a car that was evidently following rather too closely. Sam Schwartz, who visited the site, says it looked as though a new exit ramp had been built. By sheer chance, nobody was killed—a rare miracle in the history of road collapses.

But it did cause an almighty traffic jam, at least on the day itself. The West Side Highway was not a lightly used route. Each day it carried around 70,000 vehicles up and down Manhattan. In a moment of immense, if accidental, foresight, just three months before, Mayor John Lindsay had begged drivers to try to avoid it, as it was so jam-packed. "If you try to use the West Side Highway in the next three months," he warned prophetically, "you'll regret it." Hundreds of vehicles had to reverse their way back off the road, over a period of several hours, with the drivers presumably wondering if their section of the tarmac might be next to falter. The City of New York then immediately closed the road, and for the next couple of decades it sat, derelict. Before it was finally replaced, in the 1990s, it was practically a perfect symbol of the Big Apple's decline.

What it also could become, however, is a symbol of how more roads do not solve congestion. When the road collapsed, one of the immediate fears of New York's traffic engineers was that the 70,000 vehicles it carried each day would reappear elsewhere in Manhattan, clogging up streets with more traffic. But in fact, after that initial jam caused by all of the cars trying to back up off the broken bridge, there were no more. The reality, as Schwartz wrote, was that "the predicted traffic disaster never appeared." The cars "went somewhere, but to this day we have no idea where." Over the next few years, even though the road had disappeared, the number of people traveling into Manhattan's southern business district actually increased. It just happened that fewer of them were doing so in cars.

This reveals something about traffic, and the problem of what is usually called "induced demand." At the margin, whenever they set out on a journey, people choose between different forms of travel. In a city like New York, where walking, bicycling, or taking the subway or bus are all plausible options for getting somewhere, most people have alternatives to getting in their cars. If you think that there will be a traffic jam, you might choose to take the subway instead. If you know that the road will be clear, you might decide to get into your car instead of taking the subway, or cycling, or whatever.

The result is that the level of congestion on a particular road is essentially priced in. How many lanes a road has does not actually have that much of an impact on how jammed up it gets. Instead, what determines the traffic level is what other options drivers have. Traffic jams stop growing at the point at which the marginal driver decides it would be better to walk, or to hop on a train, or to simply go somewhere else instead. So what happens if you expand a road by adding more lanes? Initially, people carry on with their old travel habits, and so traffic on the road speeds up a lot. But over time—perhaps just a few months—what happens is that people notice that they can get somewhere a lot faster on the new, wider road. Pretty quickly, congestion is just as bad as it was before—because that is the level of congestion needed to deter more people from driving.

There is relatively reasonable academic evidence for this effect, though the scale and context is often disputed. A study commissioned by the British Department for Transport (an organization which rather likes building roads) tentatively found that a 10 percent increase in road capacity probably induces about a 2 percent increase in the amount of driving, overall—that is, 20 percent of the growth is used up by more cars. That, however, was based on other studies that looked at whole highway networks (in this case, of the United States and the Netherlands), rather than specifically urban roads. It makes sense that induced demand is less likely to be a problem in rural areas, where everyone drives anyway, and cannot switch to taking a subway train instead. In urban areas, other estimates put the figure as high as 40 percent after six months and 100 percent after four years. That is, over four years, the entire extra capacity generated by a road expansion is used up again. Even the Department for Transport study found that "induced demand is likely to be higher for capacity improvements in urban areas or on highly congested routes."

Induced demand is not inherently a bad thing, obviously. If you build a road to, say, a rural village in Tanzania, you would hope that as a result, more people would use it, and so more residents of that village would be able to get jobs farther away from their homes, or more farmers would be able to sell their produce at higher prices in the city. But looking at congestion is a terrible way to measure the need for more roads, largely because using roads is generally free. If you give away something that costs money to provide, you will almost always get more demand than you can ever possibly meet. And if driving is too cheap relative to other ways of getting around, there will always be more demand to drive. That is why congestion is a problem in almost every big city on earth.

And when we look at cities in rich countries, the reality is that overall, we have almost certainly oversupplied the amount of road needed already. To take another American example, look at Louisville, the biggest city in Kentucky. There is a bridge there, called the John F. Kennedy Memorial Bridge, that crosses the Ohio River, on the I-65 Interstate highway, connecting Louisville to Jeffersonville, a smaller city in Indiana. In 2010, around 120,000 vehicles crossed the bridge daily, which had six lanes of traffic (three in each direction), and routinely got completely clogged up with drivers using it. So the highway engineers at the Kentucky and Indiana departments of transport decided that they needed to widen it. As reported by the City Observatory, a think tank based in Portland, Oregon, together the departments of transport put up $1 billion to build a new, second bridge (this one named for Abraham Lincoln), adding six more lanes. In 2017, when the bridge opened, to pay back the cost, they introduced a toll to cross both bridges—$2 for each crossing, with discounts for regular commuters.

And guess what happened? The number of drivers using the bridges fell, dramatically, to around 60,000 cars per day. It has never risen back up to its previous level. What this meant was that the extra lanes proved completely pointless. As the City Observatory reported, "the two states spent a billion dollars doubling the size of I-65, only to have half as many people use the bridge. That money was wasted." What happened to the extra cars? Much as with the collapse of the West Side Elevated Highway, it is almost impossible to know. But the most plausible explanation is that most of them switched to using the Second Street Bridge, another bridge across the river just a few hundred yards away, which had no toll. That adds several minutes to the typical commute, and more at rush hour, but it saves drivers a few bucks. The state departments of transport thought they were helping drivers by speeding up their commutes, but the drivers actually didn't care. When charged even a modest fee, traffic dropped away. There was already plenty of road to begin with.

There are plenty of other cases that show this is not a one-off. In the UK there is only one major toll road in the whole country, the M6 Toll, which bypasses Birmingham. This motorway was first proposed in the 1980s, when the original M6 motorway was already handling more than twice the traffic it was constructed for. In 2003, the M6 Toll opened to great fanfare, having finally been built by a private consortium, with the tolls intended to cover the cost. In a touch almost perfectly designed to appeal to tabloid newspapers, the construction involved pulping 2.5 million Mills & Boon novels (a brand of racy romance fiction sold in Britain) into the tarmac to aid with its water absorbability. It was expected to carry about 75,000 vehicles per day. In fact, even though traffic in the UK has increased consistently over the past twenty years since it opened, it has never got much above a level of 50,000 vehicles per day. During the great financial crisis of 2008, usage dropped to just 30,000 cars per day.

Studies of toll roads show that they almost always underperform the anticipated usage. America now has plenty of toll roads—mostly outside of urban areas. In the past thirty years, the revenue generated by the federal gas tax, which funded the original Interstate system, has declined dramatically in real terms, as politicians have refused to raise it even once in line with inflation. And so states have tapped into private money to build new highways. To fund them, the developers have to issue bonds—debt—which means that they have to reassure the investors that the road will generate enough revenue. Between 1994 and 2006, public-private partnerships spent $21 billion on toll roads in America. But according to Standard & Poor's, a debt rating agency, traffic is invariably overestimated by around 30 percent on average. "Optimism bias is a consistent trend in toll-road traffic forecasting," the firm reported in 2002. More recent studies agree. In 2014, the journal *Transportation* reported that "With rare exception, actual toll road traffic in many countries has failed to reproduce forecast traffic levels."

Traffic engineers cannot resist trying to fix congestion with one more road. The reason is exactly why you should not put engineers in charge of social problems, like how to get people around. They tend to want to simplify things down to single measures that they can try to change. In America, the key measure used is typically the speed of a journey. The logic is that if people can get from A to B faster, then they have more time left over to work, or spend, or whatever. They can also go farther distances, meaning that more people can realistically reach any given job. When a lot of people already drive, this produces a logic that always favors widening roads, or building new ones, because it speeds up the time spent in traffic. And time spent in traffic is straightforwardly time wasted.

Following this logic, lots of firms try to estimate the costs of traffic congestion. In America, INRIX produces estimates of how congested various cities are; TomTom, a Dutch firm that sells satellite navigation technology, produces its own index of congestion, looking at 416 cities. The most congested cities on Earth are generally in poorer places—Mumbai, Istanbul, and Bangkok all feature highly on TomTom's list. But some richer cities come up fairly high too, such as Moscow, Paris, and London, as well as Los Angeles and New York. INRIX estimates, for example, that congestion costs the US $88 billion per year, or around $1,500 per driver. In the UK they put the figure at £21 billion, an even more staggering figure than the US one, given that the UK's economy is so much smaller. From this, we might conclude that there is not enough road space for people to get around, and that the most congested cities in particular need more of it. That's what Elon Musk has concluded, for sure.

But what the reaction to road tolling—whether it is that bridge in Kentucky or the M6 Toll—shows is that these estimates do not really stand up. The actual "cost" of congestion is what people would pay to avoid it. If so many people refuse to pay even a relatively small toll to avoid being trapped in a traffic jam, then that suggests in reality, their productivity is not really being damaged anywhere near as much as the estimates suggest. Perhaps their journeys were not actually that important to begin with, or else there were perfectly good alternatives they were choosing not to use. This is an example of what economists called "revealed preference." It applies a lot to transport. Poll people and they say that they want wider roads to reduce congestion. And yet if you actually build those roads, you discover that they will not pay for them—their preference is revealed, and either people don't actually mind congestion, or they would prefer not to drive.

And so trying to solve traffic congestion by endlessly building more roads is not a good use of resources. There are almost no big cities on Earth where traffic congestion is not at least an occasional problem. For sure, in a few cities, the population has declined so much and the road space available is so high that almost no road ever gets jammed. Detroit, for example, is wonderfully easy to drive through, at least outside of downtown, because almost nobody else is there. But congestion is, to a point, a symptom of success. If you have it, it means that people live in your city and want to get around it. And it is people, not cars, that need to move around cities.

So the question is, when faced with congestion, what should we do about it? In general, the best way to reduce congestion is to charge a reasonable price for using the roads. If the price of using a road is put at a level where the people who need them most, and have no other realistic way to get around, can afford to reasonably use them, and there is still crippling congestion, then roads are probably in short supply. But if, as with the bridge in Kentucky, the result of charging is that congestion falls significantly, then you already had enough road space to begin with, or possibly too much. And even if it does not, you can then invest the money raised in improving public transport options, so that they do not need cars anywhere near as much. And would we not be better off trying to shift some of the traffic off the roads onto other forms of transport?

And yet that is almost never how city engineers and politicians think. As Jeff Speck, an urban planner, puts it, induced demand is "the great intellectual black hole in city planning, the one professional certainty that everyone thoughtful seems to acknowledge, yet almost no one is willing to act upon." The reason is because it is so bloody hard to think otherwise. Traffic congestion is one of those truly democratic things, in that it ruins people's lives all over the world. Whether you live in Manhattan or Mumbai, Jakarta, or Jacksonville, it sucks sitting in traffic. Even Elon Musk, who owns two private jets, knows it. And when you are sitting in a car, surrounded by other cars, the idea that a wider road would make things easier makes intuitive sense. It happens to be nonsense though. What would actually help you move along faster is if the other drivers were not there. And a relatively small toll is far more likely to achieve that than a wider road. When we give people extra road space for free, we are encouraging them to get around in a way that they would not pay for, for the most part. And we are effectively subsidizing the wrecking of our cities for anyone else.

As the experience with the West Side Elevated Highway showed, taking away road space does not necessarily reduce people's mobility. In fact, more people were able to get into Manhattan than before. If roads were limited to the sorts of trips that cannot realistically be done any other way—transporting heavy goods or machinery for example, or disabled people who cannot realistically get up and down subway platforms, or frankly, just transporting really rich people willing to pay the actual market value of the space they are using, then there would be much less congestion.

Any sane transportation policy would think in these terms—what transport do people value, and what would they be willing to pay for. We know that access to good public transport is something that people are willing to pay money for. Ridership on the London Underground did not change much with price increases. We can also see that people are willing to pay more for public transport, because the cost of housing in places with good public transport is so expensive. Roads, by contrast, are simply, well, not that valuable—at least relative to their cost—because we already have so many. That is why private businesses almost never propose to build them anymore, even though they're easier to toll than ever.

But then the problem of the overprovision of road space goes beyond just the roads that vehicles move on. After all, 95 percent of the time, most vehicles are not moving at all.

10

FREE PARKING, DO NOT PASS GO

When most people think of Los Angeles's architecture, they probably imagine some of the city's gems. There is Frank Gehry's concert hall downtown, a wonderful construction of curved steel intended to look something like a ship. There is the Getty Center, high up on the hills of Brentwood, overlooking the city. There is the Bradbury Building, a late Victorian wonder of ornate iron walkways featured in the final scenes of Blade Runner. And then there are any number of grand, modernist palaces of the sort that dot the Santa Monica seafront or rise up into the hills of the Pacific Palisades.

And yet, for many architects at least, the characteristic building of Los Angeles is none of these. It is in fact a far humbler building, known as the "dingbat." This is essentially a squat block of apartments, sitting on top of what Americans call a "carport." The lower floor is occupied by cars; the upper one or two floors by modest-size apartments, typically one or two bedrooms. The buildings are boxy, with wooden frames and stucco exteriors. Often they come with 1950s Americana stylings, with names such as "the Hansen" or the "Pink Flamingo" emblazoned on the outside in stylized italics. You see them often in movies set in Los Angeles, if you know what to look for. The

1998 comedy *The Slums of Beverly Hills* features a family forced to move constantly between dingbats.

The name was first put into print by Reyner Banham, a British architectural critic who fell in love with Los Angeles and its automotive spirit in the 1970s, though he credited it to Francis Ventre, another architect. In the 1950s and '60s, tens of thousands of these buildings were thrown together by developers to create cheap housing for the inflow of workers to California, drawn to jobs in the aerospace and manufacturing industries flourishing there. They are typically near roads, especially the freeways, which were also spread across LA during that period. They represent perhaps the archetypical automotive sort of property. They are both compact, in terms of the living area, while being sprawling, because of the space taken up by the roads and car parking.

They also owe their existence, in large part, to a prominent feature of LA's postwar planning. In 1958, the city required new apartments with more than "three habitable rooms" to have, on average, 1.25 parking spaces. So a block of twelve apartments would require fifteen car parking spaces. This restraint, strictly enforced, compelled architects to plan their construction not around the needs of the people who would live in the apartments, but more around the needs of their cars. According to Steven Treffers, an architectural historian, "Architects would typically work backward from these regulations, determining how many parking spaces could be provided based on the number of automobiles they needed to accommodate." And so the dingbat was born.

Hundreds of thousands of them had been built, sprawling out into the San Fernando Valley. They illustrate one of the quiet but enormous ways in which the car has shaped cities worldwide, especially in America. In the United States, as a rule, nothing is provided for free, with one major exception: parking. In almost every city in the country, planners work on the assumption that buildings need a certain amount of parking, and mandate it by law. The result is that entire cities are shaped around the storage of cars. Of course, this parking is not actually free. It costs an extraordinary amount of money. It is just not often paid for, at least directly, by the people using the cars. It is loaded on everybody else, in higher rents and less space.

Ironically, urbanists now praise the dingbat. Relative to what came after, it was actually rather efficient, and did provide relatively cheap housing, something now extraordinarily rare in Los Angeles, where the median rent for a one-bedroom apartment is around $2,100 per month. In 1965, the city raised the parking requirement again, to 1.5 spaces per apartment, bringing to an end much of the dingbat boom. Many apartments in the city are now required to have two parking spaces, not one. It is not just apartments. Office buildings come with parking minimums, as do retail stores. There are parking minimums for almost anything, in fact. It is not the free market that results in American buildings being surrounded by oceans of tarmac for storing vehicles, it's the law.

Read Los Angeles's planning documents and you get a sense of how this works now. It is exhausting. The West Hollywood municipal code dictates that, for example, "senior housing" (nursing homes) must have 0.5 spaces for every resident, as well as one space for guests for every 10 residents. How many nursing home residents should be driving? One-bedroom apartments must (on average) have 1.5 spaces, two-bedroom apartments two spaces, and homes with four or more bedrooms at least three. "Artisan shops" must have two spaces for every 1,000 square feet of floor space; it is the same for cannabis retail. Service stations must have a space (not including the one by the pump) for every single gasoline pump. Even ATM machines come with parking minimums: one space for every machine. Perhaps most insanely of all, points out Matthew Lewis, a Californian pro-housing activist, even bars have mandatory parking. "One law says you're not allowed to drive drunk, but another says you can park free at the bar," he exclaims.

Los Angeles provides, all in all, an astonishing amount of parking. According to one study, Downtown Los Angeles has 107 parking spaces per acre. If each one is around 250 square feet, that would be equivalent to two-thirds of the land. (Obviously, there are a lot of multi-level garages.) A majority of Downtown LA, in effect, is given over to cars.

There is one man, a softly spoken, bearded academic economist at the University of California, Los Angeles, who has documented this madness. His name is Donald Shoup, and I interviewed him at the UCLA campus, a lovely, green expanse that is only marginally—by the standards of the city—wrecked by its plentiful car parking (which is, as Shoup notes, not free but in fact carefully priced). I had been wondering why LA, a city that these days is dominated by liberals, had so struggled to persuade people to use its public transport network. From 2013 to 2019, even before the pandemic hit, the ridership on LA's buses and light rail systems fell by one-third. That happened even as the city opened several new rail links, such as the Expo Line, a fancy light rail system that links downtown LA to Santa Monica. Remarkably, LA's voters have repeatedly approved ballot measures to spend more money on public transport. What they seemingly will not do, however, is use it.

This was puzzling to me, but when I asked Shoup why, his answer was simple. Driving is just too easy, because by law, you can park near enough anywhere for free. "The city continues to morph toward at least one parking space per household, and sometimes one space per person," he told me. What these regulations do, he says, is make it seem as if driving everywhere is normal, indeed, what the market provides. "We're able to hide the cost of so many things through zoning regulations," he says. For all the money that the city pours into public transport in LA directly, it is a drop in the ocean compared to the implicit subsidy spent on cars, through the means of free parking.

In certain niche circles, Shoup is seen as a sort of urbanist prophet. A Facebook group for fans of his work, who call themselves "Shoupistas," has more than 5,000 followers. Interviews he does occasionally go viral online—one, with Vox, the D.C.-based policy website, hit more than four million views on YouTube. It begins with a clip of Steve Jobs, the founder of Apple, from 2011 talking about the firm's then new campus in Silicon Valley, and how it would be surrounded by gardens. What he did not mention was that it would also include 14,200 parking spaces for Apple's 14,000 workers, hidden in two enormous garages. They use up 325,000 square meters of space, or slightly more than the actual space occupied by the offices, laboratories, and the like. These were not part of Jobs's vision at all. They were mandated by the city of Cupertino.

Cities insist on the provision of free parking at offices and businesses so that cars do not clog up the streets, where parking is also often free. In the United States, these laws, known as "mandatory parking minimums," date back to 1923, when Columbus, Ohio, implemented the first one. They have proliferated ever since. To decide how many parking spaces to supply, planners often rely on the *Parking Generation* handbook, produced by the Institute of

Transportation Engineers (ITE), a Washington, D.C.-based group that was formed in 1930 to try to come up with solutions to congestion.

ITE does research essentially to establish the peak demand for parking for any number of different businesses and then sets guidelines to provide it. It is used not just in America but worldwide. There are parking minimum standards even in cities where car ownership is relatively low, such as Singapore, and in cities we think of as being relatively difficult to drive in, such as Rome or Milan. Even in cities that have abolished explicit minimums and replaced them with maximums, as in most of Britain, parking provision is still dictated by planners, who usually aim to hit certain "standards."

And yet, much like the estimates of traffic demand that highway planners come up with, the figures for parking are essentially based on pseudoscience. As Shoup notes, the engineers guide cannot tell you how much parking costs, or anything about how much drivers can pay. The studies they use are invariably taken at suburban businesses where almost every customer will arrive by car, and they are not even based on reasonably sized samples. Typically they overestimate the amount of parking that is needed to provide anyone arriving in a car with an empty space, even if you assume that parking is free. They do nothing to account for the fact that people can arrive at businesses by other means, such as walking, or cycling, or on a bus. Their assumption is basically that cars are a bit like liquid. For any given amount of liquid, you need a container that fits it. If you do not have a big enough container, it will spill out somewhere else. So they go and work out how many cars a particular business might generate if parking is free, and decide that is the demand.

The reality though is that cars are not like a liquid at all. They are like a gas. They inevitably expand to fill whatever container they are put in. Fast-food restaurants in, say, the center of Manhattan or London have no parking spaces at all, but they thrive—people walk to them, occasionally after taking a train or a bus. But in Los Angeles, people do not walk because parking is plentiful and free. For sure, a business in the middle of nowhere that does not have plentiful parking will probably fail. But in a big city, people have other ways of getting around. The more parking you provide, the more people will choose to drive everywhere. The result of parking minimums is a stupendous oversupply of parking spaces, to the detriment of literally everything else.

I have often met people in America—and elsewhere—who worry about the huge cost of subsidies for public transport projects. Angelenos are often skeptical of the city's light rail projects. The idea of building more railways is often dismissed as a way to throw away tax revenue on white elephants. Occasionally they are right. There are plenty of public transport projects you can point to that have not worked anywhere near as well as they should. Washington, D.C.'s new streetcar, in the Northeast of the city, has been a failure, doing extremely little to encourage public transport use even at spectacular cost. Dallas and Houston both have streetcar systems that are underused. Tram systems in America are often a problem for the same reason the old ones died—they have to share space with cars. In the UK, many worry about the ballooning cost of HS2, the first new intercity railway to be built since the nineteenth century, and about Crossrail, the latest new London underground railway, which opened more than two years late and went significantly over budget.

But this public transport investment is dwarfed by the enormous subsidy that governments everywhere give to driving, not only through free roads, to drive on and park on, but also through zoning regulations that force businesses to provide free parking. In America, 99 percent of car journeys involve free parking at the destination. According to Shoup's calculations, the cost of providing free or subsidized off-street parking in the US in 2002 was between $127 and $374 billion. As he points out, the total spending on every other aspect of transportation—road, buses, aviation, boats, and nearly everything else you can think of—was $190 billion that year. So free parking costs America somewhere between two-thirds and twice as much as it spends on all other transport infrastructure combined. As mad as it may seem, if you think about how valuable urban land is, it is not obviously wrong.

If you subsidize driving, people will do it. If you know you can park somewhere at the other end cheaply or, better yet, for free, why not drive? It is generally quicker and more comfortable than walking or cycling. If you have already invested in owning a car, it is probably quite a lot cheaper than using public transport too. Generously, if parking and the use of roads is free then driving a car two miles to go shopping may cost you sixty-five cents: twenty cents in gasoline, the rest in buying and insuring the car (costs that must be paid whether you drive it or not). A bus ticket the same distance could be two dollars.

But the actual cost of driving those miles is in reality far higher, in the cost of using land for parking that could be used for something else, such as housing. And because this enormous subsidy is hidden, people do not realize how much it costs them. You may not pay for parking when you actually park your car, but you pay for it in a thousand other ways. Shops and restaurants are more expensive because they have to have more land than they otherwise would to provide parking. Rent is more expensive because fewer homes fit onto any given plot of land.

According to one 2016 study of a number of large American cities, based on 2011 census data, the cost of providing parking adds roughly 17 percent, or about $1,700 to the average person's annual rent. Some of this is loaded onto people who cannot afford cars anyway—they pay for parking they cannot even use. If developers could use the land they use for parking instead of for housing, they could make more than the parking spot costs to provide. Housing would be cheaper. A win-win.

This pseudoscience of "planning" for traffic has spread across America, and indeed large parts of the rest of the world. Part of it is simply that the ITE presents its data very confidently, and planners often do not have much else to work with. Brent Toderian, formerly the chief planner of Vancouver, in Canada, says that in the early part of his career, he felt like he had to defer to the technical expertise of transport engineers. Later, he realized that in fact their precision masked a misunderstanding about how cities work. Engineers like relatively simple relationships, but society is not simple. That is why social science is not like physics, however much some economists would like it to be.

It is not only bad data that explains why free parking has spread so far. It also comes about because politicians are scared of drivers. When cars were few in number, it was relatively easy to provide street parking for free. Nobody thought to charge for it, and the parking meter had not even been invented. Almost by accident, rich countries invented a right to park your car wherever you want on the street for free.

The trouble with rights, though, is that it is much harder to take away something than it is to not give it out in the first place.

As Shoup told me, you do not need to think that there is some conspiracy of car manufacturers to force cities to provide free parking. People do it themselves. "What is genius is that their customers demand parking requirements and wide roads," he says. "They are demanding a world in which the automobile manufacturers are necessary. It worked out extremely well for the automobile manufacturers." In particular, he says, drivers are especially likely to attend public meetings to oppose new housing developments or changes to parking rules. That is because they benefit directly from free parking, whereas the costs for losers—the residents who might have lived in a new development—are indirect.

The provision of free parking has become almost a public-policy religious tenet in America. But people do not even realize that the near universal free parking available outside of cities like New York or Chicago or Washington, D.C., is the result of deliberate public policy. I told some friends of mine who lived in Los Angeles for years about parking minimums, and they had no idea. Most Americans I know seem to just take it for granted that businesses provide ample free parking—they think it is natural, because of course, everyone drives, so how could they not? But in fact, the causation goes the other way around entirely. Everybody drives because parking is free, and parking is free because politicians do not have the guts to say that maybe things should be otherwise.

In fact, for all of its automotive reputation, Los Angeles is not actually so bad, in terms at least of sprawl. It is at least constrained by geography—the mountains mean the city can only stretch so far. Measured over its full metropolitan area (not just the city proper) it is one of America's denser cities. Its core is sprawling, but compared with other cities, the outer suburbs are crowded. When cities get big enough, even if they rely on the car, they densify at least a bit just from sheer gravity—people have to live closer together because the alternative is driving for hours to do anything. Los Angeles is doing so because its businesses are so successful, and because it is such a glamorous, exciting place to live that people move there even though the cost of living is so extraordinarily high, and they cram into homes far smaller than anyone living in, say, Oklahoma, would accept. That in turn means that it can just about support public transport that, by American standards at least, is not completely awful, even if the vast majority of the population does not use it.

But many American cities do not feel much like cities at all. Cities are meant to be busy places, with people bumping into each other on the pavement. Go to somewhere else that developed mostly after the Second World War, such as Columbus, Ohio, or Lake Charles in Louisiana, and you will find essentially oceans and oceans of car parking space, and almost nothing else. Even large swathes of Chicago, where I live, are like that. I have visited cities where the parking lots are so large that the distance you need to walk from your car to wherever you need to be can actually be larger than the distance from a bus stop or a train stop would be in a place like Manhattan or Paris, which rather undermines the idea that driving is a convenient door-to-door solution.

As William Whyte, a sociologist, wrote in 1988, "in some American cities, so much of the center has been cleared to make way for parking that there is more parking than there is city. Some cities, such as Topeka, Kansas, have gone so far as to reach a tipping point. If they clear away any more of what's left, there would not be much reason to go there and park." It may sound like a joke, but that actually describes the reality of what has happened to many historic downtowns, in places such as Columbus or Milwaukee. Planners cleared more land for drivers, to be able to provide the parking necessary to compete with the suburbs, and in the end, they tore out the heart of the cities they were hoping to save.

The cost of having so much parking is not only the loss of land to use for other things. There are less tangible but still real costs too. When cities are spread out they work differently. In a place like Tokyo or Paris, you have the sense of being in a connected whole; businesses and homes sit cheek-by-jowl and interact with each other. You can go out for dinner and then walk across the street to a bar afterward. In cities dominated by parking that is not the case, because the businesses are surrounded by empty space and cars. Instead, each building is turned into a standalone entity, which people drive to and then drive away from without ever interacting with any of the other businesses nearby. Such places have less vibrancy; they are less cool. They are, I would also say, much uglier. There is a reason relatively few young people aspire to move to Dallas, whereas millions grow up wanting to live in New York, Paris, or Berlin.

In a walkable city, a supermarket on a commercial street also supports barber shops, cafes, pubs, and so on, because people combine their trips and visit several businesses at once. That does not happen when you have to drive between each one. Ironically, that is why businessmen invented the shopping mall, and the strip mall—so that people can re-create the experience of shopping in lots of different places after parking once. Until the rise of the internet, that was enough to make them powerfully successful.

When I spoke to Shoup more recently, I asked him whether it can be fixed—can the takeover of cities by free parking be undone? He pointed me to a lot of things that have changed, such as SF Park, a scheme in San Francisco where street parking prices are routinely updated to reflect how much people actually use the spots, so as to ensure that there are always parking spaces available at the right price, and that people do not have to spend hours driving around looking for an empty space, burning up gasoline, creating traffic jams, and polluting the atmosphere. During the COVID-19 pandemic, many parking spaces were given over to other uses, such as for outdoor restaurant space. Shoup does not think that will be reversed. "It leads to greater employment, greater sales taxes, and it looks great," he says.

His ideas have never been more in vogue. Even the ITE, after Shoup's decades of needling, has begun to question whether cities really need as much parking as they have been advising for half a century. Fears about global warming in particular are helping to press people to think about how to do without driving as much, something that Shoup finds strange, since climate change is surely less visible to people than air pollution and congestion. Across America, more and more cities are beginning to replace parking minimum rules with parking maximum rules—something most British cities did in the early 2000s. Even California has removed parking minimums near public transit stops.

But the trouble, in much of the world, is what Shoup and other economists call "path dependency." Or in other words, the decisions to prioritize driving were made long ago, and now American cities are so sprawling it is hard to pack them back in again. "What's on the ground is already so auto-oriented and people enjoy driving wherever they want to go," he says. "A place like Los Angeles, the total is so much less than the sum of the parts. There are so many wonderful things here but they're so far apart and the congestion is so terrible you just don't go there," he says. The change will happen, he thinks, but it will be gradual.

Nonetheless, it can happen. There are places in the world that are beginning to find ways of at least starting to reduce the number of car trips, lower their CO_2 emissions, and free their centers from endless choking traffic jams. Many of the most successful are in Europe, where it is simpler—a matter of restoring pre-car models as much as it is of finding new ones. I will come to that. But first, I want to take you on a diversion. Because I want to illustrate why the car industry will not help.

11

EVIL CARMAKERS

If you were a screenwriter trying to come up with a parody corporate scandal to illustrate the evils of a particular industry, you would struggle, I suspect, to imagine anything much worse than the one that engulfed Volkswagen in the early part of the 2010s. In summary: A company founded by Hitler, which was boosted by the use of slave labor during World War II, decides that to grow even further, it needs to create a gas chamber. Yet in 2015, in a lab in Arizona, that is exactly what happened. The victims, mercifully, were not humans, but monkeys, and the gas was exhaust fumes from diesel engines. In ten airtight glass boxes, ten macaques were exposed to the fumes created by a Volkswagen Beetle running on rollers—a sort of vehicular treadmill. To keep them calm, they were shown cartoons. Afterward they were sedated and their blood was tested.

    This was not a cruel joke. It was "research," commissioned by a lobby organization called the European Research Group on Environment and Health in the Transport Sector, known by its German initials, the EUGT, which in turn was funded by German car manufacturers, including Volkswagen. No results were ever publicly published, nor were the experiments ever acknowledged by the company—at least not until they were revealed in legal documents uncovered by the *New York Times* anyway. They were done as secretly as possible, because they were essentially part of a propaganda campaign. The point of this "research" was for Volkswagen to show that the cars it was selling in the United States in the 2010s generated only the purest air.

Car manufacturers do not normally commission such research. They are responsible for knowing what gases their cars produce and how much, but not what damage those gases do. But in 2015, Volkswagen was facing a growing crisis. For decades the firm had pioneered the use of diesel engines, usually used to fuel long-distance trucks, buses, and ships, in passenger cars. In 1999, the firm introduced the TDI engine, or Turbocharged Direct Injection, which promised the performance of a normal gasoline car, but with the much higher fuel efficiency of diesel. As concerns about cars' contribution to global warming was growing, this was a way to sell to environmentally conscious consumers. Because diesel engines run hotter than gasoline engines, and inject fuel instead of using spark plugs, they get more out of combustion. Essentially, the higher temperature means the fuel expands more quickly as it burns and turns into a gas, and so it pushes the piston harder. As a result, they generate less CO_2 per mile driven.

The trouble is, the same process that makes diesel more fuel-efficient also generates more polluting emissions of other sorts. The primary problem is nitrogen oxides. These form when nitrogen, which makes up about three-quarters of the Earth's atmosphere, fuses with oxygen to form nitric oxide and nitrogen dioxide, known together as "NOx," or just nitrogen oxides. Hotter engines turn more of the stored energy into movement. But at higher temperatures, more oxygen fuses with nitrogen. Nitrogen is harmless; nitrogen oxides, however, cause inflammation, and are particularly bad for children, elderly people, and asthmatics. A large study in California, published in 2016, that looked at 350,000 cancer patients over a period of fifteen years, found that exposure to nitrogen oxides drastically shortened their survival. When exposed to sunlight, nitrogen oxides also form smog. The earliest smogs in Los Angeles, in the 1950s, were clearly linked to the growing generation of nitrogen oxides by automobiles.

So why were scientists gassing monkeys? It was in part an attempt to try to demonstrate that nitrogen oxides are not actually dangerous to monkeys, and so by extension, human health. Helmut Greim, the scientist who chaired the EUGT's research advisory group, had repeatedly claimed to Germany's parliament that there was no proven link between nitrogen oxides and lung damage. The research was intended to rebut a 2012 decision by the World Health Organization that classed diesel exhaust fumes as a carcinogen. But it also went further than that. The researchers were always trying to show that their cars barely produced any nitrogen oxides anyway. In fact, the Volkswagen Beetles being used in the monkey gassing experiment had been deliberately rigged to produce less pollution than they would in normal operation on the road.

To understand why, you have to go back a few decades. In the 1990s, Volkswagen had built up sales of its diesel cars in Europe, where NOx emissions controls are less strict than in the United States, and fuel is much more heavily taxed. So when car firms began producing diesel engines for ordinary passenger vehicles, they were an attractive prospect, on fuel economy grounds. But as the number of diesel cars on the road grew, so too did concerns about exhaust fumes and pollution. Volkswagen needed to reassure people. So they claimed they had adopted new technology that allowed them to have diesel engines that were just as efficient, but still able to filter out the NOx and other emissions. The technology was the Lean NOx Trap, or LNT. A sort of beefed-up catalytic converter, of the type found on gasoline cars, an LNT pushes exhaust gases through a porous material that captures carbon particles and NOx.

Government officials were keen on the idea. An early enthusiast for "clean diesel" was Sir David King, then Britain's Chief Scientific Advisor. In 2001 he visited an emissions testing lab outside Cambridge where a catalytic trap had been developed by the chemical-technologies company Johnson Matthey. He saw that, despite his own asthma, he was able to breathe freely as cars ran on rollers. "I think they had about ten cars all up on ramps, and they were testing how much exhaust they produced. And it smelled like the cleanest room you can imagine," he says. Sir David, who was at the time working on a project within the British government to try to reduce CO_2 emissions from the transport sector, as part of the 1997 Kyoto agreement, advised the government to do more to encourage people to buy diesel cars instead of gasoline ones. That helped encourage Tony Blair's government to cut fuel tax and vehicle excise duty (an annual tax on owning a car) for diesel in 2001.

Volkswagen also wanted to break into America. From around 2006, a huge advertising campaign started to help sell the message. In one spot, shown, inevitably, at the Super Bowl, an American suburb was shown overrun by totalitarian "green police," arresting people for not recycling properly or for heating their houses too much. The ad ends with an Audi (part of the Volkswagen Group) driver being waved through a checkpoint where other drivers are being searched, because his car is "green" TDI diesel. By buying a Volkswagen, the marketing went, you could have the moral purity and fuel efficiency of driving a hybrid, like Toyota's Prius, or some other lightweight small car, while still having the sporty power of a big German car.

The trouble was, it was all a lie. Volkswagen had not in fact invented technology that made their cars effortlessly green while remaining powerful and efficient. An LNT does indeed clean up a diesel engine. But as Sir David explained to me, it comes at a cost. The problem with pushing exhaust fumes through a catalytic trap is that it slows the operation of the engine down. Every one hundred miles or so, you have to flush the buildup out of the catalyst, typically using fuel. "If you put an exhaust catalyst on a motorbike it slows it down. With a trap catalyst it's even worse." If you reduce the NOx emissions, you make a car less efficient, and give up the fuel economy benefits of diesel.

There is a way around this: As well as an LNT, you can use a urea tank to flush the catalyst instead. BMW had done that with its diesel cars. But that adds another thing for car owners to maintain—the tank has to be refilled every 10,000 miles. It also uses up space and adds several hundred dollars to the costs. Volkswagen, which was trying to compete with manufacturers like Toyota in a cheaper section of the market than BMW, did not want to do that: It would have made their cars more expensive, and added another bit of fiddly maintenance for buyers. So they came up with an easier solution: They cheated.

What Volkswagen had done was install "defeat devices" on their cars. In America, emissions testing is done by the Environmental Protection Agency (EPA). Cars are driven while their exhaust emissions are measured. But they are not driven on the road, because that is fussy and difficult. Instead the cars are tested on rollers, like the ones the cars gassing the monkeys ran on. On the rollers, the testers try to simulate road driving—hill climbs, stopping and starting, highway driving, et cetera. But what you cannot do when you are driving a car on a treadmill is turn. So Volkswagen installed a simple fix.

If the steering wheel was not turned, the pollution control in the computer—which determines how much fuel is used and how often to inject it into the engine—was fully operational, and the car hit its emissions targets.

The moment you started steering, however, the computer recognized that it was operating on a road, not on rollers, and so the pollution control stopped working. The NOx trap was in effect disabled the moment you turned the wheel at all, so as not to hit the efficiency of the vehicle. What this meant was that while "clean diesel" was filling up the roads—helped by tax incentives in Europe—they were in fact polluting the lungs of millions of people. In London, where car use is still relatively high for a densely populated city, and lots of people live near main roads, nitrogen oxide levels—as well as levels of general particulate matter, such as tiny particles of soot, which are also created by diesel engines—increased rapidly from around 2008 to 2016. That happened even as cars were supposedly getting cleaner. Emissions were meant to be falling, but instead they climbed. Thousands of children with asthma were admitted to hospital. It was the same across Europe.

The scandal was uncovered by researchers at West Virginia University, home to the Center for Alternative Fuels Engines and Emissions. They were commissioned by the International Council on Clean Transportation, an NGO, to look into how clean diesel cars were under real road conditions, rather than in a laboratory. With a budget of just $70,000, the investigators—mostly a bunch of graduate students, led by Dan Carder, an academic who heads the center—built a contraption designed to measure emissions on the road. It sat in the back of the car, with a small gasoline generator to power it (so as not to tax the engine and skew the test), while one student drove and another followed the readings live on a laptop computer. They procured three cars—two Volkswagens and a BMW—by borrowing them from owners in California, and drove them around Los Angeles.

The results were staggering. In the two Volkswagens, vehicles A and B, which were equipped with "lean nitrogen traps"—the fuel-flushing model of NOx control—emissions exceeded the legal limits "by a factor of 15 to 35," reported the 117-page paper. Only the BMW, vehicle C, which had a urea system, did not significantly out-pollute the laboratory standards. (And even it pumped out quite a bit of NOx while driving up hills.) As the report wryly noted, this did not seem to be the result of a flaw. Rather, "Vehicles A and B were operating as intended and did not have any malfunctions." They had been deliberately designed to pollute more under real-world driving conditions than when they were being tested.

California was a good place to test the cars. The state, under a deal struck with the federal government, is allowed to set even more stringent emissions standards than other American states. California's geography is the reason. Los Angeles sits in a basin, surrounded on one side by mountains and on the other, the ocean. That creates natural temperature inversions (where air higher up is warmer than air on the ground), which trap pollutants. As early as the 1940s, LA was already beginning to suffer from punishing smog. Sometimes visibility would drop to as low as just a few blocks. Look at photos from the city from the 1950s and you can see it, even in black and white—a low gray fog hanging on the city's new skyscrapers. Initially people blamed coal power plants and factories (which certainly cannot have helped). But by the 1960s it was obvious the real culprit was cars. In 1967, before the Clean Air Act compelled automakers elsewhere to clean up, California's leadership came together to impose its own rules.

WVU's paper was published in 2014—just a few months before the monkey gassing project began. For more than a year, Volkswagen stonewalled it. They claimed that the results were caused by a software error, and promised a recall. In November 2015, following measures taken by the state of California, the EPA released a short press release noting that Volkswagen had been served with a Notice of Violation. It was the beginning of an ongoing process that would cost the company tens of billions of dollars. More than eleven million cars, mostly in Europe, but several millions in the United States, were affected. Volkswagen eventually paid out $35 billion—$2.8 billion in a fine imposed by the EPA and the rest in buying back 500,000 cars in the United States. The costs are still mounting, as diesel owners in Europe begin to fight lawsuits of their own about the cars they were sold on false premises.

For a small edge in competitiveness—a working urea tank system could have been installed for perhaps $500 a car—Volkswagen had poisoned hundreds of thousands of people and sold a spectacular lie: that diesel engines could help fight climate change without compromising on performance. From March 2015 to October of that year, VW's share price fell by around 50 percent. When the details of the monkey gassing emerged in 2018, Germany's chancellor, Angela Merkel, expressed her horror. "These tests on monkeys or even humans cannot be justified ethically in any way," she said. Martin Winterkorn, VW's CEO, gave a speech in which he said that "millions of people around the world trust our brands, our cars, and our technologies. I am so sorry that we have betrayed this confidence."

And yet in the long run, what did it actually cost VW? For all of their shock, the German authorities were certainly not going to do anything that would damage the viability of one of their biggest industries. Volkswagen employs some 670,000 people, almost half of whom are in Germany. Its headquarters, in Wolfsburg, in Lower Saxony, includes the world's biggest car factory, and the city has the highest GDP per capita of any in Germany. Almost as soon as the scandal emerged, the German media began to worry about what it would mean for the German economy. *Wolfsburger Allgemeine Zeitung*, Wolfsburg's local newspaper, argued quickly that the scandal was the work of a few bad apples. "It would be wrong, if because of the grave errors of a few, the honest hard work of 600,000 people would be questioned . . . our employees do not deserve this," they argued.

And ultimately, it seemed as if the German government agreed. At the time of writing, WV's share price is back up above where it was in 2015, before the scandal emerged. Though the American authorities charged nine men with federal crimes, only one executive, Oliver Schmidt, who had headed VW's emissions group in Michigan, was actually locked up—and only because he was foolhardy enough to fly back to America for a vacation in Florida after being charged. He pled guilty and was sentenced to seven years in prison, of which he served a little more than half before being released in January 2021. The other eight men charged by the American authorities escaped, simply by staying in Germany, which refused to extradite its citizens to America. Winterkorn in particular has so far escaped justice. A trial in Germany began in September 2021, but without the most prominent defendant—he is in poor health and was deemed unable to attend. At the time of writing, it remains unclear whether he will ever face justice.

By 2017, even as the scandal was unfolding, just under 40 percent of new cars sold in Britain were diesels. And air pollution in Britain's biggest cities was soaring. Sir David told the BBC that year that he had been wrong to advise the fuel-tax cut. "I was convinced that they could manage the problem," he said of the car manufacturers. But in fact, he tells me now, "What we had was a kind of conspiracy among the automotive industry which was causing a very large number of deaths, particularly children picking up asthma, particularly close to high traffic roads."

These are not just hypothetical children. One of them was Ella Kissi-Debrah, a little girl who lived near the South Circular, a main road in Lewisham, south London, who died of complications from asthma in 2013 at the age of just nine. In 2020, a coroner ruled that a failure to control emissions, or to adequately warn parents of how damaging they could be, contributed to her death.

There are other losers too. In Europe, because VW were not forced to pay compensation or to buy back old vehicles, as they were in America, the buyers of the original cars are stuck with vehicles that do not have the promised performance or efficiency and indeed are increasingly strictly regulated. They are having to go through costly lawsuits in their countries to force VW to pay them for selling them polluting cars. In Germany there are 60,000 lawsuits still pending in the courts, and 90,000 in Britain.

The point of this story is not that Volkswagen is an especially evil company. The decision to cheat on emissions tests was indeed made by a small number of relatively senior people; most of the firm's 600,000 employees would have had no idea. Nor was it unique. Two decades before, a number of American companies selling engines for trucks were also caught out doing the exact same thing. In Europe many people suspect that other companies did similar things and have not been caught. A 2016 study by *Which?* magazine, a consumer watchdog group, found that many popular diesel cars still polluted far more in real-world driving conditions than they are meant to. Cars from Subaru, Hyundai, and Jeep all massively exceeded European standards too, by as much as the Volkswagens had. Quite probably, Volkswagen was just unlucky, because it got caught, and in the United States.

So why do they do it? Sir David described to me a meeting he had with a Volkswagen executive after the scandal emerged, in which he asked why they had sought to cheat. Apparently the response was simply that they were "maximizing profits," fulfilling their fiduciary responsibility to shareholders. And governments were desperate to believe that automakers had discovered a miracle way of providing "clean" cars, profits, and jobs all at once.

The point is that car manufacturing is a vicious, competitive industry. You have to be ruthless to survive in it. I learned this myself a few years ago on a visit to the Nissan factory in Sunderland, in England's northeast. Nissan is the jewel of the economy in Sunderland—it provides the best paying jobs by miles in the region, which has otherwise been suffering industrial decline since the Great Depression, if not before. When you walk around the factory, you meet workers who are paid far above the average wage for the area, for work that is interesting and fulfilling. But the executives who took me around explained that every year, they have to find a new way to produce more cars with fewer workers, less material, and less money. If your manufacturing process gets more expensive, you will go out of business. So you have to innovate constantly.

Gross margins for carmaking—that is, the profit that a firm makes relative to the cost of producing a car—rarely exceed about 6 percent. By contrast, Apple's gross margin is 42 percent. Lower margins make you vulnerable. If you fail to keep your productivity increasing, you will go bust. When one firm improves productivity dramatically, as Toyota did in the 1980s and '90s, other firms have to copy them or they will lose sales and, fairly quickly, have to close plants. Over the past fifty years, the car industry has become a marvel of increasing manufacturing expertise. Things such as just-in-time production—where parts are shipped to factories at exactly the moment they are needed—were pioneered by the car industry. And the firms that cannot keep up, such as MG Rover, once Britain's biggest car maker, go bust.

That means that cars are continually getting faster, more comfortable, and easier to drive. It is why modern cars almost never break down as they used to, and why they get more efficient. But it also creates the incentives for cheating. Because in such a competitive industry, often there is almost no other way to get ahead. Today, diesel cars' software apparently does genuinely limit emissions. As a result, pollution levels in many European cities have begun to fall again. But sales of diesel cars have dropped back to around 10 percent of sales in Europe and less in the United States. The competitive advantage of diesel has gone.

When it comes down to it, manufacturers will always do what helps their bottom line most. They always have. Almost a century before the NOx cheating scandal, an emissions scandal orders of magnitude worse began to unfold: that of leaded gasoline. NOx emissions are extremely bad, especially for people with asthma or other respiratory conditions. But lead is far deadlier. Yet from the mid 1920s until the mid 1990s, and later in some poorer countries, gasoline was routinely mixed with tetraethyl lead, a particularly poisonous chemical variant of lead invented by German chemist Carl Jacob Löwig in the 1850s.

In the 1920s, GM was trying to beat the enormous success of Henry Ford's Model T. But the firm needed a competitive edge. In the 1920s, climate change was not a concern, but fuel efficiency was—many feared that America's oil wells, then being newly exploited, would run out quickly, and gasoline prices were rising. Scientists paid by General Motors discovered that by mixing tetraethyl lead with gasoline, you could increase the "octane," and so reduce the engine-damaging "knock" that gasoline then on sale inflicted on engines starting up. Putting lead in gasoline not only reduced engine knock, it also made the cars more efficient. General Motors had powerful allies, particularly in Franklin Roosevelt, who saw car manufacturing as a way out of the Great Depression. By 1936, 90 percent of gasoline in America had lead added to it.

Everyone knew that lead was poisonous. When a factory producing tetraethyl lead opened in New Jersey, dozens of its workers fell sick, experiencing delusions and loss of consciousness—typical of lead poisoning. The building was quickly nicknamed the "loony gas building." Several died. For a while, the additive was banned in several states. Yet much like Volkswagen's "clean diesel" marketing, an incredibly clever PR campaign covered it up. Thomas Midgley, the GM scientist who pioneered the additive, made a show of washing his hands in tetraethyl lead; one newspaper even reported that he bathed in it. Dodgy studies were sold to the press about the safety of tetraethyl, while the fact that its key ingredient was lead was quietly avoided. When it became clear that lead was the key ingredient, GM and Standard Oil insisted that, while obviously lead was poisonous in large quantities, the amounts emitted from gasoline cars were too small to do any harm.

This was, even at the time, obviously nonsense. Now it is painfully so. The World Health Organization reported in 2002 that leaded gasoline "has caused more exposure to lead than any other source worldwide." Young children and babies are especially vulnerable. Even very small doses, as low as 5 micrograms of lead per deciliter ($\mu g/dL$), can do permanent brain damage. From 1976 to 1989 the amount of lead used in gasoline in America fell by 99 percent. And recorded levels of lead in blood fell soon after. But the costs of putting lead in gasoline for so long were enormous, and we are still discovering them even now. One of the effects of lead poisoning in childhood is the reduction of people's self-control when they grow up, and some studies suggest that leaded gasoline may even explain as much as 30 percent of the enormous crime wave that grew through the postwar period in the United States. That the murder rate began dropping in the early 1990s, 20 years after most lead was phased out of gasoline, is pointed to as evidence of the effect.

The concentration of lead in the average child aged one to five fell from 15 µg/dL in 1976 to 2.8 µg/dL in 2016. But it took until the first years of the twenty-first century to phase it out in poorer countries. Indeed, leaded gasoline was sold up until July 2021. Algeria, in North Africa, was the last holdout. It had significant stockpiles built up that it did not want to throw away. Worldwide, according to the United Nations, the final phaseout of leaded gasoline is saving 1.2 million early deaths a year, as well as $2.4 trillion in social costs. That suggests that tens of millions of people went to early graves in the intervening century, and tens of trillions of dollars of damage were done.

So why did it happen? Leaded gasoline was, in the words of one Standard Oil executive, a "gift from god," too good to ignore. And for a highly competitive industry desperate to sell more cars and more gasoline, it was. Leaded gasoline helped GM sell more cars, and because the firm also became the biggest supplier of the lead, GM made profits on that too. Americans—and then later Europeans—wanted ever faster, more powerful, more efficient cars, more convenient cars, and would buy whichever company offered the best ones. The pollution they emitted was not a concern, because it did not directly affect the buyers—and they might not even realize it. In the car industry, if you skimp on something that the driver notices, you will sell fewer cars. You may even go bankrupt. Plenty of car companies have. But if you skimp on something that affects the entire world, but is not really noticeable by the driver, you might just make a bit more money.

The car industry gets, for some reason, insanely good press. Its own propaganda has been incredibly effective. People remember that Volkswagen invented the Beetle, intended to be a car for the masses. They tend to forget the idea was Adolf Hitler's. Similarly, they remember that Henry Ford paid his workers enough to be able to afford to buy a Model T. For some reason they seem to forget that he also sponsored some of the most virulently anti-Semitic propaganda in American history and lobbied against America's entrance into World War II. Big Pharma, for all of its flaws, literally sells and develops drugs that save lives, but it generates far more protesters than "big auto." Perhaps it is because the car industry provides good, well-paid, unionized jobs. But then, so too do oil companies.

Car manufacturers are really not much different from the oil industry or Big Tobacco. They will, if it helps the industry, sponsor dodgy research. They form lobby groups and sponsor astroturf campaigns. They will bribe and cheat their workers. Indeed, around the same time that the Volkswagen gassing scandal was being revealed, it also came out that the firm had repeatedly paid cash bribes and even brothel trips to union representatives. That is something other manufacturers have done for years. They also stymie the press who look into these scandals, while providing endless freebies to journalists who write positively about cars. It is, frankly, a crooked industry. Like many.

The craziest thing is that, even in the 1920s, there was already a well-known alternative to putting lead into gasoline to reduce vehicle knock: ethanol, the raw alcohol produced from crops. Back then, America was still a very rural society, and farmers routinely used home-brewed booze to supplement gasoline in their Ford Model Ts. But unlike tetraethyl lead, ethanol was not cheap or easy to produce on the scale that the car industry needed then, nor was it available in the urban areas where GM hoped to compete with Ford. So they chose the poisonous version and, for decades, covered it up. So it goes in the car industry. Unlike GM and lead, Volkswagen was punished for its emissions cheating, so that will probably not happen again. But the next scandal is already around the corner. There are new ways in which car companies are pushing the limits of acceptability.

12

GAS GUZZLER NATION

If you want a sense of what the next scandal in carmaking is, you could do worse than I did in November 2021. That month, I went to a monster truck rally in Madison, the state capital of Wisconsin. I even took my wife, Evelyn, because what better date is there than inhaling gasoline fumes and having your ear drums blown out by overly large cars?

I knew what to expect: huge vehicles, lots of American flags, rock music, and noise, enormous amounts of noise. But it was still a fairly overwhelming experience. My wife and I entered the stadium a few minutes late, as the show had already begun, and as we entered, Evelyn immediately clamped her hands over her ears to try to block out the noise. It was snowing outside, but inside the Alliance Energy Center, where the show was being hosted, earth had been piled up to create three large dirt ramps, each perhaps twelve feet high. Buried underneath the ramps were several ancient cars, presumably salvaged from a scrap yard somewhere. And then waiting at the door of the stadium were the monster trucks themselves: vehicles at least fifteen feet tall, with names like Kamikaze, Jurassic, and Jailbird emblazoned on them together with garish paint jobs. The monster trucks themselves are not really like normal cars, but more like overgrown dirt buggies. The bodywork is strapped onto a roll cage, so that if they topple over, the driver inside will not be crushed.

What happens at a monster truck rally is not exactly sophisticated. In theory, it is a competition. The drivers take turns launching their huge vehicles at the ramps, crashing over them onto the puny cars beneath, revving like something from *Mad Max*, while the announcer calls out things like: "I know we have some big-time monster truck fans! Are you ready?"

Music like Queen's "We Will Rock You" and Bruce Springsteen's "Born in the USA" blares out of the speakers. This goes on for around two hours, and at various stages, the audience members are called to vote for the best "performance" by shouting the name of their favorites. Eventually the winner is determined by the loudness of the shouts. Within an hour, the overpowering scent of exhaust fumes fills up the entire stadium, which is largely packed with families with small children. To protect their ears, young men walk around selling earmuffs in the shape of giant tires for twenty-five dollars each.

Monster truck rallies have been going on since the 1980s. The first monster truck ever created was called Bigfoot, a modified Ford F-250 pickup truck whose owner, Bob Chandler, kept adding more and more height and power to it, building an obscene off-road machine. By the late 1980s, competitions were being organized across the country, and they were broadcast on ESPN. It is a form of entertainment mostly unheard of anywhere outside of North America, and it is incredibly American. It also operates with a basic contempt for human life. The Monster Trucks Wikipedia page has a whole section on casualties caused at events. On more than a dozen occasions, spectators have been killed by trucks veering into the stands, or by parts breaking off and flying into the audience. At one event in Mexico in 2013, a single crash killed eight people and injured seventy-nine when a monster truck plowed into a crowd. The driver had apparently been drinking.

I went to the rally to see America at its most auto-obsessed. And I wanted to understand the appeal, because the interest in huge vehicles in America goes beyond Bigfoot and Kamikaze. For the past couple of decades, something has been happening to America's car industry, in that it is producing more and more vehicles that resemble monster trucks, but for ordinary use, by ordinary people. The parking lot around the stadium in Madison was packed full of them, vehicles like the Ford F-150, a truck produced at the Ford River Rouge factory in Dearborn, Michigan, that is almost as large as the Sherman tanks used in World War II, and is America's best-selling vehicle. In the past decade the car industry has come up with a fairly simple mantra, it seems: Bigger Is Better. In 2018, Ford even announced that in North America they would stop producing ordinary passenger cars entirely, so as to focus exclusively on trucks and sport utility vehicles.

For a glimpse of why Americans choose to drive such enormous vehicles, it is worth considering the ads that show during the many stoppages that seem to characterize American football. During 2021's Super Bowl, the longest ad with the biggest budget was for Jeep. It was an all-American ad, narrated by Bruce Springsteen. "Freedom is not just the property of the fortunate few," The Boss told us. And freedom, of course, means owning a giant Jeep. "There is hope on the road up ahead," he went on, talking over footage of an America very far from the urban centers in which most Americans spend much of their time driving.

Nothing, bar none, is more patriotic than driving a Jeep Cherokee or a Jeep Wrangler (descended from the vehicles that won World War II) along an endless straight road through mountains and desert. And it does look magical. If I were going camping in the wilderness of the mountainous West, I would want a Jeep too. (Though in the past I have found a Toyota Prius works perfectly well.) There are dozens of these ads, not just during the Super Bowl but on TV all of the time. GM had one in which a man buys two enormous cars as a present for him and his wife. "One for me, one for you." The joke is that she takes the pickup truck, leaving him with the presumably girlier SUV. But of course, they're both enormous. Another, this one from Audi, shows somebody driving their SUV up to a sign that clearly says the road is closed. "Is any road really closed to Quattro?" asks the narrator, inevitably a pretty young woman. "I guess I'll just find my own road," she says, as she prepares to flagrantly disobey traffic laws and zoom off into the sunset.

One thing you almost never see in car commercials is people driving in thick traffic on city streets. Even when they are filmed in cities, rather than up remote mountains or on beautiful western ranches, invariably there are no other cars around to spoil the driving pleasure. However, most of the people buying Jeeps or Ford F-150s are not using them for glorious road trips on empty highways through mountains and desert. They are driving them from their suburban house to the office, and to the supermarket, in thick traffic. In 2019, SUVs outsold traditional sedan cars by two to one in America.

Overall, SUVs made up 47 percent of sales, and when "light trucks" are added, 72 percent. That figure has been growing; IHS Markit, a market research firm, projects it will reach 78 percent by 2025. That is, four in five cars sold in America will be either rugged four-wheel drive SUVs or pickup trucks. If you come from abroad and spend time in any American city, you will be shocked at how big the cars are. Everyone seems to be driving something the size of a small house.

Pickup trucks have not taken off to the same extent in Europe, but SUVs have. In the UK, they now make up 30 percent of all sales. Indeed, the Jeep Cherokee, that symbol of American glory, is rather popular in Britain too. In the European Union, SUVs make up 37 percent of sales. Globally, the annual number on the roads has gone from around 50 million in 2010 to 280 million last year. It is not just that there are more SUVs and pickup trucks. They are also getting bigger. Take, for example, the Toyota RAV4, a car that has been in production for thirty years. Except the 2018 version of the RAV4 is 34 percent larger than the 1994 version. With greater size comes greater weight. From 1980 to 2018, the weight of an average American car increased from 3,260 pounds to 4,093 pounds, or a 25 percent increase. The same has happened in Europe. In 1980 the average European car weighed a little less than a metric ton (1,000 kilograms, or 2,204 pounds). Now it is 1,390 kilograms (3,064 pounds), an even bigger increase than in the US.

The bigger and heavier a car is, the more fuel it uses. Perhaps the most outrageous car on America's roads is the Chevrolet Suburban. It is absolutely hideous. It looks like something your eight-year-old son might design on Roblox: no curves at all, just a giant metal box. You wonder how it steers. It sells for $55,000 and weighs more than 6,000 pounds. Even with four adult passengers weighing 160 pounds each, there are still well over 10 pounds of car for every one of passenger carried. By comparison, an unladen Boeing 747 weighs about 180 tons—or sixty Suburbans—and can carry 450 passengers and their luggage comfortably, or more than a pound of payload for every pound of plane.

According to Chevrolet, the Suburban gets about 21 miles to the gallon. (Or, it consumes 5 gallons to drive 100 miles.) A typical American driver using one will burn roughly 4,000 pounds of gasoline a year, or their own body weight worth every sixteen days. In doing so, they will emit about six metric tons of CO_2, or more than the average Ethiopian emits in their lifetime. On average,

SUVs use about 20 percent more fuel per mile driven than a sedan car. Pickup trucks use even more than that. At the Ford factory outside Detroit, where the F-150 is assembled, there is a hilarious attempt at greenwashing for the visitors. They talk extensively about the green roof the factory has, and how it lowers the need for air conditioning in summer and sucks up pollution. They do not talk about the sheer volume of CO_2 emitted by the hundreds of cars that exit the facility every single day.

According to research published by the International Energy Agency in 2020, SUVs accounted for 813 megatons of increased CO_2 emissions from 2010 to 2020. As they reported, "the reduction in oil demand from the increased share of electric vehicles in the overall car market in 2020—around 40,000 barrels a day—was completely canceled out by the growth in SUV sales over the same period." Of course car companies are now beginning to produce electric SUVs too. But they too require more energy. It is a staggering waste of resources to have a slightly more comfortable vehicle with larger cup holders and enough space to carry a bit of furniture home once a year.

This has been especially bad in America, where these tank-like vehicles are most popular. From 1995 to 2019, the average fuel efficiency of American vehicles grew by 20 percent. In France, it grew by 45 percent. This is almost certainly because France has for years imposed higher purchase taxes on less fuel-efficient vehicles, whereas America, in many places, incentivizes their purchase. In 2020, France added a new tax of ten euros per kilogram on the purchase of any car that weighs more than 1,800 kilograms. For a fully kitted out Chevrolet Suburban, weighing 6,000 pounds, or 2,700 kilograms, that would add 27,000 euros, or around $27,000, to the price. These days there is almost no chance of a tax like that being introduced in America at a federal level: The car industry in Detroit would collapse. (At a local level, there may be more modest hope: Washington, D.C., has increased the cost of registering cars weighing more than 6,000 pounds in the city).

This in turns helps to explain in part why French people produce on average a third of the CO_2 emissions of Americans. In the past decade, the amount of CO_2 emitted by American vehicles has grown by 10 percent, even as CO_2 from other sources, such as power generation and construction, has fallen. That higher fuel consumption also explains why Americans are hurt so much more than French people when gasoline prices rise.

There are other downsides too. These tank-like cars do not just burn more gasoline, they are also more dangerous. Heavier cars are far more likely to kill people. A study by the Insurance Institute for Highway Safety (IIHS) that looked in detail at eighty crashes in Michigan, found that SUVs "caused more serious injuries than cars when impacts occurred at greater than 19 miles per hour." At speeds between 20 and 30 mph, 30 percent of crashes involving an SUV resulted in a death. For ordinary cars, it was about a fifth. More than 40 mph, 100 percent of crashes involving an SUV killed the pedestrian, against just 54 percent of those involving an ordinary car. Though the group admitted that their study involved a small sample size, they speculated that the rise of SUVs may explain why the number of pedestrians killed in road traffic accidents has been trending upward for the past decade, after falling for decades before that.

Sometimes crashes involving pickup trucks can be extraordinarily deadly. Take one example, from Texas in 2017. A Dodge Ram 3500 pickup truck, a vehicle that weighs 3.5 metric tons, driven by a twenty-year-old man, veered across the highway and crashed into a minibus driven by a church group. All twelve passengers of the bus and its driver were killed. An investigation by the National Transportation Safety Board (NTSB) concluded that the deaths were the result of the pickup driver being high on marijuana.

What the NTSB did not see fit to mention was that the sheer height of the pickup truck almost certainly contributed to the deadliness of the crash. Driving drunk or high is bad, but it is worse when you are driving a vehicle like these pickup trucks. These days the fronts of modern vehicles have deep crumple zones, intended to absorb the impact of collisions, so that passengers are more likely to survive. But in the crash in Texas, because the truck was so much higher up than the minibus, the crumple zones did not have a chance to work. Essentially, it just went straight through the vehicle, crushing the passengers. Photos taken at the scene look like something from a monster truck rally—the top of the bus was simply shorn off by the taller vehicle.

That is not even the only problem. When people are taught to drive, everyone learns to check their blind spots before turning—that is, the areas to the side of the car that you cannot see in the mirrors. It is important to do so, because if you do not, you could turn into another car, a cyclist, or a pedestrian. When I was learning to drive at the age of seventeen, I was terrible at it. (Thanks to sheer paranoia, I am better now). The problem with SUVs is that they have another, bigger blind spot: directly in front of them. The higher up you are in a car, the less you can see of the road immediately in front of you—this is why school buses have mirrors mounted on the hood. According to tests done by Kids and Cars, a nonprofit organization based in Kansas, almost all SUVs and pickup trucks for sale in the United States have a front blind spot of between five and ten feet. Sedan cars, which are lower, have a blind spot of only a few feet.

What that means is, even if a child is ten feet in front of the car, you may be unable to see them over the hood, because you are simply too high up. According to the research published in 2019, over the preceding ten years, 575 children were killed by what they call "frontover" accidents—usually somebody pulling out of their driveway or on a street without realizing that a child is standing in front of the car. That was an 89 percent increase on the preceding decade. Some Americans, perhaps the ones who like monster truck rallies, think that isn't even enough. An increasingly popular trend is for "lifted" pickup trucks: that is, customized pickup trucks that are even higher above the ground than factory ones.

So why are car manufacturers so desperate to sell these cars? The answer is essentially that the car industry has found a way to make more profit from them. Big cars tend to be more profitable than smaller ones. Take the Ford F-150. Ford makes around a 25 percent margin on the sale of each one, at $45,000. By contrast, a smaller car probably has a margin of less than 10 percent, on a sticker price of half of the pickup truck. In 2018, a low point for Ford's share price, Adam Jonas, an analyst at investment bank Morgan Stanley, said that the F-150 might actually be worth more than the entire rest of the company combined.

Explaining this is difficult. Surely huge pickup trucks should be vulnerable to the same cutthroat competition that holds down the prices of other vehicles? Part of why they aren't is probably because Japanese and Korean car manufacturers are so efficient at producing smaller cars, that the market for trucks is less competitive. (And in America, there are import tariffs on "light trucks" that do not apply to smaller cars.) It is also possible for some workers to write off the taxes of extremely large vehicles like the Ford F-250 (an even bigger pickup truck than the F-150) in a way that they cannot smaller ones, because they are classified as work vehicles. And there is another big incentive in the fact that the "gas guzzler tax," which America has imposed on passenger cars with a fuel efficiency of less than 22.5 miles per gallon since 1991, does not apply to pickup trucks and SUVs, so if you want a big powerful vehicle, it is cheaper to get one that is not a normal car.

But I also suspect that their popularity is not only about the cost, because these enormous cars are also still extremely expensive, even with all these hidden subsidies. Rather, I suspect it is because when car companies sell people a small car, they are mostly selling a means of transportation. When they are selling a big one, they are selling a lifestyle. People like bigger cars. You can fit more stuff in. Being higher up gives people a sense of power and safety. They are, I am told, more fun to drive. (I don't see it myself; if I have to drive, I like small cars with powerful acceleration and nifty steering.) But most of all, they appeal to an idea people like to have of themselves, in a way that driving something like, say, a Nissan Altima, does not. Owning a pickup truck suggests you are a rugged sort of individual, ready to conquer mountains, even if in reality you are mostly using it to pick up groceries at Walmart and drop the kids off at soccer practice.

In the past, when pickup trucks were designed to be purchased by actual blue-collar workers, they were almost always sold with a "single cab": that is, just two or three seats at the front. These days almost all pickup trucks have double cabs; that is, a back seat too. The reality is that, as Ford's own employees admit, they are mostly purchased as family vehicles. According to the New Vehicle Experience Study, a market research survey, three-quarters of pickup truck owners use their vehicles at most once a year for towing something, and 70 percent only go off road once a year or less. These pickup trucks are not workhorses, but "luxury cars with a pickup box," as one Ford worker told a journalist from Jalopnik, a car news website. Toyota has even advertised this, selling their Tundra pickup truck, a 5,000-pound behemoth, with an advert in which a very smartly dressed man drives into a city that looks like Paris, but apparently has no parking issues, to get a coffee.

All of the costs—in climate-changing emissions, traffic deaths, and so on—are imposed on other people, who are not the purchasers. Even insurers do not seem to charge pickup truck owners much of a premium for driving such dangerous vehicles. Car manufacturers will defend themselves by saying that they are just serving their customers. But the fact is, they are going to a lot of effort to sell these trucks and SUVs. Manufacturers are not only responding to their customers, they are also responding to the same incentives that they are being given by regulators that want cars to become more efficient. Indeed, one of the reasons that these manufacturers are currently selling electric cars is to give them the space from regulators to sell more gas guzzlers. It is practically built into law that sales of electric cars or lightweight cars will be canceled out by sales of heavier, less efficient machines.

Under the Corporate Average Fuel Economy (CAFE) standards originally set in the 1970s, in response to the Arab oil embargo, American car manufacturers are meant to sell cars with an average "fleet-wide" fuel efficiency of 35 miles to the gallon, or 250 grams of CO_2 for every mile driven. The European Union has similar, if somewhat stricter, rules, targeting an average fuel efficiency of 95 grams of CO_2 for every kilometer (or 152 grams per mile) that their cars drive. The tricky part is that "fleet-wide" bit. For every electric vehicle that the manufacturers sell, they lower their fleet-wide average a bit. That, in turn, frees them up to sell another monstrous gasoline-burning SUV. In fact, perversely, one of the gains of Volkswagen's diesel aim was that—while they convinced people that their cars were better for the environment—the sales of NOx producing cars also gave them the space to sell lots of big Porsche Cayenne SUVs.

They do not even have to sell the electric cars themselves. In the first quarter of 2022, other automakers in the United States paid Elon Musk's firm $679 million in credits that it earned from overshooting the overall fuel efficiency targets, or about $2,200 for every car the firm produced. Every Tesla on America's roads creates a little bit more regulatory space for another Chevrolet Suburban. Before 2022, Tesla was making more from selling the right to pollute to other car firms than it was in profit from selling its own cars.

That is not inherently bad, of course; it means that there is an extra cost to selling more polluting cars, and an incentive to sell clean ones. The whole point of the regulation is to encourage the manufacturers to invest more in electric cars, and they are doing it. If the targets tighten, manufacturers will be required to sell more electric or otherwise fuel-efficient cars to balance out the monster trucks. But it does mean that if you buy a Tesla, or another electric car, you are not in fact taking a whole car's emissions off the road. Rather, you are just giving somebody else a license to pollute a little more. As long as the CAFE standards remain as they are, individuals buying electric cars cannot do much to improve the overall level of climate change emissions, because the car industry will continue to aim the overall target.

In essence, the car industry has discovered that if they can sell one more electric vehicle to a liberal worried about climate change, that means they can sell one more monster truck to a couldn't-care-less-about-the-planet Trump voter. (These stereotypes are not wrong; Republican voters are eight times more likely to own a pickup truck than Democrats, according to one poll. And while Elon Musk may seem like a right-wing troll, Tesla owners are still more likely to be Democrats than Republicans.) So as long as there remains a market for big, powerful vehicles that consume enormous amounts of gasoline, electric cars will do little to reduce overall fuel consumption. For that, we need the fuel efficiency standards to improve—and that will take action by the government.

And if Republicans are in office, good luck with that. When Donald Trump came to power in 2016, he quickly started on plans to roll back the emissions standards for cars imposed by Barack Obama, and began a war on California, which imposes its own standards above the federal level, to stop it. Elaine Chao, Trump's transportation secretary, said as a result of the move, "more jobs would be created." But the request came most from car manufacturers, who wanted to sell more SUVs and pickup trucks without having to sell as many cleaner, smaller vehicles. In March 2020, the Trump-era rules were finalized: The efficiency of American cars has to improve by only 1.5 percent each year, compared with the 5 percent Obama imposed. On taking office, Joe Biden reversed the change—but a future Republican president might well undo it again.

We cannot trust car manufacturers to produce cars that are safe, or good for the environment, or even good necessarily for their drivers, without pressure. When it comes down to it, the car industry is about profit, and not much else. They are ruthless extractors of government subsides, which they get by also being firms that will happily close factories, destroying communities, unless they are paid off. I don't really say this as criticism. That is capitalism. Companies are meant to work for their shareholders. But so many people seem to believe that car companies are something special, that they are national champions and providers of good jobs.

It is not worth it. Working in a car factory is better than working in a sandwich factory, but it is still often tedious, repetitive work. The car industry is always working to produce cars with fewer people than it did before. If you have a good job at a car factory, you should look over your shoulder. Whether it is Detroit or Flint in Michigan, or Janesville in Wisconsin, or Birmingham in Britain, the car industry inevitably shrinks. Trying to bring those jobs back is hopeless. There are now 1,300 robots for every 10,000 workers in the American car industry. As artificial intelligence improves, the number of robots could overtake the number of workers.

Car manufacturing is not some noble pursuit. It is a business. And as long as customers want newer, bigger, more powerful cars, manufacturers will endeavor to supply them. As long as those customers want enormous new highways to be able to drive their enormous cars on, the car industry will lobby for that too. If their customers are annoyed by rules intended to protect pedestrians, or prevent crashes, they will work against them too.

Indeed, one of the things that shows this is traffic deaths. In newspaper reports and on television, these are often called "accidents": unavoidable acts of God. But what the next chapter will reveal is that they are anything but, and the car industry has played its own lamentable role in ensuring that these accidents keep happening.

13

WHAT CAUSES TRAFFIC ACCIDENTS?

Years ago, when I lived in Africa, friends at home would often ask me if I ever felt in danger. It was a reasonable question. I covered wars and riots, in places like Congo and Somalia, and spent my time hanging out in slums where murder was unfortunately commonplace. On one occasion I was robbed, together with two other journalists, by a group of drunk Congolese policemen clutching AK-47s. Yet the honest answer was that the most fear I ever felt was sitting in the back of a car, on a trip from Abidjan, the commercial capital of Ivory Coast, to Bouaké, a city in the middle of the country where there had been a major army mutiny I was heading to cover. The mutiny was not what scared me. It was the driving. I was working with a young Ivorian journalist who had hired the driver, who was in turn also about twenty-five years old. Three young men in a car, and he had a point to prove: that he could get us from Abidjan to Bouaké, a distance of about 200 miles, in under four hours.

That may not sound like a huge challenge to people used to driving on American or European motorways. In much of Africa it is quite a different thing. The continent has few segregated, separated freeways of the sort we have gotten used to. Instead, most roads are simple two-lane roads, so to overtake slow-moving traffic, you wait for a gap, then cross into the opposite lane, dodging potholes, and accelerate quickly. And there is a lot of slow-moving traffic. My driver was determined to prove his ability, and at every opportunity, he jammed down the accelerator on the ancient Toyota Corolla and pushed it straining past. On each overtake we would duck back into our lane just moments before an oncoming vehicle hit us, its driver having been forced to brake to let us through.

Many of my most memorable experiences from reporting and traveling around the world involve hairy drives. They make for fun stories, but they also help to explain why 1.35 million people worldwide are killed each year in car crashes, the vast majority in the developing world. Numerically the biggest victims are not people inside cars, but outside them. More than half of those who die are either motorcyclists, cyclists, or pedestrians. Worldwide, more people are killed in traffic crashes than are killed by HIV/AIDS, or by malaria. According to data from the Centers for Disease Control, there was not a single low-income country in the world in which the number of deaths fell from 2013 to 2016. Lower- and middle-income countries account for 90 percent of the world's car crash deaths, despite accounting for a far smaller share of the world's vehicles. The reason is a toxic mix of far poorer infrastructure, worse driving, and less well-maintained vehicles. But undoubtedly poor infrastructure is the leading cause.

This amount of death, which generates far less attention than that caused by disease, is atrocious in itself. But it also reveals something about traffic death in the rich world too. In the first few decades of the rise of the automobile, it was almost as deadly in rich western countries as it is in poor ones now. Around 7,000 Britons were killed by cars every year before the Second World War, and in 1941, with blackouts in place, more than 9,000 were, the highest figure yet recorded. In the Netherlands, where cars came more slowly than in Britain, deaths peaked in 1970, at around 3,500. In France in the early 1970s, deaths peaked at around 16,000 per year. In all of those countries, the number of deaths has subsequently fallen dramatically. Britain now has less than 2,000 deaths per year; France has around 2,500; and the Netherlands around 600.

In the rich world, there is one exception to this pattern: the United States. There, by 1940, around 40,000 people were being killed on the roads each year. In 2021, 43,000 were killed, according to the CDC, the highest figure in more than a decade. For sure, America's population has grown substantially since 1940, so the rate per million people has fallen. But whereas in the 1970s, Americans were slightly less likely to die in car crashes than French people, now they are three times more likely to. Compared with the UK, they are five times more likely, and compared with Norway, the safest country for traffic deaths excluding the city state of Hong Kong, six times more likely.

The gap can only partly be explained by the fact that Americans drive further than Europeans. Americans cover roughly twice the distance as Brits in their cars each year, so per mile, they are still more than 2.5 times more likely to die. In a typical year, more than 4.8 million Americans, or 1.5 percent of the population, are involved in a car crash serious enough to require them to seek hospital treatment. That implies that over an 80-year lifetime, the average American has a 65 percent chance of being in a car crash that puts them in a hospital. More than a million Americans are living with life-altering disabilities sustained in a car crash. According to research published by the American Medical Association, the higher level of traffic deaths shorten the average American life by roughly three months compared with 12 other countries. In some states, such as Wyoming, Louisiana, and Texas, the death rate is at levels comparable to far poorer countries, such as those in Africa.

So what causes all of these crashes? According to the National Highway Traffic Safety Administration in the United States, 94 to 96 percent of car accidents are caused by "human error," of various types. These include speeding, aggressive overtaking, driving drunk or distracted, or driving sleep-deprived. Drunk driving in particular accounts for about 11,000 deaths per year. They are, in short, at least in the view of the NHTSA, "accidents": unavoidable mistakes. And in a way, they are. Male drivers are roughly three times more likely to be involved in a fatal car crash than women, which does rather suggest that aggressive driving also has something to do with it.

Indeed, it would be easy to conclude that the high rate of traffic deaths is largely the result of Americans being god-awful drivers. On the occasions that I am forced to drive in America, I often find myself convinced of this.

There is a culture of reckless driving in the States you do not find as much in Europe. On freeways people tailgate you before overtaking you on the inside. People veer across lanes in a way that is, frankly, insane. Driving in Los Angeles, I was once passed by a young woman with one knee lifted up against the steering wheel, as she applied nail polish to her toes at 30 miles per hour.

According to a survey done by the CDC, around 2 percent of Americans admit to driving over the limit in the previous thirty days. Another survey suggests almost half of Americans admit to having driven after drinking too much at least once in their lifetime. In Louisiana there are even drive-through daiquiri bars. More than 1.5 million people are arrested each year for it, but that must be a tiny fraction of the number doing it. Driving without a license or insurance in America is also extremely common; a fifth of car crashes that result in a death involve drivers who do not have a license, or about 7,000 a year. So too is driving and texting, which most people in America seem to think is hardly a crime. Indeed, in quite a few places, it is not. Only twenty-four states prohibit any use of a handheld phone while driving, while two states, Montana and Missouri, do not even prohibit texting while driving.

Enforcement of road rules in America is often extremely weak. Speed cameras, for example, are still rare. Only nineteen states allow their use to punish dangerous driving, and eight explicitly ban it. In Missouri in 2015, the state Supreme Court came to the utterly bizarre conclusion that automated traffic enforcement is unconstitutional, on the basis that it is unreasonable for a driver issued a ticket to have to prove that they were not the one driving their car to get out of it. As a result, the chance of being punished for speeding in America is much less than in Europe, because in many places, cops have to pull you over to ticket you.

But poor driving exists everywhere, so I am not sure that it fully explains America's especially high death rates. In Britain, 8 percent of drivers who have consumed alcohol in the past year admit to having driven over the limit, according to a government survey. And punishment of bad driving is hardly any more severe than it is in America. If you Google the words "Dangerous Driver Escapes Jail," you will find dozens of cases in British local newspapers of people getting suspended sentences or community service for crimes like driving at 90 mph in a 20 mph zone around a school, or crashing into people while trying to overtake at 60 mph on a normal city street. Dangerous drivers who kill people are only extremely rarely sent to prison.

In fact, it seems unlikely that Americans are actually twice as bad at driving, or twice as likely to drive aggressively, as, say, Irish people. Similarly, I doubt that people in Texas are twice as reckless as drivers in Rhode Island. The idea that 96 percent of car crashes are caused by human error is not exactly wrong, but it is misleading. No doubt, if everyone drove perfectly, there would be far fewer crashes. But people make mistakes all the time, everywhere. What matters is how easy it is for that mistake to turn into a deadly crash.

The real reason traffic deaths are so much higher in America than they are in Europe is also the same reason traffic deaths are so much higher in countries like Ivory Coast or India than they are in America. It is that the roads are built in such a way that they encourage dangerous driving, or even make it necessary. And America, unlike poor countries, does not have the excuse of limited resources. Its roads are deadly by choice. In America, eight-lane highways run through the centers of cities, with pedestrian crossings protected only by red lights. Instead of roundabouts, which force drivers to slow down to enter, there are intersections, which a drunk or distracted driver can simply blast through on red. In Britain you almost never hear of a car being T-boned, because there are fewer roads where it's even possible. In many American suburbs, the roads do not have sidewalks for pedestrians at all.

Jeff Speck, an urban planner who has written extensively about traffic safety, notes that roads in American cities tend to be much wider than in other countries. This is largely because states require it. The Federal Highways Administration rules that highways ought to be wide enough for each lane of traffic to be twelve feet across. In urban areas, that can drop to ten feet, but that is a relatively recent bit of advice, and so most city streets still have twelve-feet lanes. By contrast, in the UK, the guidance published in the Department for Transport's *Manual for Streets* suggests that urban roads should be 5.5 meters, or eighteen feet wide for a street with traffic in either direction, or just 4.8 meters for a one-way street with car parking on one side. American streets are roughly one-third wider than British ones.

The logic for these wider lanes in America has been, at least in theory, to make driving safer. According to the National Association of City

Transportation Officials (NACTO), wider streets have historically "been favored to create a more forgiving buffer to drivers, especially in high-speed environments where narrow lanes may feel uncomfortable or increase potential for side-swipe collisions." Narrower streets are thought to increase traffic and make crashes more likely.

The key phrase there, however, is "high-speed environments." If you assume that drivers will be traveling at a particular speed, then wider roads are indeed safer, because it gives more space for error. But in fact, drivers adjust their speed according to how safe the road feels. But as *Manual for Streets* points out, in typically bureaucratic language, "when long forward visibility is provided and generous carriageway width is specified, driving speeds tend to increase. This demonstrates that driver behavior is not fixed; rather, it can be influenced by the environment." In other words, the wider (and straighter) the street, the faster people drive. And what America's wider streets mean, in effect, is that drivers feel safer going faster. And the faster they are going, the more likely it is that if they do crash into somebody, it will kill them. I have written this already, but just to repeat it: When a driver hits a pedestrian at 20 mph, 5 percent of collisions will result in death. At 30 mph, 45 percent do.

In highway standards, like in parking standards, engineers have smuggled in essentially a subjective judgment, which is that it is more important for people to be able to drive their cars reasonably fast and without a lot of stress than it is for people to be able to walk safely. Per mile driven, highways are indeed the safest places to drive in America (and everywhere). In 2007, there were 0.54 deaths per one hundred million miles driven on highways, against 0.92 on urban arterial roads, and 1.32 on urban streets. (Rural roads are the least safe, at a rate of almost two deaths per one hundred million miles.) Superficially, then, making urban roads more like highways is the way to make them safer.

This sort of thinking has led roads in many American suburbs and newer cities to be designed like highways. The most common type of new urban form is what Charles Marohn, an urbanist highway engineer, calls a "stroad." This is halfway between a road and a street. That is, it is designed for cars to move fast (to get somewhere, along the road), but it also has businesses, homes, and the like all along it (like a street). Stroads are essentially highways within cities. If you have driven anywhere on the edge of a big American city, you know what they look like: six or eight lanes of traffic, lined by fast-food joints, big-box stores, and gas stations, all with plentiful parking.

And stroads are insanely dangerous. As Speck notes, when you think about it, what makes highways safe is precisely that pedestrians and cyclists cannot use them; exits and entrances are rare, and everyone is going in the same direction. That is incompatible with city driving. The most dangerous places to drive (or to be a pedestrian in America) are all in places where the population has grown most in the past fifty years or so. Floridian cities are especially bad. Places like Tampa, Jacksonville, and Orlando have some of the highest crash death rates in the country. In Dallas, the traffic death rate is ten times what it is in New York State. Old cities, designed by chance, are safe to walk in. New cities, designed with all of the scientific expertise of an entire profession dedicated supposedly to safety, are far more dangerous.

The fact that old cities in America are where driving is safest is proof that improving safety is possible. In New York State, for example, the traffic death rate is half what it is in Britain. That is hardly surprising, since the state is dominated by New York City, where traffic is slow moving by necessity. But deliberate policy has also helped a lot. Since 2014, the city has run a program called Vision Zero, which was originally pioneered in Sweden, and is intended to reduce the toll of car violence. It involves a mix of speed cameras and more enforcement, but also, more importantly, the redesigning of dangerous roads. From 1990 to 2018, the number of deaths in New York City fell from 700 to 200. (It has risen sharply again since, but nowhere near previous highs.) Boston and Washington, D.C., have had similar successes.

In Britain too, where death rates have long been much lower than in America, policy works. Under the last Labour government, which was in office from 1997 to 2010, local councils were given money to introduce safety measures. Residential neighborhoods of British cities were suddenly covered with an array of speed bumps, miniature roundabouts, and the like intended to slow drivers down. And it worked. Over the period in which Labour were in power, the number of people killed each year fell by almost half, from a little more than 3,000 to around 1,700. But then the Conservatives got into power and cut local council funding to the bone, and these efforts mostly stopped. In the twelve years since, traffic death rates have remained stubbornly at their 2010 level.

So why do governments and highway engineers not do more? The problem is not that traffic engineers are stupid, though it is tempting to believe. It is that their incentives, created by politicians, are in favor of drivers. Drivers like to be able to go fast and not have to concentrate too much. One poll of Americans that asked them why they liked driving found that the principal appeal was "time to be alone" and "quiet." There is such a deeply ingrained idea in America that driving ought to be easier or more comfortable, which comes from the fact that people have to do it so much. You see it not only in the size of the lanes (and the cars), but also in the size of parking spaces; you can drive every day in large parts of America and never once have to learn to parallel park. You can see it in the fact that almost all cars sold in America have automatic transmissions. You can see it in the way that in many states, drivers turning right at an intersection are allowed to continue through a red light, a dangerous habit that American drivers consider to be completely ordinary.

In the eyes of motorists, who make up a majority of voters in almost all of America, pedestrians do not seem to count as real people in the way that car drivers do, probably because their journeys cannot be measured in the same way that car traffic can be. And so in aid of speed, and the safety of car drivers, streets are routinely redesigned in more dangerous ways. A classic example is turning a two-way street into a one-way. That helps cars move down it faster, since it means you have more lanes in one direction and more opportunity for passing. It also makes it scarier to cross for pedestrians, because the cars are going faster, and the drivers are less likely to be paying attention to what is in front of them.

Unfortunately, and predictably, the car industry has played a long role in this. As I wrote earlier, back in the 1920s and 1930s, they encouraged the building of highways and the criminalization of "jaywalking" to segregate drivers from pedestrians, as a way to reduce the death rate without reducing speed. Later, by the 1950s, as Jessie Singer notes in her book, *There Are No Accidents*, the industry blamed "accidents" on bad drivers, rather than on badly designed cars or roads. Instead of admitting that the vehicles they sold and the roads they drive on were in any way unsafe, they promoted the idea that car crashes were caused entirely by "the nut behind the wheel." For years, this argument was used to justify not installing seat belts, or steering wheels that would not impale drivers in a crash.

Just as the gun industry today promotes the idea that "guns don't kill people, people do," the car industry promoted the idea that "cars don't kill people, drivers do." And just as the gun industry does this even as it sells assault rifles to teenage boys with video-game marketing, the car industry does it while running ads in which drivers race or pull crazy stunts at high speed. Ultimately, it is drivers using cars exactly how they are intended to be used by their designers—driving fast and furiously—that kill people. Cars that are safe to drive are boring, and roads that force you to slow down are also boring. Boring, for the most part, does not sell cars, and it certainly does not sell the giant trucks, SUVs, or exceptionally powerful sports cars on which carmakers make their biggest profit margins.

But the paradigm does not work perfectly, because the car industry is also, these days at least, trying to offer something else by promising technological improvements that will supposedly make fast driving safer, such as more cameras fitted to cars and automatic blind spot readers. Many have invested heavily in autopilot systems, designed to keep cars in their lanes if drivers are losing concentration. The problem with all of this is that it basically encourages dangerous driving, because people think the machine will make them safe. And they are simultaneously encouraging precisely the sort of distracted driving that is most dangerous, because it makes driving more comfortable and pleasant for their passengers.

In the spot where you might expect a radio, modern cars now feature ever bigger touch screens, which drivers can use to choose music, look at maps, and even watch television (at least when the car is not moving). Apple has launched its own in-car system, which is also expected to run across a whole dashboard. Throughout the car industry, manufacturers are signing deals with entertainment firms, such as Amazon, to provide in-car media. Given that the typical car journey in America features a solo driver and no passengers, it is a little disturbing.

The one thing car manufacturers seem utterly uninterested in is anything that slows drivers down. Speed limiters have been available for vehicles for literally a century. (Remember that Cincinnati wanted to introduce them in

1922.) And yet, they are never fitted to private vehicles. There are now much smarter versions, known as "intelligent speed assistance," that use sign-reading cameras and GPS data to automatically adjust a car to the maximum speed limit on a particular road. According to the European Transport Safety Council, a Brussels think tank, forcing its introduction on new cars could eventually reduce traffic deaths by 20 percent. But the car industry, obviously, hates it. When the European Union proposed making such systems mandatory, the European Automobile Manufacturers' Association lobbied aggressively and successfully against it. At best, new cars will be mandated to have systems that warn drivers when they are speeding but do nothing about it.

The reality is that when you are driving in a built-up area, it ought to be difficult. You should not be able to look at a screen if you are moving, because you should need to focus on what is happening on the road ahead of you. You are, after all, maneuvering a ton or more of metal at a dangerous speed, powered by explosions happening under the hood. Driving in a place where the lanes are narrow and there are pedestrians and cyclists everywhere is really stressful. And ironically, that is why it is safer, because the stress comes from the fact that drivers are forced to concentrate. A basic rule of cities is this: If it is a relaxing place to drive, then it is invariably a god-awful place to walk. Does anyone really want to live in a city where pedestrians are advised to wear a high visibility vest to cross the street, as they are in Texas, or to walk along strictly in single file, as they are in Utah?

Ironically, we probably need to stop blaming drivers for car accidents. It is a little like the climate-change debate. For years, big oil and gas firms have tried to frame it in terms of individuals and their carbon footprints. But they did that precisely because they knew that individuals will struggle to reduce their own use of fossil fuels if society does not change to make it easier. The car industry is the same. It wants us to blame bad driving for crashes. But we will not reduce the level of traffic violence by just hoping that individual drivers can be persuaded to behave better. Rather, we collectively have to create an environment in which safety comes ahead of driving ease.

In *The Great Gatsby*, Jordan Baker, the golfing socialite friend of Jay Gatsby, opines that driving recklessly is fine, because "it takes two to make an accident." Later that is exactly what happens—Myrtle runs into the path of a car being driven by Daisy Buchanan. Both are in the wrong. Sadly, the adage is not true: One driver not paying attention can easily kill somebody, even somebody behaving sensibly. But it should be true. If our roads were designed properly, it would be extremely difficult for drivers to make dangerous mistakes. And if that were the case, I suspect that when drivers did behave dangerously, public sympathy for them would be a lot less than it is today. We would have fewer "accidents," and those we did have would be punished severely.

14

BRING IN THE BIKES

For a picture of how cities can change, there are worse places to go than the Right Bank of the River Seine, in Paris, the capital of France. Just south of the Place de la Bastille, there is a motorway exit ramp at the Port de l'Arsenal that leads down to the riverbank. Until the 1960s, these were industrial quays for barges. Then they were converted into a motorway, the Voie Georges-Pompidou, named for the prime minister who opened it in 1967. Pompidou, a leader during the "Glorious Thirty" years of France's postwar economic boom, saw it as a way to help newly wealthy French people drive. For the next fifty years, it funneled 43,000 cars per day along the Seine. Pompidou, who airily proclaimed in the 1970s that the French "love their cars," actually thought it was rather too modest. He had originally wanted a road at least twice as wide, with the space to be found by concreting over the river.

In 2009 a paperback guidebook to the city, in its section on cycling in Paris, advised that the Georges-Pompidou should be "avoided at all times," so dangerous and polluted was the road. For the past few years, however, the entrance to the road has been obstructed to cars by concrete blocks, and signs indicate that only pedestrians, cyclists, and people on electric scooters are allowed in. In 2017, the entire expressway was closed to motorized vehicles (well, except for the scooters). The concrete tunnels that make up parts of the expressway now provide an eerie calm for cyclists to zoom through. The emergency telephone boxes and escape staircase that existed for motorists who broke down are still in place, but the fumes are gone. The open areas have become a sort of urban park along the river, with trees and benches. The Voie Georges-Pompidou feels a little like the High Line in New York. Where before there was constant traffic, now there are several open-air pop-up bars where you can buy a beer and watch families zoom past on bicycles. It is lovely.

And yet closing the road was incredibly controversial and took more than a decade. The first to try it was Bertrand Delanoë, who served as mayor of the city of Paris from 2001 to 2014. In 2002, he closed the road for a full month to turn it into a beach, covering the tarmac in sand: the Paris Plage. Motorists complained that traffic was backed up through the city as a result, but that summer two million Parisians visited, and it proved so popular it became an annual event. In 2010, Delanoë proposed turning it permanently into a pedestrian space, but the backlash was stronger—closing the road in August, when all wealthy Parisians have snuck off on *les vacances* is one thing; closing it year-round quite another. Nonetheless, he persevered, and in 2013 he succeeded on the opposite side of the Seine, closing a section of the Left Bank permanently to cars. But the closure of the Pompidou was held up, first by François Fillon, the prime minister from 2007 until 2012, and then by the police.

It took until 2017 for the road to be closed, not by Mr. Delanoë but by his successor, the socialist Anne Hidalgo. Even then, she almost failed. First she had to persuade the police department, which had the right to reopen the road if it judged that the closure was displacing traffic elsewhere. (After conducting a study, they were persuaded—another example of how roads induce demand.) Then in 2018, a year after it was first shut, a bunch of pro-car activists, who claimed to speak on behalf of France's forty million drivers, managed to get a court decision ruling that the city had not followed the correct procedure in closing the road. The Republicans, the leading opposition on the right at the time, hailed it as a victory for motorists. They were eventually overruled. But it was dicey.

It took guts to keep the road closed to cars—and open to people. "For them, car traffic takes priority over public health: An urban motorway is worth more than a park in the center of the city," said Hidalgo at the time, of her political opponents. She called the pedestrianization a "reconquest" of the city that would alleviate air pollution—then killing 48,000 French people per year—and give back space to ordinary Parisians.

It is difficult to find people who regret the closure. Polling suggests 55 percent of Parisians supported it at the time; more recent figures suggest it is now more like 75 percent. Chantal Glasman, a costume designer who I met on the riverfront, told me how incredible the change has been. "This route is marvelous," she said. "We are at the edge of the water. You can sit, watch the people, it is quiet." Before it opened, she rarely came down to the river. Now she comes often. Everyone I spoke to said essentially the same thing. A father and son standing on what used to be the edge of the motorway tossed powerful magnets into the river to fish up treasure accumulated in the water over centuries. It would never have been possible before, the father told me. Magnet fishing is now so popular that the riverfront hosts a mini exhibition of things pulled out of the river in the past few years. It includes, predictably, rusted bicycles and scooters, but also ancient weaponry, coins, and other trinkets. It is amazing to think that for decades, cars, not people, had priority on the banks of the Seine.

I went to Paris to get a sense of somewhere that is managing to break the mold on car dependency. Because what Paris shows is that you can change transport a lot by introducing technology. Not, however, fancy new technology like self-driving cars or hyperloops. Actually the technology that Paris is using to transform itself is rather old: the humble bicycle. The key benefit of closing roads to cars in Paris has come from the fact that they are reopened to people on bikes. And that has the power to radically transform cities for the better.

When the roads closed, many feared that the result would be backed up traffic elsewhere in the city. Instead, the cars simply disappeared. The people who were using the road mostly switched away from driving through Paris entirely. Many took up walking and started using public transport more. But the biggest change was that people took to cycling. Nicolas Duchie, a young father I met near the Champs-Élysées, told me that his family now almost never uses their car anymore, despite living in the suburbs, not in the city of Paris proper. "We keep it uniquely for going out of Paris, on holidays," he said. Instead, he and his wife get around by electric bicycle. To carry their two small children, they have two trailers that attach to the back. Almost all journeys are faster by bike than by driving, he told me, including his commute into the city.

Bicycles, after all, are a rather magical invention. According to an article published in *Scientific American* in 1973 and written by S. S. Wilson, a lecturer at Oxford University, traveling by bicycle is essentially the most efficient way to move, in both the human world and the animal one. Wilson's piece is a classic. Unlike much written by scientists, it is a joy to read, which is perhaps why so many people still cite it. It begins with a brief history of wheeled transport. "When one considers how long the wheel has served in transportation (more than 5,000 years), it seems odd that the first really effective self-propelled wheeled vehicle was developed only about 100 years ago," he noted, before taking readers through the history of the first "hobby horse" bicycle devised in Germany in 1817, and leading through to the invention of Henry John Lawson's safety bicycle in Coventry in the 1870s.

The key conclusion of Wilson's piece, however, is this: "When one compares the energy consumed in moving a certain distance as a function of body weight for a variety of animals and machines, one finds that an unaided walking man does fairly well (consuming about 0.75 calories per gram per kilometer), but he is not as efficient as a horse, a salmon, or jet transport. With the aid of a bicycle, however, the man's energy consumption for a given distance is reduced to about a fifth (roughly 0.15 calories per gram per kilometer). Therefore, apart from increasing his unaided speed by a factor of three or four, the cyclist improves his efficiency rating to No. 1 among moving creatures and machines." Compared with a car, per calorie of energy used, bicycles are roughly eighty-five times more efficient at moving a person. And the energy comes from food, not from fossils.

This is why, as Wilson noted in his paper, bicycles were actually radically transformative of human transport long before freeways came along. In World War I, most European armies introduced bicycle corps, as a way of transporting large numbers of troops quickly to battlefields. Japanese soldiers conquered Singapore in 1942 traveling on bicycle. Long before the Brompton, a British bicycle model popular with commuters because it folds up, one of the first folding bicycles was invented by the French and issued to its soldiers in World War II to carry on their backs. Warfare was, of course, only a tiny (and lamentable) part of it. Look back at photos from factories in Europe in the early part of the twentieth century and you can easily find footage of thousands of workers arriving by bicycle. A favorite clip of mine shows the workers arriving at the Morris Motors car factory in Oxford, England, just after the end of the Second World War. They come on a swarm of bicycles to build cars.

Indeed, most of the earliest macadamized roads were built not for cars but for bicycles. In the late nineteenth century, it was bicyclists who lobbied for smooth roads to be built, mostly in the countryside, so that people could get out of the city and explore. Sadly, a few of the same cyclists went on to become the world's first car enthusiasts. But it started with bikes, a far more democratic means of travel. In the late 1890s, an ordinary British worker could afford to buy a bicycle with roughly six weeks' wages—something like six pounds sterling. That may sound expensive in today's terms, but in the nineteenth century, that meant that for less than two months' labor, people could gain access to a device that would allow them to travel tens of miles quickly, opening up the possibility of better-paid jobs, better marriage prospects, and a better quality of life. Cars, by contrast, were only for the superrich.

Bicycles also have other advantages that Wilson barely got into. The primary one is that, much like cars, and unlike most public transport, they will take you door-to-door. They also provide exercise, which the residents of most big cities in the rich world could frankly do more of. According to the *British Journal of Sports Medicine*, cycle commuters typically weigh around four pounds less than non-cyclists, and they have a lower risk of heart disease and stroke. If you feel safe, a deeply important "if" that I will come to, it is fun. There is also a more recent improvement, which is the electric bicycle. Nowadays, you do not even have to provide the power to push yourself uphill. Electric bikes will do so for you, far more efficiently than an electric car.

For cities, however, the biggest advantage is that they occupy extremely little space, at least relative to cars. And they require essentially no new infrastructure. According to another study, done by academics at the University of the Andes in Santiago, Chile, one single one-meter-wide bicycle lane can transport 4,657 people on bicycles per hour before any of them have to slow down. A single car lane, which is generally a minimum of three meters wide in cities, can transport around 1,500 cars per hour. So if every car has four passengers, cars can, at most, transport roughly half of the number of people as bikes can in a single lane of traffic. If cars have 1.5 passengers on average, a more realistic figure for cities, bicycles can transport six times as many people.

Now in fairness, buses and trains can transport more people than bikes. But they do not go door-to-door, and you have to invest in them. By converting roads to bicycle lanes, however, as Paris has done, cities can instantly increase the capacity of their road infrastructure sixfold at essentially zero cost.

From 2010 to 2018, the number of people using bikes daily to get around Paris, including in the suburbs, increased by 30 percent. In the past twenty years, the proportion of Parisian households (in the city proper) who own a car has fallen from 60 percent to 35 percent. Air pollution, which peaked in 2016, has been gradually falling. And since the start of the coronavirus pandemic, the transformation has accelerated dramatically. When the city shut down in March 2020, Hidalgo quickly realized that with public transport off limits for safety reasons, the city needed to make sure that Parisians did not all get back into their cars. Pretty much overnight, it installed 60 kilometers of new bicycle lanes, quickly nicknamed *coronapistes* by locals. Another 150 km are planned. The national government also started giving out €500 subsidies for the purchase of an electric bike, and €50 vouchers toward bike repairs. Bike shops were inundated with people bringing in their ancient frames to get them useable.

The coronapistes are not always pretty—many are separated from the road by crude concrete blocks, which local graffiti artists have already made their own. But they are great for cyclists. Separated from car traffic, they feel far safer. When I visited Paris, even on a blustery October morning, with the rain pouring down, I saw whole families in rain jackets cycling along happily. According to figures released in May 2020, at the end of the first French lockdown, in just three months the number of cyclists in Paris had jumped by 44 percent over pre-pandemic levels—a bigger leap than the entire previous decade. The city now sees more than one million cycle journeys per day. Bicycles have overtaken the number of journeys made by that distinctly Parisian mode of transport, the motor scooter.

Not everyone is happy, for sure. Bicycle accidents have risen, in particular in places where pedestrians are not always ready for people hurtling around on electric bikes. (Parisians are not always keen on following traffic rules.) One elderly lady, walking her dog, told me that cyclists are "insane" and crossing the road now unnerves her. The *New York Times* rather breathlessly called it "anarchy." But even those who are concerned about being hit by somebody on a scooter or a bike admit that traffic congestion has not got worse, and the air is cleaner.

Ms. Hidalgo's ideas have turned her into a darling of urbanists. Underpinning this cycling transformation is a big idea called the "fifteen-minute city," which she took from Carlos Moreno, a French Colombian scientist at the Sorbonne. According to the theory, most necessities should be reachable within fifteen minutes by public transport, cycling, or walking. The idea is that most car journeys can be rendered unnecessary by making it easier not to drive. The idea has caught on elsewhere. Shaun Donovan, who served as secretary of US Housing and Urban Development under Barack Obama, proposed it in New York City as part of his (unsuccessful) run for mayor in 2021. Boulder, Colorado, one of America's great cycling cities, has flirted with it. The mayor of Cleveland, Ohio, Justin Bibb, has explicitly backed it too. Other cities, such as Portland, Oregon, and Melbourne, in Australia, and even Detroit, Michigan, have proposed twenty-minute variations, albeit with varying degrees of commitment.

What the fifteen-minute (or twenty-minute) city idea stands for, above all else, is creating the space for people to get around without needing cars. It is a model for nudging people away from their automobiles without having to radically transform entire cities. So can Paris become a model for change? For sure, Paris is not the easiest place to copy. There is a reason it is the world's most visited city by tourists. Being built mostly in the nineteenth century meant that the central city is dense and easy to walk around. The apartment buildings are tall and set up for urban living. The weather, as in much of northern Europe, is mild most of the year. It is much harder to imagine that what works in Paris being made to work so easily in a place like Houston, Texas, where the city is so much less densely populated, and where, at the moment, there are not always decent pavements for pedestrians to walk along if they want to. And cycling there would be intensely scary.

And yet I do think that Paris has lessons for other cities. I asked Christophe Najdovski, Hidalgo's deputy mayor in charge of transportation policy, and a member of the Green Party, about what Paris can teach the world. He told me that the key is not really about having an ancient city, or any particular geographical advantages. The recipe is simple: political will. In the 1950s and '60s, there was an enormous amount of political will to turn even ancient cities with cobbled streets into motorway cities. In Paris, not only were the expressways built along the Seine, but almost every spare patch of land was devoted to car parking space. It is easy to find old photos of places as famous as the Notre-Dame Cathedral and the courtyard of the Palais-Royal with the shocking sight of hundreds of cars parked out front. Now we need to do the opposite, removing the cars from our public spaces. And climate change and air pollution, combined with the shock of the pandemic, have created a moment for change.

Indeed, as Najdovski pointed out to me, Paris is actually coming belatedly to what a few other European cities, in particular those in the Netherlands and Denmark, discovered decades ago. The reason bikes are so common in Amsterdam or Copenhagen "is not a question of genetics, or the fact that they are flat cities," Najdovski told me. "It is that at a time in the 1970s and 1980s, these cities gave priority to active mobility instead of giving space to motorized traffic."

In Copenhagen, as in Paris with the coronavirus pandemic, it took a crisis. In 1973, in the wake of the Yom Kippur War, the Arab oil-producing states introduced an embargo on oil shipments in protest of American and European support for Israel. The price of a barrel of oil quadrupled from $2.90 to more than $11. With it, the price of gasoline shot up, and the world plunged into an economic crisis. The embargo was lifted a year later, but by then, the oil-producing states had realized their market power, and the Organization of the Petroleum Exporting Countries (OPEC), a cartel formed in 1960, began to exercise its might to keep oil prices high. Throughout the 1970s, the oil price kept rising. And with it, the enormous, inefficient cars of the day began to look pretty wasteful. In America, gasoline stations imposed rationing, and drivers often had to wait for hours to fill up. The federal government imposed a 55-mile-per-hour speed limit nationwide to try to reduce fuel consumption.

In Copenhagen, however, the city government had a better idea. It started with a ban on driving on Sundays. But then officials noticed that when people could not use their cars, they began getting out their bicycles. So the city started creating cycle lanes. Over the next thirty years, Copenhagen started adding more and more to its cycle infrastructure, and cycling started climbing back up. And Copenhagen is a pretty good place to show that, with the right infrastructure, cycling can be appealing even when the climate is not. Unlike

Paris, Copenhagen, if you have not visited, is not a place with especially wonderful weather. It gets twenty-three days of snow per year, compared with just twelve in New York City. And yet today, 62 percent of people travel to work, school, or university by bicycle. In 2016, for the first time since the 1950s, there were more bikes in the city center than cars.

Amsterdam is a similar story. In the Netherlands, there are 1.2 bikes per capita and fully a quarter of the population cycles every day. There, it was the sheer numbers of deaths from traffic accidents that motivated the change. In 1967, a group of anarchist youths called Provo announced that, "The car equals authority. Suffocating carbon monoxide is its incense. Its image has ruined thousandfold streets and canals." Their adherents introduced the first bicycle-sharing scheme, painting old bicycles white and leaving them around Amsterdam unlocked for anyone to use. It didn't work, as the police confiscated the bikes. But by 1971, as the number of child deaths in the city hit 500, their message had become mainstream. A campaign called Stop the Child Murder persuaded politicians to begin closing some streets to cars, so that children could once again play in them. As driving became harder, the Dutch, like the Danes, got out their bikes.

In both cases, what it took was a leadership that decided enough was enough. The Dutch have now so enthusiastically embraced cycling that their prime minister makes a point of traveling to meetings by bicycle. So too do many of its ambassadors overseas. In 2022, Donald Trump's former ambassador to Denmark, Carla Sands, tweeted that in Denmark, people are so poor that they cannot afford to drive, citing her diplomatic driver's daily cycle to work. Danes responded by noting that if money were the problem, then their royals must be poor as well, as the Crown Prince routinely cycles his children around in a cargo bike.

Najdovski told me he reckoned that almost any city could do at least some of what Paris is doing, and what Amsterdam and Copenhagen have already done, if they just have the will. When I spoke to him, it was in the middle of the COP26 climate talks in Glasgow, Scotland, and he told me he was dismayed that the world's leaders, including Emmanuel Macron, the president of France, seemed obsessed with electric cars, instead of trying to change the incentives about how people live. "If you replace one million fossil fuel cars with one million electric cars, you will still have the same congestion, and the same traffic, and the same shit. You won't change anything at all." By contrast, even relatively modest changes, like closing some roads and installing protected bicycle lanes, hint at a way of doing things differently. Paris's success shows that if you make it even just a little easier for people to not use their cars, they will move away from them in huge numbers. Because cycling is, frankly, better.

The basic problem is that the marginal cost of using a car is simply far too cheap. That is not to say that owning a car is cheap. Overall, owning a car is extremely expensive, and getting more so. Running vehicles costs the poorest fifth of Americans nearly a third of their pretax income. But the trouble is, once you have bought it, paid your insurance, taxes, and everything else, suddenly using it for one additional journey is very cheap, even when gasoline prices are relatively high. The key costs of using a car—the roads and parking—are subsidized enormously by governments. Most extra journeys require the driver only to pay for gasoline and perhaps parking. And given that you have paid for it, you want to use it. For tax purposes, the American government estimates the cost of owning a car, on average, to be around sixty-five cents per mile (an estimate that does not include the price of parking, road space, or anything else). The cost of gasoline is more like ten cents per mile. Even if you include the extra maintenance and depreciation costs that driving more entails, the marginal cost—that is, the cost of taking your car for a mile's drive—is probably more like twenty cents.

The greatest thing about bicycles is that if you own one, the marginal cost of using them is not just cheap, but literally free. The overall cost is extraordinarily cheap too. I spent $450 buying my bike, its lights, and its lock. It gets me to most places in Chicago as quickly as a car, for nothing. And at least insofar as I can trust the lock, I do not need to worry about parking.

The main reason people do not take up cycling in bigger numbers, despite all of these benefits, is simple: The danger people face from cars. Safety concerns are why cyclists in cities in the United States, and indeed much of Britain, tend to be Lycra-clad young men who thrive on the adrenaline rush of weaving through traffic to get around. Think of New York City's bicycle couriers, or the people in London's Richmond Park on weekends. But that is not what cyclists look like in Amsterdam or Copenhagen. The typical Dutch bike is not a low-slung racing model, but a high-seated, elegant, and heavy thing with a basket, a rack, and probably a child seat too. They are vehicles for getting around on.

Courtney Cobbs, a cycling activist in Chicago, told me that she moved to the city from her hometown in Arkansas in 2011 precisely because she did not want to have to drive everywhere. "It wasn't as busy as New York, it's not as expensive as New York. So I was like, Chicago. Perfect." Working as a social worker, she kept a car initially. But as soon as she was able to get a job that didn't require her to drive, she gave it up. Then in 2014, Chicago introduced its bike-sharing scheme, Divvy. And Courtney quickly realized that biking could work as a means of transport. "It started with, 'oh, I missed the bus. So I'm gonna, you know, bike to my destination,'" she says. Then the biking started to become her first choice for getting around.

The trouble is, biking in Chicago was—and often remains—pretty miserable. It is not primarily the weather that is the problem—even with Chicago's bitter winters, there are still probably only a dozen or so days a year in which the ice makes taking a bike outside foolhardy. For recreational cycling, the city has some of the best trails in America—the nineteen-mile Lakefront Trail is used year-round by bikers, even when it is well below freezing. The problem is the safety on the roads. The Lakefront Trail is gorgeous, but getting to it on your bike is not, which is why, depressingly, a lot of people drive their bikes to the trail, park up, and then cycle. There are some bike lanes, but they often end suddenly, pushing cyclists out into the path of cars. Many of the bike lanes that exist run alongside parked cars, from which drivers will open their car door straight into your path without bothering to look.

In my experience as a white man cycling in Chicago, I have had drivers hoot at me and overtake me too close, and I have had to pass hundreds of them parked in bike lanes. Courtney, a Black woman, has had far worse. "I've had people threaten to harm me," she says. Once, when she remonstrated with a driver who had parked, illegally, in a bike lane, his passenger got out and chased her down the road, before pushing her off her bike so that he could try to smash it up. Driving seems to bring out people's deepest racial hatreds. Other people have told her that she does not belong in the neighborhood she lives in and should get off the road. Courtney cycles everywhere, but she admitted to me that she often underplays how miserable it can be when talking to friends, lest it discourage them.

The sheer entitlement of drivers is perhaps the main reason cycling feels unsafe. It is not that drivers are inherently bad people. It is that driving literally changes your perception. At the wheel, you develop a sort of tunnel vision, and going at any speed lower than, say, 30 mph, can feel like a crawl. If you are in a rush to get somewhere, somebody on a bicycle ahead of you, traveling at, say, 12 mph, can feel like an affront. Road rage comes on quickly, and the idea that cyclists are the problem is easy. The late conservative satirist P. J. O'Rourke argued in a 1987 essay in *Car and Driver* magazine that the "very existence of the bicycle is an offense to reason and wisdom," mostly on the basis that he hated having to avoid them. He concluded the essay by arguing that soon, bicycles would be extinct anyway, because "law-abiding citizens like me" would deliberately murder enough cyclists that nobody would ride bikes anymore.

Sadly, he came close to being right. The sheer hatred of cyclists is the main reason cycling almost died out in the decades after the Second World War, and why it is only fitfully recovering now. You can see it in the vociferous campaigns against bike lanes that are mounted almost anywhere they are proposed. In Chicago, the local councilors, known as "aldermen," invariably oppose many new bike lanes on the basis that they will supposedly cause congestion. One alderman, Leslie Hairston, who represents a chunk of the South Side, argued that a protected bike lane was a bad idea precisely because the cars go too fast. "The traffic speed on most of Stony Island does not lend itself to sharing the road with bikes," she said, obliviously. Her views are sadly not rare—there is a widely held view on both sides of the Atlantic that cycling is not really a form of transport, but rather an activity people do for fun, and so bike lanes are a luxury.

But bicycles can be made safe, without having to persuade drivers to be safer, if just a small amount of the available road is given to them in the form of protected cycle lanes. In London, the first segregated routes began opening in 2016. As the network has grown, the number of cyclists has soared. From 2005 to 2020, the number of cyclists entering central London more than doubled, to 160,000 per day (despite the pandemic reducing the need to go into central London). In 2021, after the opening of several more lanes during the pandemic, the number of people cycling on weekends doubled that of 2020. Cycling deaths have slightly declined to around ten a year, but, per mile, cycling is sadly still more dangerous than driving. But the health benefits of the exercise more than outweigh the risk.

When the lanes were introduced in London, they were fiercely opposed by many. The Embankment cycle lane, opened in 2018, which runs along the River Thames, was denounced by a group of business interests, including haulage firms and taxi drivers, calling themselves Unblock the Embankment. They produced research arguing that the new lane was costing the London economy £5.7 million. Their calculations assumed that every driver delayed by more traffic on the road cost the economy a chunk of money. The increased numbers of cyclists using the road, however, were not counted at all—apparently their journeys were literally worthless. This lobbying effort, thankfully, failed. Polling showed that nearly nine out of ten Londoners supported keeping the bike lane. The idea of removing it now would rightly be seen as insane.

If only people in Chicago—or indeed many other cities—would get the message. More cyclists now die annually in Chicago than they do in London, a city more than three times larger. The same is true of New York, which has, in recent years, totted up thirty or so deaths a year of cyclists. In per capita terms, that's similar to Chicago. So is it any wonder we cyclists are relatively rare? But that is easy to change. As the experience of Paris and London show, if you built protected bike lanes, which cars cannot enter, people will use them. In fact, much as with motorways and cars, they induce demand rather effectively.

This is particularly true if driving is made slightly more expensive. Stockholm and London introduced their congestion charges more than fifteen years ago; following Singapore, which introduced one in 1975. The result was that a lot of people simply chose to stop driving. Birmingham, my hometown city, has introduced a daily charge for drivers using older, more polluting diesel vehicles to drive into the city center. When it was introduced, my dad, who refuses to replace his aging car, gleefully bought an electric bicycle, which he described to me as a brilliant wheeze to avoid the tax. In fact, that is exactly what the tax is meant to produce. Birmingham is also introducing an annual levy of £500 for every car parking space that employers provide in the city center. If people have to pay for parking, they may realize they do not need it.

The past few years have been good for this sort of thinking. Paris was not alone in opening more cycle lanes during the pandemic. London has done plenty too, creating new lanes for cyclists by closing off lanes of Waterloo

Bridge as well as much of the Embankment, which runs along the north bank of the River Thames. The result is that now at the start and end of the working day, there are literally thousands of people on bicycles making their way to and from work. One big silver lining of the pandemic was the realization that some of this can be quite easy to do. A shock, even as terrible a one as the pandemic, can be a good opportunity to make changes that would have been unthinkable before. About the coronapistes, Najdovski told me: "We just drew these bike lanes in one night, and put some concrete blocks and just some paint, and it went very fast. I can say also that some taboos fell. It was an incredible moment," he says.

Even in America, change is happening. In New York, part of the roadway across the Brooklyn Bridge was turned into a protected bike lane, and data suggested that it wasn't just pulling cyclists from other bridges but encouraging new riders. Over the past few years, Minneapolis has built some of the best urban bike lanes in America. And despite its appalling winters, the number of cyclists using them has soared.

In Chicago, I met a man, Jon C. Lind, who set up a shop a decade ago in Lincoln Park, a fairly fancy neighborhood north of downtown, to import Dutch-style bicycles to his home city. He says initially it was a challenge—most Americans looking for bicycles want to buy fast racing bikes, for fun and sport. But, he says, change is happening. "There's been a slow warm-up over the past decade or so toward the idea of transportation biking," he says. The big change recently has been the advent of electric bikes. "We've sold more electric bikes in the last year or two than I could ever have really imagined," he told me in late 2021. The reason, he speculates, is because "it limits the number of excuses people have not to cycle." The city has promised to build 200 miles of cycle lanes over the next two years, spending $17 million on them. That is both pathetically little and also evidence of how fantastically cheap cycling is as a way to add to transport infrastructure.

In 2021, the United States imported 790,000 electric bicycles, according to the Light Electric Vehicle Association, an industry group. That is 100,000 more than the number of electric cars purchased that year. And that is despite the fact that electric cars qualify buyers for as much as $7,500 in federal tax credits, and sometimes more in state tax credits, whereas for the moment, electric bikes qualify for none at all. In Europe, the figure for sales is now more than three million, while in Asia, it is more than thirty-five million. Electric bikes are probably not fully replacing cars for many Americans. But Jon tells me that they are making a difference in replacing urban trips—the most damaging sort of driving—and in helping families avoid owning two cars.

With an electric bike, you can still turn up to a meeting in a suit without being sweaty. They are wonderfully fast, zooming along at 15 mph (or as fast as most cars manage in a dense city center). In London and New York City, almost every food delivery rider rides one; various firms rent them out for around £40 a week, or $150 a month in New York. Electric motors also make other types of bikes, such as cargo bikes, which have enormous front boxes capable of carrying children or quite a lot of groceries, far more plausible as a means of transport. You see a lot of them in London and Paris these days too, carrying much larger deliveries around—the sorts of quantities you would otherwise need a van to carry—at much higher speed.

But you even see cargo bikes in Chicago, New York, and Los Angeles nowadays—in Chicago, versions that were mostly likely sold by Jon. On the 606, a former elevated railway track now converted to a park in Chicago, I counted nine parents carrying their children in cargo bikes or in bike trailers on one summer's day. It is faster than taking public transport and cheaper than driving and parking. One thing that has helped people realize that bikes can be better than cars has been the proliferation of flexible bike rental systems. In Chicago, despite owning my own bike, I also use the Divvy bikes. It costs $120 a year, but residents on lower incomes can sign up for $5. In a city where one in five people lives in poverty, and many neighborhoods lack good public transport options, it is a pretty good alternative way to get around that simply did not exist a decade ago.

With a bike, the number of jobs that a person in, say, the South Side of the city, which is mostly poor and Black, can reach within an hour without needing to own a car soars. One big advantage of bikes is that, unlike most public transport systems, they are quick at getting between different neighborhoods, as well as into city centers. The problem is, as things stand, it is just not reasonable to expect many people living in on the South Side to cycle to work. It is simply not safe. A study by researchers at Harvard and Boston University found that Black cyclists are roughly 4.5 times more likely to be killed per mile traveled than white ones in America. That undoubtedly reflects the fact that the fastest, most dangerous highways tend to have been built through majority Black neighborhoods, so that wealthier drivers can zoom through quickly, whereas many protected bike lanes tend to be built in affluent white districts. But it means that the people who are most in need of alternatives to owning a car have the fewest non-driving options.

That said, even with the right infrastructure, it will take time to change attitudes. As well as better road infrastructure, we also need secure places for people to store their bikes while at work and at home. We need more workplaces to offer showers, as a growing number in London now do, so that cycling does not mean you have to turn up to the office sweaty. Workplaces also need secure bike storage. That sort of thing will take an attitude shift as much as policy changes. In Britain, moaning about cyclists is practically a national pastime. We are, it is said, smug, self-righteous lunatics, putting ourselves in danger and clogging up the roads. On the first part I don't entirely disagree. I am rather smug. But the only times in my adult life that I have been physically assaulted have all been by drivers, in London. One was a middle-aged BMW driver who parked illegally in a cycle lane and then, when I took a photo of his car so that I could report it, chased me half a mile down the road hurling abuse at me and literally steering his vehicle at me to scare me. I remember it distinctly, not least because one of the things he shouted at me was that cyclists had "ruined the city." We haven't; BMW drivers have, but it will take time to persuade people of that.

It is worth trying, however. Walking and cycling are not only convenient, and often cheaper, but they are also much healthier than sitting still behind the wheel of a car. We live in increasingly sedentary societies. A 2010 survey by the Centers for Disease Control found that 38 percent of Americans say that they have not walked for more than ten minutes at a time in more than a week. At a typical walking pace, that means more than a third of people have not walked half a mile in a week. The average Briton walks only around half a mile per day to get anywhere (so, not counting walking from the sofa to the fridge), or 181 miles a year, according to the Department of Transport. That is down by 83 miles since 1986. And so it should hardly be a surprise that we are getting fatter. Around 28 percent of Brits are clinically obese, and another 35 percent are overweight. In America, 41 percent of people are obese, a figure that is higher still in states like Texas or Iowa, where almost everybody gets around by car.

Driving everywhere is not only making our cities ugly and polluted, it is also making us fatter. It is easy to moralize about that, but it is mostly not because people are lazy that they do not exercise enough. It is because they follow the incentives society creates. And those incentives are to drive everywhere, rather than to walk. Our ancestors did not spend much time in the gym, or even eat especially healthy diets, but they stayed slim because their day-to-day habits involved walking. It would do us good to rediscover that.

Telling people that they do not need to drive is not always easy. But the best thing that we can do is simply to alter our preconceptions. Over the past few years, as cities like London and New York have taken space away from cars to give it to bikes and pedestrians, many drivers are initially affronted. In Britain, arguments over low-traffic neighborhoods, where cars are blocked from driving through certain streets (though not from parking on them), are perhaps as politically controversial as almost anything else that government, whether local or national, does. Much as with the Pompidou in Paris, when they are introduced, initially, drivers tend to be unhappy. But what they learn after a while is that, actually, if you have to drive a car somewhere, the worst thing is being surrounded by other people running errands in their own cars that they could do just as easily on foot or by bicycle. Reducing the number of cars on our streets is not only good for people who walk and cycle. It is also good for the drivers who remain.

The greatest way in which drivers delude themselves is by imagining that driving is the pleasant option. Even I sympathize with drivers. It is miserable enough trying to get around in a car without having to feel guilty too. Sure, you do not get rained on as much as you do on a bicycle or by walking. But otherwise, it sucks. According to Everytown for Gun Safety, an American lobbying group, there are around forty-five shootings every month in America linked to road rage. That is one every eighteen hours. Sitting in traffic is miserable. If you do not need to do it, why not consider the alternatives? And if everyone else does too, then on those occasions where you really do need to drive, you might hate it a little less.

15

GO EAST: LESSONS FROM JAPAN

For cities that want to reduce the number of cars, bike lanes are a good place to start. They are cheap, usually city-level authorities can introduce them, and they do not require you to raise taxes on people who own cars. What if you want to do something more radical though? What would a city that genuinely wanted to get the car out of its citizens' lives in a much bigger way do? A city that wanted to make it possible for most people to live decent lives and be able to get around without needing a car, even without needing to get on a bicycle? There is only one city on Earth I have ever visited that has truly managed this. But it happens to be the biggest city on the planet: Tokyo, the capital of Japan.

In popular imagination, at least in the west, Tokyo is both incredibly futuristic, and also rather foreign and confusing. Before I first visited, in 2017, I imagined it to be an incredibly hectic place, a noisy, bustling megacity. I was on holiday and trying to escape Nairobi, a rather sprawling, low-height and green city, and I picked Tokyo largely because I wanted to get as far away from Africa as I could. I needed a break from the traffic jams, the power cuts, the constant negotiation to achieve anything, and the heat. I was looking for an escape somewhere as different as I could think of, and I wanted to ride trains around and look at high-tech skyscrapers and not worry about getting splattered by mud walking in the street. I was expecting to feel bowled over by the height of the buildings, the sheer crush of people, and the noise.

Yet when I emerged from the train station in Shibuya, blinking jetlagged in the morning light after a night flight from Amsterdam, what actually caught me off guard was not the bustle but rather how quiet the city is. When you see cliched images of Tokyo, what invariably is shown are the enormous crowds of pedestrians crossing the roads, or Mount Fuji in the background of the futuristic skyline. I expected something like Los Angeles in *Blade Runner*, I suppose—futuristic and overwhelming. From photos, Tokyo can look almost unplanned, with neon signs everywhere and a huge variety of forms of architecture. You expect it to feel messy. What I experienced, however, was a city that felt almost like being in a futuristic village. It is utterly calm, in a way that is actually rather strange.

And it took me a little while to realize why. There is simply no traffic noise. No hooting, no engine noise, not even much of the noise of cars accelerating on tarmac. Because there are so few of them. Most of the time you can walk in the middle of the street, so rare is the traffic. There are not even cars parked at the side of the road. That is not true of all of Tokyo, of course. The expressways are often packed. Occasionally, I was told, particularly when it snows, or during holidays when large numbers of people try to drive out to the countryside, jams form that can trap drivers for whole days. But on most residential streets, traffic is almost nonexistent. Even the relatively few cars that you do see are invariably tiny, quiet vehicles.

Among rich cities, Tokyo has the lowest car use in the world. According to Deloitte, a management consultancy, just 12 percent of journeys are completed by private car. It might surprise you to hear that cycling is actually more popular than driving in Tokyo—it accounts for 17 percent of journeys, though the Japanese do not make as much of a big deal out of it as the Dutch do. But walking and public transport dwarf both sorts of vehicles. Tokyo has the most-used public transport system in the world, with thirty million people commuting by train each day. This may sound rather unpleasant. You have probably seen footage of the most crowded routes at rush hour, when staff literally push people onto the carriages to make space, or read about young women being groped in the crush. It happens, but it is not typical. Most of the trains I rode were busy but comfortable, and I was able to get a seat.

And what makes Tokyo remarkable is that the city was almost entirely built after the original city was mostly flattened by American bombers in the Second World War. Elsewhere in the world, cities built after the war are almost invariably car-dependent. Think of Houston, Texas, which has grown from 300,000 people in the 1950s to ten times that now. Or England's tiny version, Milton Keynes, which is the fastest-growing city in the country. Or almost any developing world city. Since the advent of the automobile, architects and urban planners worldwide have found it almost impossible to resist building cities around roads and an assumption that most people will drive. Tokyo somehow managed not to. It rebuilt in a much more human-centric way.

It may come as a surprise that Japan is home to the world's biggest relatively car-free city. After all, Japan is the country that gave the world Mitsubishi, Toyota, and Nissan, and exports vehicles all over the world. And in fairness, a lot of Japanese people do own cars. Overall car ownership in Japan is about 590 vehicles per 1,000 people, which is less than America's rate of about 800 per 1,000, but comparable to a lot of European countries. On average, there are 1.06 cars per household. But Tokyo is a big exception. In Tokyo, there are only 0.32 cars per household. Most Japanese car owners live in smaller towns and cities than the capital. The highest rate of car ownership, for example, is in Fukui Prefecture, on the western coast of Honshu, one of Japan's least densely populated areas.

And car ownership in Japan is falling, unlike almost everywhere else on Earth. Part of the reason is just that the country is getting older and the population is falling. But it is also that more and more people live in Tokyo. Annually, Japan is losing about 0.3 percent of its population, or about half a million people a year. Greater Tokyo, however, with its population of thirty-seven million, is shrinking by less than that, or about 0.1 percent a year. And the prefecture of Tokyo proper, with a population of fourteen million, is still growing. The reason is that Tokyo generates the best jobs in Japan, and it is also an increasingly pleasant place to live. You may think of Tokyoites as being crammed into tiny apartments, but in fact, the average home in Tokyo has

65.9 square meters of livable floor space (709 square feet). That is still very small—indeed, it is less than the size of the average home in London, where the figure is 80 square meters. But the typical household in London has 2.7 people living in it. In Tokyo, it is 1.95. So per capita, people in Tokyo actually have more space than Londoners.

Overall in fact, people in Tokyo have one of the highest qualities of life in the world. A 2015 survey by *Monocle* magazine came to the conclusion that Tokyo is the best city on Earth in which to live, "due to its defining paradox of heart-stopping size and concurrent feeling of peace and quiet." In 2021 *The Economist* ranked it fourth, after Wellington and Auckland in New Zealand, and another Japanese city, Osaka. Life expectancy overall is eighty-four years old, one of the highest levels of any city on the planet. A good part of this has to do with the lack of cars. Air pollution is considerably lower than in any other city of equivalent size anywhere in the world. Typical commutes are, admittedly, often fairly long, at forty minutes each way. But they are not in awful smoggy car traffic.

So how has Tokyo managed it? Andre Sorensen, a professor of urban planning at the University of Toronto, who published a history of urban planning in Japan, told me that Japan's history has a lot to do with it. Japan's urbanization happened a little more like some poorer countries—quickly. At the start of the twentieth century, just 15 percent of Japanese people lived in cities. Now 91 percent do, one of the highest rates of urbanization in the entire world. That rapid growth meant that Tokyo's postwar growth was relatively chaotic. Buildings sprawled out into rice paddies, with sewage connections and power often only coming later. Electricity is still often delivered by overhead wires, not underground cables. And yet somehow this haphazard system manages to produce a relatively coherent city, and one that is much easier to get around on foot or by public transport than by car.

Part of the reason, Sorensen explained to me, is just historical chance. Japanese street layouts traditionally were narrow, much like medieval alleys in Europe. Land ownership was often very fragmented, meaning that house builders had to learn to use small plots in a way that almost never happened in Europe or America. And unlike the governments there, the government in postwar Japan was much more concerned with boosting economic growth by creating power plants and industrial yards than it was with creating huge new boulevards through neighborhoods. So the layouts never changed. According to Sorensen's research, 35 percent of Japanese streets are not actually wide enough for a car to travel down them. More remarkably still, 86 percent are not wide enough for a car to be able to stop without blocking the traffic behind it.

Yet the much bigger reason for Tokyo's high quality of life is that Japan does not subsidize car ownership in the way other countries do. In fact, owning a car in Tokyo is rather difficult. For one thing, cars are far more enthusiastically inspected than in America or most of Europe. Cars must be checked by officials every two years to ensure that they are still compliant, and have not been modified. That is true in Britain too, but the cost is higher than what a Ministry of Transport test costs. Even a well-maintained car can cost 100,000 yen to inspect (or around $850). On cars that are older than ten years, the fees escalate dramatically, which helps to explain why so many Japanese sell their cars relatively quickly, and so many of them end up in East Africa or Southeast Asia. On top of that there is an annual automobile tax of up to 50,000 yen, as well as a 5 percent tax on the purchase. And then gasoline is taxed too, meaning it costs around 160 yen per liter, or about $6 a gallon, less than in much of Europe, but more than Americans accept.

And even if you are willing to pay all of the taxes, you cannot simply go and buy a car in the way that you might in most countries. To be allowed to purchase a car, you have to be able to prove that you have somewhere to park it. This approval is issued by the local police, and is known as a *shako shomeisho*, or "garage certificate." Without one, you cannot buy a car. This helps to explain why the Japanese buy so many tiny cars, like the so-called Kei cars. It means they can have smaller garages. Even if the law didn't exist though, owning a car in Japan without having a dedicated parking space for it would be a nightmare. Under a nationwide law passed in 1957, overnight street parking of any sort is completely illegal. So if you were to somehow buy a car with no place to store it, you could not simply park it on the street, because it would get towed the next morning, and you would get fined 200,000 yen (around $1,700). In fact, most street parking of any sort is illegal. There are a few exceptions, but more than 95 percent of Japanese streets have no street parking at all, even during the day.

This, rather than any beautiful architecture, explains why Tokyo's streets feel so pleasant to walk down, or indeed to look at. There are no cars filling them up. It also means that land is actually valued properly. If you want to own a car, it means that you also have to own (or at least rent) the requisite land to keep it. In rural areas or smaller towns, this is not a huge deal, because land is relatively cheap, and so a permit might only cost 8,000 to 9,000 yen, or about $75 a month. But in Tokyo, the cost will be at least four times that. Garages in American cities can cost that much too, but in Japan there is no cheap street parking option, as in much of New York or Chicago. Most apartment buildings are constructed without any parking at all, because the developers can use the space more efficiently for housing. Only around 42 percent of condominium buildings have parking spaces for residents. Similarly, even if you own a parking space, it is almost never free to park anywhere you might take your car. Parking in Tokyo typically costs 1,000 yen an hour, or around $8.50.

This is a big disincentive to driving. Sorensen told me that when he lived in Tokyo, some wealthy friends of his owned a top-end BMW, which they replaced every few years, because they were car nuts. But because they did not have anywhere to park it near their home, if they wanted to use it, they had to take public transport (or a taxi) to get to it at its garage. As a result, they simply did not use their car very much. In their day-to-day life, they used the trains, the same as everybody else, or took taxis, because that was cheaper than picking up the car. This sort of thing probably helps to explain why the Japanese, despite relatively high levels of car ownership, do not actually drive very far. Car owners in Japan typically drive around 6,000 kilometers per year. That is about half what the average British car owner drives, and less than a third of what the average American does.

Parking rules are not, however, the limit of what keeps cars out of Tokyo. Arguably, an even bigger reason is how infrastructure has been funded in Japan. That is, by the market, rather than directly by taxes. In the 1950s and '60s, much like Europe and the United States, Japan began building expressways. But unlike in Europe and America, it was starting from a considerably more difficult place. In 1957, Ralph J. Watkins, an American economist who had been invited to advise the Japanese government, reported that "the roads of Japan are incredibly bad. No other industrial nation has so completely neglected its highway system." Just 23 percent of roads were paved, including just two-thirds of the only highway linking Osaka, Japan's historical economic hub, to Tokyo.

But unlike America, the idea of making them free never seemed to cross politicians' minds, probably because Japan in the postwar era was not the world's richest country. Capital was not freely available. To build the roads, the national government formed corporations such as the Shuto Kōsoku-dōro Kabushiki-gaisha, or Metropolitan Expressway Company, which was formed in greater Tokyo in 1959. These corporations took out vast amounts of debt, which they had to repay, so that the Japanese taxpayer would not be burdened. That meant that tolls were imposed from the very beginning. The tolls had to cover not just the construction cost, but also maintenance and interest on the loans. Today, to drive on the Shuto Expressway costs from 300 to 1,320 yen, or $2.50 to $11 for a "standard-size" automobile. Overall, tolls in Japan are the most expensive in the world—around three times higher than the level charged on the private autoroutes in France, or on average, about 3,000 yen per 100 kilometers ($22 to drive sixty-two miles).

What that meant was that, from the beginning, roads did not have an unfair advantage in their competition with other forms of transport. And so in Japan, unlike in almost the entire rest of the rich world, the postwar era saw the construction of enormous amounts of rail infrastructure. Indeed, at a time when America and Britain were nationalizing and cutting their railways to cope with falling demand for train travel, in Japan, the national railway company was pouring investment into the system. The world's first high-speed railway, the Tokaido Shinkansen, was opened in 1964 to coincide with the Tokyo Olympics, with a top speed of 210 kilometers per hour. That was almost double what trains elsewhere mostly managed. From 1964 to 1999, the number of passengers using the Shinkansen grew from 11 million annually to more than 300 million.

Sorensen told me about how in the 1950s and '60s, the trains were a huge point of national pride for the Japanese government, a bit like car industries were elsewhere. "And justifiably! It was a fantastic invention. To say we can make electric rail go twice as fast. What an achievement." Thanks to that, the railways ministry became a huge power center in government, rather than a neglected backwater as it often had become elsewhere. In rail, the Japanese "built up expertise in engineering, in bureaucratic resources and capacities, and political clout that just lasted," he told me. "Whereas the road-building sector was weak." Elsewhere, building roads became a self-reinforcing process, because as more was poured into constructing them, more people bought cars and demanded more roads. That did not happen in Japan. Instead, the growth in railway infrastructure led to growth in, well, more railway infrastructure.

If you visit Tokyo now, what you will find is that the most hectic, crowded places in the city are all around the train and subway stations. The reason is that Japan's railway companies (the national firm was privatized in the 1980s) do not only provide railways. They are also big real estate investors. A bit like the firm that built the Metropolitan Railway in the 1930s in Britain, when Japan's railway firms expanded service, they paid for it by building on the land around the stations. In practice, what that means is that they built lots of apartments, department stores, and supermarkets near (and directly above) railway stations, so that people can get straight off the train and get home quickly. That makes the trains more efficient, because people can get where they need to go without having to walk or travel to and from stations especially far. But it also means that the railways are incredibly profitable, because unlike in the West, they are able to profit from the improvement in land value that they create.

What this adds up to is that Tokyo is one of very few cities on Earth where travel by car is not actively subsidized, and funnily neither is public transport, and yet both work well, when appropriate. However, Tokyo is not completely alone. Several big cities across Asia have managed to avoid the catastrophe (cartastrophe?) that befell much of the western world. Hong Kong manages it nearly as well as Tokyo; there are just 76 cars per 1,000 people in the city state. So too does Singapore, with around 120 per 1,000 people. What those cities have in common, which makes them rather different from Japan, is a shortage of land and a relentless, centralized leadership that recognized early on that cars were a waste of space.

In Singapore, for example, congestion charging was introduced in 1975, almost thirty years before anywhere else managed it. It was motivated by a growing traffic problem; in the decade before, the number of cars owned in

Singapore was increasing at a rate of 9 percent per year, and traffic jams were beginning to choke up the city. This, said Singapore's communications minister at the time, Yong Nyuk Lin, was "slowly eroding the economic well-being of Singapore." So they did something about it. To enter the central business districts, drivers were made to buy a special license for their car, at a cost of three Singapore dollars per day, which they displayed in the windscreen. It was an astonishing success. From March to October 1975, when the scheme was introduced, the number of cars entering central Singapore fell from 43,000 per day to a little more than 11,000. In 1998, the system was replaced with electronic road pricing. Now if you drive in Singapore, you are automatically charged a fee that is fixed according to how busy the road is. The busier it is, the higher the fee, thereby ensuring that traffic jams do not form. It is the sort of thing that makes economists slaver with envy.

Singapore's traffic control measures get more dramatic than that, however. Only cars that are less than three years old can be imported, so you essentially have to buy a new one. You also need to buy a Certificate of Entitlement, which entitles you to own and operate a car for ten years. For a smaller car (with an engine of less than 1,600 cubic centimeters), these currently cost around 57,000 Singaporean dollars ($41,000). For larger cars, it is twice that. The number of permits is fixed; it is only allowed to increase in line with road capacity, and they are sold at auction. In Hong Kong, there is no cap on the number of vehicles, but buyers of a car have to pay a "First Registration Tax," which starts at 46 percent of the value of the vehicle (on the first HK$150,000, or US$20,000) and rises to more than 132 percent of the value. That makes importing cars expensive. As in Japan, parking is also expensive, and rare, while roads and bridges are tolled.

Similar policies in recent years have been adopted in mainland China—in particular in Shanghai and Beijing. Frankly, they came a bit late. In the 1980s, cyclists made up 65 percent of the users of roads in Beijing; old film footage of Chinese cities shows streets thronged with two wheelers, and only the occasional government official in a stately limousine. That had declined to 16 percent by 2010 and further still since. Now, the city's roads are choked with traffic, and the air is appallingly polluted. Some cities have even adopted some American-inspired policies designed to stop pedestrians from slowing down vehicular traffic, with a typically totalitarian spin. In Shenzhen, the electronics-producing megacity on the other side of the Hong Kong border, China's terrifying facial recognition technology is being used to fine jaywalkers. As well as being fined, they are publicly shamed, with their photos displayed on a giant LED screen above an intersection in the city.

But some parts of the Chinese government have also realized the downsides of expanding car ownership and roads forever. In Beijing, the municipal government makes people enter a lottery to win a permit to own a car. Cars from outside of Beijing are allowed to enter the city—but only with a permit that lasts seven days, and drivers can only buy twelve permits in a year, meaning that it is not a very practical solution for wannabe car-owners who live in the city. In Shanghai, as in Singapore, license plates are sold by auction, and typically cost the equivalent of around $10,000. Even the Communist Party of China, with its relentless focus on raising the living standards of Chinese people to make up for the crushing of their freedom, has realized that there is a limit to the number of people who can realistically own a car before it begins to ruin cities.

As Japan did, the Chinese have also, in little more than two decades, built out a high-speed rail infrastructure to make anywhere else in the world envious of, meaning that there are alternatives to owning a car. The Beijing subway now carries four billion passengers a year, or about three times more than the London Underground. The result is that car ownership, which had been rising fast, has stalled at about 200 vehicles per 1,000 people—high for a developing world country, but still far below the levels in Europe or America. China is now by far the world's biggest market for cars—but the hopes of automobile executives to sell enormous numbers of new vehicles there have been dashed. Despite GDP increasing by 33 percent between 2015 and 2020, sales of new vehicles have stayed stagnant, at around twenty-five million per year. Electric vehicles also make up a higher share of those sales in China than almost anywhere else. (Sadly, for now, they are mostly all charged with energy generated from coal power.)

Why do I bring all of this up? Unfortunately, replicating the Asian model in countries in Europe, America, or Australia from scratch will not be easy. We are starting with so many cars on our roads to begin with, that imposing the sorts of curbs on car ownership that I listed above is almost certainly a political nonstarter. Just look at what happens when politicians in America or Britain try to take away even a modest amount of street parking, or increase the tax on gasoline. People are already invested in cars, sadly. And thanks to that, there is also a chicken-and-egg problem. Because people are invested in cars, they live in places where the sort of public transport that makes life possible for the majority of people in Tokyo or Hong Kong is simply not realistic. As it is, constructing rail infrastructure like Japan's is an extraordinarily difficult task. Look at the difficulties encountered in things like building Britain's new high-speed train link, or California's, for example.

And yet it is worth paying attention to Tokyo (and to Hong Kong, and Singapore, and even Shanghai) precisely because it shows that vast numbers of cars are not necessary to daily life. What Tokyo shows is that it is possible for enormous cities to work rather well without being overloaded by traffic congestion. Actually, Tokyo works better than big cities anywhere else. That is why it has managed to grow so large. The trend all over the world for decades now has been toward greater wealth concentrating in the biggest metropolises. The cost of living in somewhere like New York, London, or Paris used to be marginally higher than living in a more modest city. That is no longer the case. And it reflects the fact that the benefits of living in big cities are enormous. The jobs are better, but so too are the restaurants, the cultural activities, the dating opportunities, and almost anything else you can think of. People are willing to pay for it. The high cost of living is a price signal—that is, the fact that people are willing to pay it is an indicator of the value they put on it.

Especially in this post-pandemic era where many jobs can be done from anywhere, lots of New Yorkers could easily decamp to, say, a pretty village upstate, and save a fortune in rent, or cash in on their property values. Actually, hundreds of thousands do every year (well, not only to upstate). But they are replaced by newcomers for the simple reason that New York City is, if you set aside the cost, a pretty great place to live. And yet, if everyone who would like to live in a big city is to be able to, those cities need to be able to grow more. But if they continue to grow with the assumption that the car will be the default way of getting around for a significant proportion of residents, then they will be strangled by congestion long before they ever reach anything like

Tokyo's success. People often say that London or New York are too crowded, but they are wrong. They are only too crowded if you think that it is normal for people to need space not just for them but also for the two tons of metal that they use to get around.

The sheer anger of motorists might mean that banning overnight parking on residential streets proves difficult. But if we want to be bold, some of Tokyo's other measures are more realistic. We could, for example, do a lot more to build more housing around public transport, and use the money generated to help contribute to the network. According to the Centre for Cities, a British think tank, there are 47,000 hectares of undeveloped land (mostly farmland) within a ten-minute walk of a railway station close to close to London or another big city. That is enough space to build two million homes, more than half of which would be within a forty-five-minute commute to or from London. The reason we do not develop the land at the moment is because it is mostly Metropolitan Green Belt, a zoning restriction created in the late 1940s by the Town and Country Planning Act intended to contain cities and stop them sprawling outward. But the problem with it as it works in Britain at the moment is that it does not stop sprawl—it just pushes it further away from cities, into places where there really is no hope of not using a car.

Developing the green belt too would not be popular. People have an affection for fields near their homes, and they do not necessarily want the trains they use to be even more crowded. But there are projects that show it is possible to overcome NIMBYism. In Los Angeles in 2016, voters approved the Transit Oriented Communities Incentive Program, which creates special zoning laws in areas half a mile from a major transit stop (typically, in LA, a light rail station). This being Los Angeles, it is fairly modest. One of the rules is that the mandatory parking minimums applied are restricted to a maximum of 0.5 car parking spaces per bedroom, and total parking is not meant to exceed more than one space per apartment, which is still rather a lot of parking. But nonetheless, it does allow developers to increase the density of homes near public transport, and it has encouraged developers to build around 20,000 new homes near public transport that probably would not have been constructed otherwise. These are small but real improvements.

Ultimately, no city will be transformed into Tokyo overnight, nor should any be, at least unless a majority of the population decides that they would like it. I am trying to persuade them; for now, not everyone is as enamored with the Japanese capital as I am. But NIMBYism and other political problems can be gradually overturned, if the arguments are made in the right way, even in the most automotive cities.

16

WINNING THE ARGUMENT

In fall 2020, around the corner from my parents' house in Moseley, a suburb of Birmingham, England, one morning residents awoke to find two large wooden planter boxes in the road. The planters were positioned to stop cars from entering the road down to Moseley Village, the suburb's main shopping street. A sign indicated that bicycles were allowed through, but no motorized vehicles of any sort. Residents could still drive to their own homes, and delivery vehicles could come in, but they would have to enter at the other end. People who simply wanted to drive through could not. They would have to find another way.

The Moseley planter boxes were there to enforce low-traffic neighborhoods, or LTNs—the technical term for new traffic control measures that have spread across England in recent years. There are a variety of different types. Some in London use cameras and numberplate recognition technology to issue fines to people who drive down roads that are closed to through traffic. Most use either bollards or planter boxes to block one end of the road. The idea is to stop "rat-running," where people drive down residential streets to avoid the ever-thicker traffic on main roads. In 2020 and 2021, under a change to the law passed during the coronavirus pandemic, local councils were given money to introduce more of them, and to reduce the length of the previously painful consultation process necessary to close a road. Quickly they proliferated all over England. More than seventy were introduced in London in just six months, from March to September 2020.

I know about the case in Moseley in more detail than perhaps I would even like to, because my mother has a singular passion for local politics. Since May 2022, she has been an elected councilor on the city government. And little has excited the residents of Moseley more than the appearance of the LTNs on their doorsteps. People really care about where they can and cannot take their cars. Mum, the astute local politician that she is, has tried to walk a careful tightrope, broadly supporting the road closures while criticizing some of the details and the lack of consultation. But she faces people on one side who think that their most fundamental rights (to drive everywhere quickly and painlessly) are being trampled on, while others think that what it is happening is long overdue.

It is not just in Moseley. Over the past couple of years, LTNs have become a hot topic all over England. Across London you will see signs erected in people's gardens that read "Stop the Road Closures." Some of the planters have been tipped over, while cameras have been spray-painted. Piers Corbyn, the conspiracy theorist brother of Jeremy Corbyn, Britain's former opposition leader, thinks that they are part of a "new normal" agenda intended to turn Britain into a dictatorship under the guise of a fake public health emergency. Or something like that anyway. Britain's right-wing tabloids, in particular the *Daily Mail*, have made campaigning against LTNs an obsession.

People are upset by LTNs for lots of reasons. For some, it means that journeys that they got used to doing by car are now trickier. Others worry about emergency vehicle access: If you look at anti-LTN Facebook groups, nothing incites more anger than a bit of CCTV footage of an ambulance stopped outside a bollard. The biggest argument against them, however, is that, at least in the views of the protesters, they mostly only displace traffic onto other roads. The *Daily Mail*'s line has been that the bollards actually cause more pollution, as people have to drive further to avoid them, and they get stuck in traffic for longer. Comments left on a government consultation website in Moseley reflect this view. "It is no longer the lovely fairly quiet residential road it was," said one resident of a street near the blocked one. "This increase in traffic is causing a major safety issue, has increased the volume, noise, and pollution from traffic, and is a major health problem."

LTNs are a fairly British phenomenon, but you can find equivalent campaigns all over the world. In Los Angeles, for example, proposals to turn lanes of traffic into dedicated bus lanes often generate heated protests. There too, the primary argument against them is that they displace traffic. Take the example of one protester interviewed by Spectrum News, a cable news channel, about protests to a new bus lane being introduced in Eagle Rock, a neighborhood to the northeast of downtown Los Angeles. She told the reporter that she did not like to drive herself, but was worried about traffic displacement from the bus lane affecting her ability to. "My greatest fear is that . . . there is going to be fatalities because people are really angry, they are stuck in traffic and they just race on through to a parallel side street."

You can see why people think this. Of course people are worried about traffic increasing on their streets. Because it has, continually, for years. Traffic on Britain's residential roads has soared in the past decade or so. A lot of streets that used to be quiet, with only the occasional car driving down them, are now often jammed up with cars. From around 2012 onward, suddenly the number of cars driving on B, C, and unlisted roads—that is, residential roads and non-main roads—absolutely soared, far more than traffic on main roads and motorways. From 2013 to 2019, traffic on these roads climbed by 35 percent, to 135 billion vehicle miles per year. You can see similar trends in America, where 2019 had the highest traffic levels in all of recorded history—some 3.25 trillion miles driven. Since 2001, traffic on rural roads has fallen somewhat, but traffic on urban roads has increased by roughly 50 percent.

But this does not have that much to do with bus lanes being taken away, or roads being closed. Rather, the causation goes the other way around. Cities are so keen to close roads precisely because traffic has grown so much. And one of the things that has helped that happen is that now everybody has a computer in their car with an app, something like Waze or Google Maps, automatically estimating the fastest route between any two destinations. The result is that vast amounts of traffic have been displaced from main roads onto side streets, as people try to skip the jams. Take an Uber now, anywhere in the world, and the likelihood is that your driver will follow a rather convoluted route to get you to your destination, because he is following a live update of traffic on his phone.

Indeed, in California, among other places, the growth of Waze caused surprisingly large protests. In Los Altos, a suburb of San Francisco, residents demanded first that Google remove their streets from Waze in protest at the number of people driving through. When that did not work, they got the city to put up "No Thru Traffic" signs, which in turn did make the company withdraw it. In Leonia, New Jersey, the city restricted the roads to residents during rush hour, with a $200 fine for drivers without a permit. In other places, people have taken more drastic measures. A man in Takoma Park, a suburb of Washington, D.C., started reporting fake crashes to try to deter drivers.

But what these protests reveal is that drivers tend to think that it is other people who are the cause of the traffic problem. They are stuck in traffic, not traffic themselves. Almost certainly the residents who protest about Waze have also used the app themselves to find quicker ways through other people's neighborhoods. And this in turn helps to produce the anger against road closures or LTNs that local politicians like my mother have to deal with. But it is not an insurmountable problem. As the experience of Paris or New York shows, in Europe and America at least, it is mostly city governments that are trying to do something about the sheer number of cars on our streets.

That should not be surprising. After all, it is in cities where the costs of carmageddon are most visible. Cities are the places where congestion and traffic pollution are the most destructive. But nationally, the voters in cities tend not to be that important, especially in first-past-the-post systems like that of the UK and America. Suburban voters are generally the swing voters—the people who politicians want to reach out to. And they use cars. That is why national politicians are so keen to keep down the cost of gasoline and to build enormous amounts of new road. It is cities that suffer the costs.

Brent Toderian, formerly chief planner of Vancouver, British Columbia, and a powerful advocate for reducing the use of cars in cities, told me that the important thing to generate change is political will. And that generally does materialize at a local level, not a national one. By European standards, Vancouver is still a pretty automotive place. But for a city built mostly after the end of the Second World War, it is not that bad. Around 50 percent of journeys in the city are made by walking, biking, or public transport. That has been achieved partly because the city never built expressways in the 1960s heyday of city-wreaking. It has also been aided more recently by a land-use plan that said the city needs to encourage walking, something that Vancouver's leadership managed to implement despite a lot of initial hostility. "We had a transportation plan that said no new street or road capacity for cars," says Toderian. "No more, right? We're going to grow the city, we're going to grow the population but there will be no net increase in capacity or space for cars. As a matter of fact, we're going to be gradually decreasing it."

In Vancouver, that meant introducing more bicycle lanes and the like, but also making sure that new housing is accessible by transit or, better yet, walking. Though the city still has plenty of sprawling, single-family suburbia, almost all new construction in Vancouver now is of apartment blocks and high-density row houses, generally without parking spaces. But achieving this took guts. Brent told me that building that sort of housing often generates a lot of complaints, because the people who tend to turn up at public meetings also tend to be older, existing residents who probably drive. And this brings new problems. Because older residents tend to think as a default that everyone who moves into a building will bring a car, they agitate against new buildings without lots of parking. The result is that while Vancouver is building exactly the sort of dense, transit-focused housing North America needs much more of, it is not building anywhere near enough of it to soak up the demand.

(Incidentally, a pleasing exception to this is a spot of land owned by the Squamish Nation, an indigenous Canadian First Nation. On roughly ten acres of land right on the waterfront, the Squamish are building 10,000 apartments in eleven towers, with several hundred reserved for members of the tribe, and the rest expected to be used to generate revenue to be distributed to the members. Remarkably, a governing authority that is run like a business for the benefit of its members, rather than as a council in which the loudest members dominate, tends to like more housing.)

For local politicians, public meetings—as well as their inboxes—are a difficult thing to ignore. Lots of complaints scare people off. And it is not just housing that this applies to. Drivers are quite likely to kick up a stink about losing a lane of traffic to a bicycle lane. Potential cyclists, however, probably will not, because until the bike lane is actually built, it might not even have occurred to them to consider cycling to school or work. But just as roads induce driving, bicycle lanes induce cycling. And so the sort of opposition often dissipates once a project has actually been completed. After the housing is built, people realize it is fine. Most bike lanes prove popular quickly enough too. And so over time, with a bit of boldness, cities can encourage walking and biking, without suffering many political consequences.

LTNs are a good example of this. Unpopular as they often are initially, the evidence suggests after a while, people come to like them. A poll conducted by Transport for London in September 2020, a few months after most LTNs were rolled out at the end of the first coronavirus lockdown, found that 51 percent of people backed them, whereas only 16 percent opposed them. Remarkably, even car owners were more likely to back them than oppose them. What the car lobby misses is that most people actually do not want to have heavy traffic on their streets all of the time. Indeed, one of the drivers of the growth of LTNs in England has been that when one is introduced, people on neighboring streets ask for their own, because they are worried by the displacement. As much as people are often upset about being stopped from driving on other people's streets, they are delighted to be able to stop other people driving on their own.

Brent is critical of people who say that they want to "ban" the car, because that is a sure way to instantly turn people off. He told me about a conversation he had with the vice mayor of Oslo, Norway, who had proposed "banning" cars from the city center, and how there was a huge backlash to it. "I asked the vice mayor, then why did you court that controversy by calling it ban the car, and she said, 'well, we really wanted to make a splash, we really wanted to get the credit.' And that's a, you know, that's an interesting one, it's good to get attention. But there is such a thing as bad attention," he says. The aim of local politicians ought to be to persuade people by showing them projects that work, rather than by confronting them with extremely radical change. "I don't want to let NIMBYs off the hook completely," he says. "But there's an element of human nature to NIMBYism. We know from actual studies what people value. They fear loss more than they value gain. And we are predisposed with a bias towards the status quo," he says.

I cannot imagine that many roads being closed soon in many American cities. (Though New York City has managed it a little, as have some more surprising places, such as Denver, Colorado.) Similarly, building lots of houses without parking is proving tricky in many cities. But even there, there are gentle policies that are making a difference. Donald Shoup, the UCLA parking supremo, proposed one idea that, though modest, actually got passed into law in California more than thirty years ago. It is called "parking cash out," and how it works is that employers who offer free parking to their employees are required by law to offer them the cash equivalent of the cost of the parking space if they do not use it. This is a slightly backward way of working—the default should be that nobody gets parking unless they pay for it—but it essentially changes the incentives in the same way. This matters. Even in Manhattan, 54 percent of people driving in from New Jersey each morning park for free. Since the cost of a parking space in a garage in Manhattan is on average $570 a month, according to SpotHero, a parking provider, that is quite a subsidy.

Give those people cash instead, and a lot of them will choose not to drive. Shoup's research in Los Angeles found that taking away free parking reduces the number of people driving to work by between 19 percent and a whopping 81 percent. A study of California's cash-out program reduced the number of people driving alone at companies that adopted it by a slightly more modest average of 17 percent. Bus use rose, as did carpooling and cycling.

Unfortunately, California's program, passed in 1992, is rather limited. Companies that own their own parking lots or garages (which, thanks to those parking minimums, many do) do not have to comply with it, for the reasonable enough reason that they are not saving money by paying for less parking. Even firms that rent their parking spaces do not have to pay people out if that rent is bundled together with their office space—i.e., if they cannot reduce the number of spaces they supply. Firms with fewer than fifty employees are exempt. And finally, unlike free parking, the cash paid out is taxable by the state. So the overall effect has been rather limited.

Nonetheless, better programs are being adopted elsewhere. In January 2022, the municipal government of Washington, D.C., passed its own cash-out law. Unlike in California, this requires companies to pay the full market value of the spot to employees who do not use it, not just what the firm saves. All firms with more than twenty employees, not fifty, are liable, which means it covers the vast majority of employers. And the cash is tax free. According to Allen Greenberg, a former federal highways official, it is a "big deal." Sadly, the law still does not apply to companies that own their parking spaces—a carve-out that will make it less effective. But it could still make an appreciable dent in the number of people driving into D.C. each day.

The big benefit of cash-out programs is that they provide an incentive not to drive (or more accurately, reduce the subsidy to drive) without offending anyone. And in America, they are the sort of policy that can have a real effect without having to win an enormous political battle. Indeed, they can evolve. In Britain, for example, free parking is a perk that, unlike, say, private health insurance, is untaxed. But some local governments have found ways of reducing the subsidy for it too. Nottingham, a small city in the East Midlands, taxes employers £415 per year (or $560) for each parking space they provide. The money generated is used to fund Nottingham's trams—one of the only light rail systems operating in a British city of its size.

Some other cities have tried alternatives. Coventry, for example, is paying people who choose to give up their cars £3,000 (around $4,000) on debit cards that they can use exclusively for transport services. If city leaders tried, they might find a surprising amount of enthusiasm for public transport. In 2016, 72 percent of voters in Los Angeles agreed to raise sales tax in the city to fund public transport. Even cities like Baton Rouge, in Louisiana, one of the most sprawly places I have ever visited, has voted to fund more public transport. Overall, in 2020 and 2021, more than 90 percent of ballot proposals to increase property taxes to fund public transport passed, according to APTA, the American Public Transportation Association.

The trouble, awkwardly, is that it is often easier to get people to pay for public transport than it is to get them to actually use it. Los Angeles's sales-tax hike paid for the building of new light railway lines, but even before the pandemic hit, use was falling. Indeed, as Bloomberg Media's CityLab reported on the Los Angeles measure, "few Angelenos viewed transit as an amenity that directly benefited them. People voted for Measure M as an expression of their political beliefs." The problem is partly how public transport is seen culturally. Often it is sold to voters as a way to reduce traffic by stopping other people from driving. But the result tends to be systems that are treated more like welfare services for the poor, rather than an actual alternative to driving. Indeed, when I was arranging to visit the people at LA Metro, Los Angeles's public transport agency, on the edge of downtown LA, they told me where I could park. They seemed slightly surprised that I arrived by train.

This view, sadly, in many American cities, that "normal people" drive and public transport users are poor, is something that can't help but turn off anybody who can afford the alternative of owning a car, even if it is cripplingly expensive. There are some pathetically modest things that cities can do to improve public transport. In Los Angeles, Jessica Meaney, an advocate for better public transport, told me that a lot of Angelinos are put off from using the buses and trains there because of things like a lack of seating or shade at bus stops, or a lack of toilet and baby changing facilities in train stations. Trains and buses can often feel dangerous, not least because of a lack of reasonable security. Los Angeles has poured a fortune into building new rail lines without fixing those things. The new rail lines are good, but helping people feel better about buses could achieve a lot, both for poorer Angelenos and for those who already own one car.

Making public transport mildly less miserable so it is actually an alternative to driving, rather than merely a deeply inferior social support network for those too poor to own a car, is one of the biggest challenges cities face. But in America too many cities have let their core system of public transport—buses—stagnate. Bus services are often set up to, in theory, provide transportation to anywhere in a city. But the service is often so irregular that it is not a reasonable alternative to driving. Transport agencies spend a fortune on buses that are so infrequent that nobody sane would rely on them to get to work or school, while major routes that transport lots of people to work are much less frequent than they could be. I see this in Chicago, where some buses are packed almost all of the time, even though you have to wait fifteen minutes for one to arrive, while other routes seem to essentially trundle around the city empty.

Worse is the fact that traffic is allowed to hold them up. In New York City, this leads to a situation where some buses average a speed of less than 5 miles per hour. That is slower than a light jog. And New York City has an extensive network of dedicated bus lanes, which car drivers are not allowed to use. It is just that they are so frequently blocked by people using them as essentially emergency parking, for deliveries and the like. The boom in online shopping has not helped, by leading to a surge in the number of deliveries. I see this in Chicago too. Many ordinary people who would probably feel guilty if they left their car abandoned in the middle of an ordinary lane of traffic seem to think nothing of parking with their hazard lights on in the middle of a bus lane, thereby slowing down the journeys of dozens of their fellow citizens.

If it were up to me, buses would be fitted with rocket launchers to blow them up or plows to shunt them out of the way. But absent my murderous fantasies, a more realistic solution would be to install cameras on the buses to automatically issue parking fines to the drivers. And yet that technology is extraordinarily rare. There seems to be a basic acceptance of the idea that the rights of one driver are more important than those of dozens of bus riders. New York, unlike Chicago, has at least tried. In 2020 the Metropolitan Transit Authority (MTA) installed cameras on 123 buses on various routes that run through Manhattan and Brooklyn. In the first ten days of operation, they sent fines to the owners of 1,500 illegally parked cars. In two years, they have issued more than 100,000 tickets. That is a sharp disincentive to deeply antisocial driving behavior that people seem to think is just fine.

Buses are the primary form of public transport for the vast majority of public transit users in America. Every survey suggests that the main reason people do not use them more is simply that they are not reliable enough. Jarrett Walker, a transport consultant based in Portland, Oregon, told me that American cities have less bus service than comparable cities almost anywhere else in the world. Canadian cities, which also have grid layouts and often look like American ones, have one and a half to twice as many bus miles driven per capita than American cities of equivalent size. Even before the pandemic, "underinvestment was already the status quo," he told me.

A study by TransitCenter, a New York–based think tank, looking at Atlanta found that a 40 percent increase in the frequency of buses there could increase the number of jobs a hypothetical worker could reach in thirty minutes from around 6,000 to around 57,000. That would radically improve the employment options for people who cannot afford a car. Another study by the Urban Institute, a Washington, D.C., think tank, suggests that $17 billion a year could literally double the availability of public transport in American cities with a population of more than 100,000 people. That is about seven times less money than Americans spend on their pets in a typical year. It is equivalent to less than 0.8 percent of total local government spending, or 2 percent of the national defense budget.

One of the great things about these sorts of policies is that, however modest they start, they can help set a city onto a positive upward spiral—essentially the reverse of what happened in the 1950s and '60s. The more people who can be persuaded to get onto buses or trains, the more money will be available for those services, and the more effective they will become. One of the problems many cities have persuading people to give up their cars is that public transport simply is not fast or regular enough to replace many trips. And yet an irony is that public transportation costs the taxpayer more the less it is used. In 2017, Americans spent $15.8 billion on public transportation fares, whereas transit agencies spent $66 billion providing those services. In other words, fares cover just 21 percent of costs. In New York City, however, fares covered more than half of the running costs of public transport, even though they are not that expensive. In London, where the tube is pricier than the New York subway, the figure is 70 percent.

The challenge that many cities in America and Britain face is not even that people own cars, but that often households have several of them. Walking around Birmingham you see countless driveways with as many as four or five vehicles cluttering up what was probably a garden when the houses were built. In Britain, seven million households (or about 30 percent of all households) own two or more cars, considerably more than the percentage who do not own a car at all. In America, it is a whopping 57 percent of households that own two cars. Getting families to give up both of their cars in most of America is a hell of a long way away. But getting them to give up one is a far more realistic ask.

The gains of doing so are more than just less congestion and less pollution, as wonderful as those are. There are also direct gains to the drivers. Running cars costs the average American household around $9,500 a year. For the poorest 20 percent, it costs almost a third of their income. This creates enormous amounts of poverty. In 2021, the amount of money Americans owe in debt on the purchase of vehicles is $1.8 trillion, or $5,500 for every person in the country. The figure doubled between 2010 and 2020. A worryingly large proportion of this is subprime debt—that is, loans made at high interest rates to people with poor credit ratings. The rates on these loans can be as high as 19 percent, at a time when mortgages cost less than 6 percent a year. Over the lifetime of a car, they basically double the price paid. When people default on these loans, their cars are taken away from them, which often means they lose their jobs, if they cannot travel to work. More than two million cars are repossessed each year.

This has real social costs. Take, for example, the effect on higher education. Something that astonished me when I first lived in America, in 2015, was discovering that many universities have ample parking lots, and a large proportion of students drive. In my own university experience, I was too hard up (or, more accurately, tightfisted) to even take the bus, and I got literally everywhere on my bicycle or by foot. In America, the College Board, a nonprofit organization, estimates that the cost of transportation accounts for 20 percent of the cost of going to university. For students at community colleges in California, the cost of transportation generally is more than the cost of tuition. And unlike tuition fees or rent, it is rarely covered by financial aid. The result is that the cost of transportation is a leading reason people drop out of college in America. If your car breaks down, and you have no money to fix it, or if it is repossessed, you may have no option but to quit.

Of course, this is one of the reasons politicians worry about anything that increases the cost of motoring. When the cost of gasoline rises, it pushes people into poverty. There is a reason polling on presidents so closely follows the price of gasoline—it is a lot of people's spending. That is why, somewhat surprisingly, Democrats are often more nervous about things like toll roads than Republicans. You might imagine Republicans to be motorheads, and they generally are—but their priority is typically reducing government spending while ensuring that drivers can get around in their monstrous pickup trucks at high speed. Democrats worry more about the cost to poorer people who also drive. And they are not wrong, at least in the short run.

Indeed, unfortunately, in some sprawling American cities—places like Houston or Atlanta or Phoenix, where public transport is practically nonexistent—simply giving poor people cars would probably be one of the quickest ways to reduce poverty, because it would significantly increase the number of jobs that they could reach. That is a mad indictment of those cities' economic models, because imagine how much better poor people could use that money if they did not need a car. We have created an economic model whereby cities sprawl out in such a way that you can only hope to get a decent job if you can afford nearly $800 a month to own a car. In some American cities you can be stuck in a place that is basically a bit like living in the countryside in Europe—at least a twenty-minute drive from anything useful. That is why keeping gas prices low is such a priority for most American politicians.

But leaning into this model in the long run is madness, because the more people have cars, as Samuel Schwartz, the former New York City traffic commissioner, says, the further away everything gets. "No matter how many roads we built, or how well, people weren't getting from point A to point B any faster, because points A and B were getting further apart . . . transportation had fallen into a vicious cycle in which more and more resources were being spent to less and less effect." You end up in a situation where poor people cannot afford to live in a city, but instead have to travel hundreds of miles each morning by car to get to work. If you think I am exaggerating, look at what happens in San Francisco, where the proportion of workers traveling more than ninety minutes in each direction more than doubled from 2007 to 2017.

If governments can tilt people away from cars, even just in a modest way at first, it could start a self-sustaining shift. But we do not always have to wait for government. One of the things that may surprise you, at least if you have gotten used to driving, is that even in America, and certainly in Europe, living without a car need not be impossible. Indeed, for a whole new generation, it is becoming less important than ever to own a vehicle. There is growing reason to think that if they had the choice, fewer people than ever would choose using their own private vehicle to get around.

17

PEAK CAR

When I reached the age of seventeen my parents bought me a rather typical birthday present for a seventeen-year-old in England: driving lessons. Growing up in Britain's motor city, Birmingham, I saw being able to drive a car as an enormously obvious first step toward adult life. I attended a school that was relocated in the 1950s from the city center to Bartley Green, an outer suburb made up of dull gray public housing constructed mostly after the Second World War. By road it was about seven miles from our house in Moseley—one of the costs of attending Birmingham's selective grammar schools—and each morning I had to get up before seven A.M. and rush to the bus stop to have a chance of arriving before morning assembly at eight thirty A.M. On a good day, by bus it took just under an hour to get to school; on a bad day, with a long wait at the stop and then at the next stop where I changed, it could take much longer. By car, the journey was about twenty-five minutes.

Thanks to this, through my school years I was almost permanently sleep deprived. Occasionally—on mornings after nights where I had attended a concert in the city—my dad would generously agree to drive me to school so that I could sleep a little longer. (My mother was much less indulgent and would never.) It felt like an extraordinary privilege. And so of course, when I turned seventeen, the chance of being able to drive there in my own car, and join my classmates who parked in a queue half a mile long on an old country lane outside the school gates, seemed incredibly alluring. I went to my first driving lesson full of anticipation.

Sadly, or perhaps luckily, the lessons went terribly. I was always a dreamy student at the best of times, and put in charge of a powerful vehicle, I exhibited the worst possible combination of arrogance and laziness. I would forget to check my mirrors before pulling out, forcing the instructor to jam on the brakes before I lurched out in front of a fast-moving truck. My blind spots remained blind. Even when I was not busy endangering myself, my driving instructor, and the other drivers on the road, I would lose concentration. At lights I would forget what I was doing and miss them turning green, or I would miss turns, driving straight into traffic jams we then had to waste time in. Quickly I realized that I found driving, especially urban driving, simultaneously stressful and boring.

After a few lessons I admitted to my parents that I was not especially interested in continuing to learn. They were a little disappointed. My father, a former police officer who worked on a traffic beat for years, saw being able to drive as an essential skill. I also suspect they had been hoping I would be able to drive them home from restaurants and the like, meaning that they could order a bottle of wine. But it was never really a problem. I carried on with my bus pass, and the next year, when I got my first job, instead of driving there, I pinched my father's bicycle to get to work. Cycling to the office each day—a journey of about five miles—took half the time it would have taken by bus, and left me feeling awake instead of dozy. Several of my friends at school who did manage, somehow, to pass their driving tests and acquire cars ended up having much worse fights with their parents after they crashed them.

In the end I did not learn to drive until I hit the age of twenty-six, when *The Economist* offered me a job in Washington, D.C., and I had to learn to be able to drive on reporting trips in America. Before then it simply was not necessary. I went to university in Oxford and then moved to London; in both cities I could get everywhere I needed to mostly by bicycle and occasionally by public transport. Even before I developed the militant anti-car tendencies that led to this book, the idea that I would ever want to spend thousands of pounds on owning and running a car seemed farcical.

And in no way am I unusual. There are millions of stories like mine. In America, in 1983, more than 90 percent of twenty- to twenty-four-year-olds had a driver's license. By 2017 the figure had dropped to 79 percent. In Britain, where fewer young people drive, the proportion holding driver's licenses has declined as well. According to analysis of government statistics by researchers at the University of Bristol, the proportion of seventeen- to twenty-year-olds holding licenses has fallen from about half in the early 1990s to just 29 percent now. For those aged twenty to twenty-nine, it fell from 73 percent to 63 percent. Young people are not only less likely to hold licenses, they also drive roughly a third as much as older people did at their age.

The reasons behind this trend are hard to pin down. A large part of it is almost certainly the enormous rise in higher education. A generation or two ago, far more people left school at eighteen and got jobs, which meant that they also bought cars. Nowadays people stay in school longer. And when they enter the workplace, the jobs they get are more likely to be based in city centers, which are better served by public transport. There is also the rising cost of certain aspects of driving. Car insurance, for example, has gotten a lot more expensive for young people, as insurers have realized how much likelier they are to crash, and as the cost of those crashes have risen. Buying a car is also trickier if you do not have a good credit rating, as most young people do not.

Then there are more cultural and political changes. From the 1960s onward, owning a car still felt like freedom. Think of the Beatles song, "Drive My Car," straightforwardly linking car ownership with good "prospects." Or the Queen song, "I'm In Love With My Car," about the "machine of a dream . . . with the pistons a pumpin'/ And the hubcaps all gleam." Think of the 1980s teen movies—*Ferris Bueller's Day Off* or *Say Anything*—where cars are linked with being cool and having sex. Think of Italy and the myth about the Fiat 500—the cheap automobile that supposedly set off a baby boom by providing private space for young people away from their conservative parents. Young people don't need cars to have sex anymore. Instead of cars, teenagers today have mobile phones. They are worried, rightly, about the effect of driving on the environment. And owning a car is a pain.

But I think the biggest thing is a broader resurgence of cities. In the 1960s, '70s, and '80s, cities were bad places to live, and not only because of congestion.

In London, even after the Clean Air Act of 1956, several coal power plants continued to pump noxious gasses into the air for decades. Bankside Power Station, now the site of the Tate Modern, was a working generator until 1981, creating noise and pollution right across from St. Paul's. Cars were not quite as numerous, but they did produce enormous amounts of pollution from leaded gasoline. Of course people wanted to leave, to live in quieter, more spacious suburbs, and that meant buying cars.

Nowadays, cities are more glamorous—they are where what the sociologist Richard Florida calls the "creative class" congregates. People want access to restaurants, bars, and culture. They want to be near other people who they can date. It is much less common for women in cities to give up work when they get married or have children, and it is far more likely for both partners in a couple to be able to find good jobs within a reasonable commuting distance in a city center than it is in a village an hour away by car. From the 1960s to the 1990s, the construction of freeways led to a hollowing out of cities. But by the 1990s, at least in a few places, it was going into reverse. Suddenly places like New York and London became fashionable again. Even the effect of the COVID-19 pandemic, which pushed many people out to suburbs again, was temporary. When the vaccines arrived, the flow dipped again.

Given this decline in driving among young people, it may seem surprising that the number of cars on the road continues to soar. The explanation lies partly in the fact that young people are a relatively smaller part of the population than before, and older generations are driving far more. A generation or two ago, people over the age of sixty had often never owned a car or learned to drive. In the 1950s and '60s in particular, it was still relatively rare—especially in Europe—for women to learn to drive. Even if their family owned a car, driving it was often seen as the husband's responsibility. That generation, however, is now mostly very elderly or dead. They are being replaced by people who were born in the 1950s and '60s, the Baby Boomers, who are the most automotive generation in history. Since 2000, the number of drivers over the age of seventy in the United States has grown by 60 percent. That is why car sales continue to rise and why the roads are ever more clogged. They are full of retired people.

But sadly, it is also true that the extent of the changing preferences of young people not to drive has also been overstated. In 2020, in the United

States, the so-called millennial generation (that is, people born between roughly 1980 and 1995) bought more cars than people of any other age bracket. I suspect this is because young people cannot afford to live where they would like to. More than half of eighteen- to twenty-nine-year-olds live with their parents in the United States. In the UK, 32 percent of men aged eighteen- to thirty-five live with their parents, and 21 percent of women do. In both countries, and in others too, the share has been rising fast in the past couple of decades.

When they do move out, or have kids, they are, much as their parents did, also moving out to car-centric suburbs, and to car-centric cities like Atlanta and Houston, because that is where housing is cheapest. They also love ride-sharing apps like Uber and Lyft, which are incredibly convenient, for sure, but have also clogged the traffic of big cities enormously. The turn away from cars is a little like the turn away from marriage and having children. People are waiting much longer to do it, but they are ultimately still doing it. Much as I did, young people may be learning to drive later, but for the most part they still seem to be learning to drive.

And yet, the millennial turn against cars, modest as it is, offers hope that we may still hit what auto executives ominously call "peak car." That is the idea that we hit a point where the annual number of car sales begins to decline, and eventually, that we begin to drive less. In the early 2010s, as high oil prices and falling incomes in the wake of the global financial crisis led driving to briefly fall, the theory that people might be turned off cars gripped the car industry. Having swallowed their own marketing about cars being equivalent to freedom, executives began to worry that maybe young people did not see it the same way. By 2015, the drop had reversed and once again the number of cars on the road soared until the pandemic caused another, temporary, slowdown in 2020. The car executives it turned out had little to fear—people drove cars because they had to, not because they wanted to.

But the idea of "peak car" is still credible, because the reason young people are moving to suburbs and buying cars now is largely because of the inflated cost of living in walkable neighborhoods, rather than because of any deep affection for big front lawns and driveways with two vehicles in them. In the 1960s and '70s, moving to the suburbs was an upwardly mobile move—it took you from a declining neighborhood in a noisy and polluted city to somewhere fresh and safe. These days it is something done reluctantly, usually because people cannot afford enough space to raise a child otherwise.

What that means is, there is an opportunity to provide more people with the chance to stay in cities, where they can use public transport, bicycles, and their own two legs to get around. I spoke to an architect and urban designer in Toronto named Naama Blonder about this. Naama works for an organization, Smart Density, that helps design the sorts of housing projects that allow people to live without a car. She told me she and her husband and their children live in a three-bedroom condo downtown, which allows them to get by without a car. Lots of people would like that. But the problem is, there is nowhere near enough suitable housing in Toronto (or almost anywhere really) for most families to be able to afford that—even rather wealthy ones. "There's a demographic of young people who have the potential to pay a million [Canadian dollars], not in cash, but with a mortgage, even to C$1.3 million, and you'd take us as a group of customers and you push us to the suburbs," she told me.

That is why it is so damaging that so much new construction happens in sprawling, car-dependent places. We are missing a massive opportunity to give people lives they would like—lives that happen to be far more sustainable, as well as more pleasant—in walkable cities, and instead pushing them out to places that are developed entirely around the automobile. Each year the Houston metropolitan area, with a population of seven million, adds 70,000 new homes, almost all of them in the suburbs, while Dallas adds 60,000. The New York metropolitan area, by contrast, with a population three times higher, covering much of Long Island and New Jersey as well as the city, manages only 54,000. The San Francisco area built a pathetic 10,000. The cities where people would most want to live, and where you can live best without cars, are simply not adding homes, while cities that depend on you driving everywhere, however unsustainable it is, are growing like mushrooms.

The result is, inevitably, that housing prices are rising fastest in walkable places and slowest in sprawling suburbs. It is the same elsewhere. The fastest-growing parts of Britain are towns like Milton Keynes or Aylesbury, a new suburb on the edge of London's green belt. They are places you need a car.

The reason walkable cities aren't building more homes is because building housing in dense cities is difficult. NIMBYish neighbors facing a new car-free property often refuse to believe that people will not bring cars and park them on the street. Naama finds it baffling; she thinks people who need a car will not buy a property without a parking space. "You're not going to make your life miserable, if your work is dependent on a car. Let's say you live in downtown and you work in the suburbs—then you won't buy a unit without a parking spot," she says. And yet, it is completely possible to live without a car, even with children, if you live in a neighborhood where there is decent public transport and where there is enough density to be able to walk or cycle to most of your daily tasks. If there were more housing built in those neighborhoods that already exist, more people could manage it.

There is an enormous underserved population of people who would prefer not to need a car, or certainly not to need two. According to polling by Pew, around 40 percent of Americans would prefer to live in walkable neighborhoods, even if it means having smaller homes. And that polling was done in 2020, when the benefits of living in a dense urban core were significantly reduced, thanks to COVID-19, meaning bars and restaurants and the like were closed. An earlier poll, taken in 2017 by the National Association of Realtors, showed that more than half of Americans would prefer to live in walkable neighborhoods with smaller homes. Millennials prefer walking to having to drive by 12 percentage points.

Far more people than are currently able to would embrace living in dense cities if only they could. Another poll conducted in 2020 by the National Association of Realtors found that one in five Americans would prefer to move from a larger detached home to a smaller one if it meant that they could walk more and have a shorter car commute, whereas only one in ten reported the opposite. People who report living in communities where "there are lots of places to walk nearby such as shops, cafes, and restaurants," according to the poll, have much higher reported levels of happiness than people who report the opposite. A study published in 2022 by researchers at McGill University in Montreal found that most car commuters want to walk and cycle more, and drive less. Almost nobody reports wanting to drive more. Car commuters are far more likely to agree with the statement "the only good thing about my travel is arriving at my destination" than anyone else.

Indeed, a thing that is often missed is that there are, even in America, plenty of people who already choose not to drive, even though their cities are so poorly served by alternative options. A lot of these people are women. In America, men account for three-fifths of miles driven, while 55 percent of public transport users are women. In Chicago, the figure is 65 percent. And yet cities that are set up for cars are generally difficult to navigate for women. As the writer Caroline Criado Perez reported in her book *Invisible Women*, cities tend to prioritize the sort of to-the-office-and-back commuting patterns—from neighborhoods to downtowns—typically made by men, at the expense of the sorts of trips, often chained together, that women are more likely to make, such as dropping children off at school, then visiting elderly parents, then doing grocery shopping. In older cities like London or Chicago, where neighborhoods tend to radiate out from a city core, one of the things that encourages people to get cars is that these trips are so difficult to do by public transport.

Investment in freeways and the like does not help with those sorts of trips even when the people making them have cars. What is needed is public transport that works better for them. In Los Angeles, a large increase in the amount of driving in recent years has come from families who have gone from owning one to two cars. And yet for thirty years, the city barely even thought about these people—almost all new investment went into rail lines, targeting commuters, while things like buses were neglected. That is now, belatedly, changing. In early 2020, before the pandemic, the city updated its bus routes for the first time in three decades to take account for the fact that many services were simply too inconvenient outside of normal commuting hours.

And neglecting these people does not just encourage car ownership. It also makes life difficult for those who would prefer not to drive, or who simply can't. I spoke to a few people about how they live without access to a vehicle. One was Abla Kan, a freelance television producer who recently moved to Lewisham, a suburb of London where car ownership is still rather common, despite having excellent train links to central London. Talking to Abla, who has never learned to drive and still relies on public transport to get around, often with her small child, gives a sense of why so many people think that they need a car. "When I had the buggy, it was a pain in the ass," she says. "You'd be, like, praying every time you're at bus stop that the bus would be empty." The problem was, if there were too many other mothers on board with strollers, she would not be able to get on. Even the trains were not as convenient as they should be, because of a lack of elevators, meaning that she would have to enlist bystanders to help her carry her stroller up and down stairs.

Abla stands out as somebody who really does not want to learn to drive. And yet, there are times when she really wishes she could, she says, because of the inconvenience of having to rely on public transport. The funny thing is that Abla and her husband do own a car, because he runs an IT business and occasionally needs to haul around expensive equipment. But they try to avoid using it, and for the most part, they manage. The trouble is, living without it is tricky, and not because public transport is inherently difficult to use, but rather because the planners and officials who run it seem to ignore the basic needs of people with children.

Other parents I spoke to mentioned that owning a car does not solve all of the problems that come with public transport. Anthony Couzens, an actor, told me that when he first had a child, getting a car seemed like it solved a lot of the problems of having to carry stuff on buses. But by the time his children got a little older, he realized the benefits of public transport—because when you are driving, unlike when you are standing on a bus or a train, you cannot take your eyes off the road to deal with your children. "When they're smaller, it is much, much simpler with the car. But when they get older, they can start to talk, and they can start testing boundaries. That then becomes a nightmare. Because if you're stuck in traffic or stuck trying to park somewhere and they're kicking off in the back, it's a headache." His family now lives without a car, and instead Anthony rents one occasionally for the sorts of journeys that are too tricky to do without one.

It is not only in London where this is possible. In Chicago, Martin Medenica, a real estate agent, told me that when his car was stolen a few years ago, he decided to see whether he could live without it, initially just for a year. In the end, he managed without for almost three years, despite the fact that his job involves a lot of rushing around the city. Because he had to take some of his trips by taxi, it did not save him that much money, he told me, but it was nearly as convenient, and he never had to worry about breaking down, or crashing, or having his car stolen again. He also got more exercise. Disappointingly, he did in the end buy a new car, but he endeavors to use it less. And he is a real estate agent. He drives all over, showing potential buyers or tenants homes. If your job requires you to move less, you could save a lot.

What the car industry does its best to downplay is that owning a car is not actually something that everybody wants. Car advertisements, TV shows, and movies tend to show happy families going on camping trips and moving around cities quickly, never worrying about finding a parking space or getting stuck in traffic. And yet public policy that assumes cars are the default way of getting around fully neglects people who would much prefer to go without the daily commute, or the daily school run, or whatever. In a car-centric world, not being able to drive in effect turns you into a second-class citizen, reliant on forms of transport that are impractical. But a large proportion of people would much prefer not to be reliant on their vehicle, and not to feel like second-class citizens.

Right now, in most rich world cities, even walking is too dangerous. Speed limits in much of the developed world are either 30 miles per hour or 50 kilometers per hour (just over 31 mph). Given how much more dangerous a car is at 30 mph than it is at 20 mph, that is the sort of policy that shows the contempt with which people who do not drive are treated when they move through cities. Fortunately, in some places it is changing. Many British cities have now implemented 20 mph limits in residential areas. New York City has 15 mph speed limits in areas with schools. They are, however, often poorly enforced. One of the few things you can say for constant traffic congestion, at least, is that it makes it safer to cross the road.

In the United States, even with its sprawling cities and suburbs, figures from the Department of Transportation show that 60 percent of car journeys are of a distance of less than six miles. Around a fifth are of less than one mile. Cycling a mile in a city is almost always going to be quicker than driving, once you include the time you have to spend parking or stuck in traffic. Six miles will depend on how fast you cycle and the road infrastructure, but it may still be quicker. That suggests that up to half of car journeys could potentially be replaced, even without a radical change in what our cities look like. In the UK, 71 percent of all car journeys in 2019 were of less than five miles, and 25 percent were less than one mile.

To shift those journeys onto bicycles, we need to make people feel safer. As Christophe Najdovski, the Paris deputy mayor of transportation, told me, even if your children's school is only a kilometer away, if the road to get there is thick with fast-moving traffic, you will still feel justly nervous about cycling it. But it will also require a shift in mentalities. A lot of people simply will not have realized that there are other options. A world in which cars are less necessary in our daily lives, and less dominant in our cities, is possible. We just have to find a way to get there.

CONCLUSION

When I started writing this book, in early 2020, the car industry was in dire straits. The coronavirus pandemic had kept many people at home; millions of people lost their jobs. The unemployment rate in the United States went up to 15 percent, far higher than it did in 2008. In Europe, millions of people were moved on furlough schemes to protect their jobs and paid to wait at home for the virus to ebb. Nobody wanted to put a lot of money into buying a car, especially not if it was just going to sit in their driveway for months at a time. But though the news was miserable, the collapse of driving was a noticeable silver lining. Suddenly the streets were clear, with wild animals flocking back into now deserted town centers. To get out of the house, I cycled all over London, for once unworried about being squeezed off the road by angry drivers in jams, or being overtaken at speed by idiots in BMWs. The quiet made it all a little more manageable.

As I finish writing this book, more than two years later, the global economy is booming, as the coronavirus, though very much still with us, has been made far more manageable by the advance of vaccines. Traffic has climbed back to pre-pandemic levels in most of the world; in some places, it has already overtaken previous levels, even as public transport systems struggle to attract riders back. Oil prices are at the highest levels they have been in more than a decade, as all of that driving creates ever more demand for gasoline, and the war in Ukraine has removed a chunk of Russian production from the market.

Even as their governments commit to reducing CO_2 emissions, Europe and America are facing an energy crunch as difficult as any since the 1970s, and they are desperate for new sources of oil and natural gas.

And the car industry is more than back on its feet, as millions of people sought to spend the savings accumulated in months of sitting at home on new vehicles. Thanks in part to a global shortage of computer chips, demand is more than factories can accommodate, setting off a huge new investment boom in manufacturing. Even though gasoline prices are as high as they have been in more than a decade, used cars are selling for more than new cars sold for a few years ago. The cost of renting a car in the United States has more than doubled, because there is so much demand for vehicles to get around. My inbox is full of press releases from firms and city and state governments all promising to capitalize on improvements in electric cars, autonomous cars, and even flying cars, to build more factories, more roads, and more ways of filling our world with fast-moving steel.

Given all this, I hesitate to speculate about what the future will look like. On the one hand, the pandemic has created the space—literally—to think about a world with fewer cars. In cities all over the world, roads were closed and parking spaces taken away, as it became extraordinarily obvious that the land they occupied was better used by people walking, cycling, playing, or simply sitting and eating at a restaurant. Though they may still be avoiding buses and trains, more people are cycling than ever before, and as a means of getting around, not just as a recreational activity at the weekend. On the other hand, a rush away from city centers and from public transport, and toward suburbs and private transportation means that the growth of the automobile is very much still with us. For workers who have taken advantage of working from home to move out into the country, the disappearance of the commute is more than made up for by more driving day-to-day. And the glut of money being spent on "rebuilding" by governments all over the world seems sure to carry us forward into a more automotive world.

That is why it is so important to make this argument now. We are at an inflection point. We can begin to unwind the investments of a century into a world dominated by the private automobile, at the expense of pedestrians, cyclists, and anyone who has to breathe the air of a city street. We can begin moving back to one where people can get around without having to own two tons of steel, and without having to emit tons more of CO_2 each year into our ever-warming climate. Or we can do the opposite, adding more and more vehicles to already jammed roads, and then building more roads, until nobody has a choice but to live in a tarmac wasteland, motoring around on whatever the latest energy consuming metal hulk looks like.

I hope if you have got this far in the book, you will already be at least somewhat persuaded that the growth of the car has gone far enough, and needs to be rolled back. But if you are not, I want to reiterate, a future with fewer cars need not mean a future with no cars. There will always be journeys that are better made by car, and there is nothing necessarily immoral about wanting the convenience or luxury of a personal vehicle. Nor does it have to mean a future in which people are made poorer, and are forced (rather than merely encouraged) to give up their cars or forgo travel. It can mean a future in which there are just better alternatives.

There are green eco warriors who believe that economic growth is inherently a bad thing, and that people ought to go back to living in smaller communities and never going anywhere, and who campaign as vociferously against new railway lines and against new homes in the center of cities as they do against new roads. I visited half a dozen countries just in the reporting of this book, and I could hardly disagree more. The urge to travel and explore is part of what makes us human. And among the main reasons I want to free people from their vehicles is so that they have more time and money left over to spend on things that are actually more enjoyable than sitting in traffic, as well as being less environmentally destructive, like eating at restaurants or visiting the theatre, or going on holiday. This is not a manifesto for making us poorer in aid of saving the planet. It is an argument that we can be both wealthier and have more sustainable lifestyles at the same time.

There are also people on the right who will dismiss this as the utopian ravings of a yuppie determined to force people to give up lifestyles that they love—big cars, big houses, and the freedom of the open road. And they have a point. But in Europe and America the reality is that there are tens of millions of people who would happily give up that lifestyle, if only they had the choice of living somewhere walkable. Why should they be forced into owning cars and driving everywhere? And if the people who would like to live in cities were given the chance, the space for those left over would be greater, perhaps the roads less crowded. Making our cities more capable of being home to more people means taking pressure off our countryside. More than thirty-three million acres of land in America is used solely to grow corn used to make ethanol to fuel vehicles. Imagine what we could do with that land if we did not need it for fuel. We could reforest it. We could turn it back into a vast wilderness, of the sort that we have spent the past two hundred years destroying.

The problem is not cars themselves. It is privileging cars over any other form of transport, so that they are not a luxury or an occasional necessity, but rather something that we are forced to rely on, day-to-day. The problem is building our homes and our cities in such a way that pavement, rather than people, comes first. Americans spend only a little less on buying and running their cars than they do on housing themselves. If we did not need them as much, we could have a lot more left over to spend on whatever we want. And not needing as many cars is not some lofty, unrealistic goal. It is frankly bonkers to think that every family spending $5,000 to $10,000 a year on their own individual vehicle is the most efficient way of getting people around. We do not have to be so reliant on gasoline, cooking the planet to be able to live decent lifestyles. The important thing is not moving metal, it is moving people. As I hope this book has illustrated, cars get in the way of our freedom to move around easily at least as much as they help it, by creating cities where everything is farther away, including opportunity.

I unapologetically think that big, densely populated cities are the best places for most people to live, both for them and for the planet. I would rather live in Manhattan or Amsterdam than I would in Houston or Dallas. I have been lucky–or rather, privileged—to have been able to spend most of my adult life living in cities where owning a car really is not necessary. Not everyone will agree with me about that preference. America's car-focused suburbs, with their plentiful green space, privacy, and security are still deeply appealing to many people, not just in America but all over the world. So too is the convenience of having your own leather-upholstered, air-conditioned movable armchair to take you from that suburb to a pleasant suburban shopping mall, without ever having to breathe the fumes you are generating along the way.

But you do not have to agree with me that cities are better places to live to accept that there are too few options for people who want to live like I do. Suburbanites too can recognize the congestion and pressure that is created in their neighborhoods by the lack of affordable options in cities. What is maddening is that the lifestyle I lead is rendered unaffordable by cars, while the suburban lifestyle is grotesquely subsidized. Indeed, it is really only affordable to me because I do not have children, and so I can afford the outsize rents that come with living in one of the few genuinely walkable neighborhoods in America.

There is simply no good reason that the sustainable option—living in a decent-size apartment or rowhouse, in a neighborhood where you can walk, cycle, and use public transport to get around—ought to be so expensive, while living in an enormous detached house and using vast quantities of natural resources is the cheap option. It is only the case because of decisions made by our leaders over decades that have compounded to create a world where wasting resources is normal, and sustainable living is rare.

So what to do about it? As much I would like it, we do not need to re-create Tokyo in every country and state. Nor do we need to start tearing up every single freeway, or imposing draconian rules like Singapore's registration lottery. At least, not straightaway. We simply need to shift the incentives back toward what they ought to be, in favor of the least damaging forms of transport. The French idea of taxing heavy cars more, and setting aside more road space for cyclists, is a good place to start. So is the Dutch model of giving priority on busy streets in order of their vulnerability—so that walkers come first, and then cyclists, and only then people in cars. So too is imposing congestion charges, like London did years ago and New York is fitfully trying to do now. Populist politicians and grumpy newspaper columnists will call it a war on the car, but it is not, not really. Charging a reasonable price for the use of a road is not forcing people to get out of their cars. Nor is forcing drivers to pay attention to pedestrians.

These are realistic measures that can be taken, often by city governments, with a dose of political courage. What is happening in Paris could easily be implemented in Berlin, Chicago, and Toronto, if the politicians in those cities just tried. It takes courage to ignore the loudest voices, but shrewd politicians ought to be able to identify the silent majority who would like their children to be able to walk to school without feeling endangered by cars, or to breathe air that is not polluted with particulates from engines and from tires. So far, no city that has closed a major road has felt it necessary to reopen it. Indeed, in most cases, the idea is unimaginable. Imagine flooding Times Square in New York or Trafalgar Square in London with vehicles again. It simply won't happen. The risks of reducing car use are far less daunting than we realize.

More and more politicians are realizing that. This is driven heavily by the realization that our automotive habits are cooking our planet. And it is not only in the places you would expect, like Paris or Copenhagen. For example, in February 2021, Pete Buttigieg, Joe Biden's then newly appointed transportation secretary, argued that "we talk about trains, planes, and automobiles, but what about bikes, scooters, and wheelchairs for that matter. Roads aren't only for vehicles." A month later, in a keynote speech at South by Southwest, the festival in Austin, he argued that "we are better off if our decisions revolve not around the car but around the human being."

In lots of places, on both sides of the Atlantic, that rhetoric is at least partially being backed by action. Cities across America, even including ones like Houston and Los Angeles, are beginning to roll back parking minimums, and to reduce the amount of suburban "single family" homes being built in favor of denser, more city-focused development near transport. Minneapolis has built thousands of new apartments since it eliminated parking minimums in 2018. In Europe, biking has taken off in a spectacular fashion, and not just in Paris. Even my hometown, Birmingham, one of the most automobile-obsessed cities in Europe, is beginning to change. The city's leaders, motivated as much by the desire to create more economic growth as by any ideas of social justice or climate, are beginning to act to encourage people out of their cars, by building bike lanes and imposing charges on more-polluting vehicles. More densely populated cities with good public transport are richer cities.

There are challenges, of course. Governments are still happily subsidizing the adoption of electric cars, without confronting the problem of congestion that cheaper electric driving will inevitably create. They are still determined to keep gasoline prices down. Attempts to discourage driving, by taxing gasoline more, for example, are met by fierce protests. In 2018, Emmanuel Macron, the president of France, backed down from increasing gasoline prices in the face of protests, just as Tony Blair did almost twenty years earlier. And road building carries on as it always has. The infrastructure bill passed in 2021, Joe Biden's signature achievement, included $110 billion for roads, more than it put toward public transport and railways combined. Austin, where Buttigieg gave that speech, is one of many cities planning to expand its central freeway, I-35, in the next few years. It will involve demolishing homes and businesses in predominantly Black neighborhoods, just as it generally did in the 1950s and '60s.

And we should not underestimate the risks that new technology poses if we are not careful. The enthusiasm of the car industry to find more ways of persuading us to buy new types of vehicles remains unbounded. If we embrace the siren song of Elon Musk's tunnels, or self-driving taxis available on demand, or even personalized electric helicopters, we will miss the chance to redevelop the world in a more sustainable, manageable, human way. Transport ought to be a way to reduce inequality, by making it easier for anyone, whether rich or poor, to be able to get around. These schemes offer instead more comfortable travel for the elite, using more resources, more energy, and more land, and, in the end, just making things worse.

Yet on balance, I think that we are beginning to make the turn away from cars. The biggest challenge may be the cultural one. I have owned one car in my life. I hope to never own another. But we have so ingrained the ideas that car ownership is tantamount to freedom and that your car is an expression of your personality, that it will take time to unlearn. I think of a friend of mine in Chicago, originally from Texas, who keeps a car. Even though she only rarely uses it, she says she would feel trapped if she didn't know it was there. It will take time for people who have gotten used to living with a vehicle at their beck and call to realize that it can be just as liberating not to have one: to never have to worry about gasoline prices, or parking, or maintenance, or insurance, or whether you can have a beer on a night out without having to worry about how to get home afterward.

It was Gustavo Petro, a mayor of Bogotá, the capital of Colombia, who argued that "a developed country is not a place where the poor have cars, it is a place where the rich use public transportation." He was right. In London it is common to see politicians and celebrities on the tube. In New York, the mayor, Eric Adams, has made a point of taking the subway to interviews at least. (One of his predecessors, Michael Bloomberg, used to take an SUV to get to the subway station.) In the Netherlands, the prime minister, Mark Rutte, travels to his meetings by bicycle. In Copenhagen, the capital of Denmark, even the crown princess is known for taking her children to school in a cargo bicycle in the midst of winter.

These are the richest, most innovative places on Earth. They are the places with the highest quality of life, the longest life expectancy, and the happiest people. That is also why they are among the most expensive places on Earth. People are desperate to live in them, in a way they are simply not desperate to live in, say, Albuquerque. The reality is that using public transport or traveling by foot or by bike does not have to be an inferior alternative to having your own motorized vehicle. It can actually be more convenient, less stressful, quicker, and cheaper. When space is made for them, bicycles, trains, and buses offer the liberation that cars promise and then fail to deliver.

That message needs to get across to the rich of the world's emerging countries, faster than it is. If we begin taking cars off the road in the west only for them to multiply ever faster in the rest of the world, it may help cities, but we will still face the problem of catastrophic climate change. Cities like Delhi, Jakarta, or Lagos will become livable to only the majority of their populations if people can get around them without needing—or indeed, wanting—vehicles. Ultimately, only transit systems that serve a majority, rather than a minority of the rich, will help alleviate poverty without ruining the planet we live on. I say this sincerely, but reducing the number of cars on the road is not just about climate change, or about urban mobility. It is about justice too. Cars are engines of inequality, because, put simply, we do not have the resources for everyone to have their own.

In 1950, Walt Disney released a film featuring Goofy, the cartoon dog, called *Motor Mania*. In it, Goofy is named Mr. Walker, and he lives in a pleasant American suburb of the type we associate with the 1950s, picket fence and all. Mr. Walker, the narrator tells us, "lives in a quiet, respectable neighborhood, he is a typical, average man, considered a good citizen, of average intelligence, a kindly man, courteous, punctual, and honest. Mr. Walker wouldn't hurt a fly." But Mr. Walker owns an automobile, "and considers himself a good driver." When he gets in it, and starts the engine, "a strange phenomenon takes place." Mr. Walker "is charged with an overwhelming sense of power." He becomes "an uncontrollable monster, a demon driver. Mr. Walker is now, Mr. Wheeler." As he drives along, he says, "of course I own the road. My taxes paid for them." But clearly he is miserable. He drives along causing chaos, fighting over parking spaces, and crashing into his neighbors—until he parks, and once again becomes "Mr. Walker."

Walt Disney saw, half a century before most other people, the basic problem. There can never be enough road space, enough parking spaces, or enough gasoline for everyone to have one, and for it not to be miserable. If driving a car is to be pleasant, other people must go without. I suspect that even Mr. Toad would have found modern motoring infuriating. The reality is that offering alternatives to driving is actually good for drivers. It is sort of collective madness that makes motorists fail to realize that what is good for pedestrians would actually be good for them too, by helping them escape the awful grind that driving is.

We sleepwalked into the automotive takeover of the world. To undo it will take conscious effort. But I think as a species, we are capable of it. As much as we continue to build roads, the lessons of the 1950s and '60s are clearer to more people than ever. In America, inspired by a podcast called *The War on Cars*, urbanists have now started putting up stickers that read "Cars Ruin Cities" on lamp posts. Protests against new roads that destroy people's homes are no longer dismissed as the views of cranks. People are actually willing to vote for more funding for public transportation, rather than just sitting back idly watching as it is demolished. We are beginning to realize that if we choose to, we can live better lives. In a way, it is a little like learning to ride a bicycle. As daunting as it might seem, once you get the hang of it, you never forget. We just need to climb out of the car and get onto the saddle. Or onto the train. Or the bus. Or your feet. You might find that it actually sets you free.

ACKNOWLEDGMENTS

Writing a book is something most journalists aspire to do. But actually doing it is something else. I am one of those hacks (a less derogatory term in the British media than in the American) who is motivated most of all by tight deadlines and sheer rush of breaking news. Crafting an argument that is intended to last years, not days, is a challenge. That you have read this far is only thanks to dozens of people who made sure I kept at it.

Most thanks of all goes to Kate Barker, my agent, who in the midst of the first COVID-19 lockdown took the time to listen to my pitch and help me shape it into something worth writing, and then worked tirelessly to sell it. Over the next year, Kate also nudged me gently but firmly, making sure that I both did the reporting and started writing without leaving it all to the last minute (though I fear I still left too much). Next comes Jamison Stoltz at Abrams Press who took on that first completed draft and whose deft editing and wise suggestions for more reporting led to a much stronger argument. I wish every author could have as much brilliant support in writing their first book.

There are many others to thank. Duncan Robinson, my colleague at *The Economist*, read an early draft and as well as proffering useful thoughts on the content, also wisely encouraged me to reduce the number of sentences I begin with the word "and." And Duncan was just one of a whole crowd of friends who kindly sent me links, observations, and ideas in a relentless WhatsApp group. I only wish I had been able to use more.

Various others made this book possible in a more practical way. Robert Guest, the foreign editor at *The Economist*, gave me the space and time to work on it while also signing off the expenses for reporting trips that I was able to extend to research several of the chapters of this book. In particular, the reporting from the Democratic Republic of Congo, a country close to my heart, is owed to Robert. Indeed, it is Robert who sent me around the world in the first place, from my first foreign posting in Washington, DC, to my latest in Chicago, and all those in between, so he is owed even more thanks. Abhishek Kumar, a colleague and friend in Mumbai, helped me with the reporting from the Maximum City.

I should also thank Joel Budd, the editor at *The Economist*, who first brought me into the paper in 2012, and whose own writing about cities, urban planning, and transportation inspired so much of my own. Joel firmly believes that I will eventually crack and buy a car. If anyone is looking for somebody to write a lengthy piece about why I am wrong, it would be him. I worry he might even persuade me.

This book would never have come to fruition without the support of my wife, Evelyn, who at every stage of this has been not only encouraging but extremely patient, even when I let writing the book interrupt holidays, lock me up for weeks at a time, and turn me into a grouch. She has joined me in my reporting, canvassed friends, and even did a few of the interviews. She is even more vociferous in her dislike of cars than I am. Now that we live in America, I am in fear of her eventually having to learn to drive and discovering that perhaps after all she rather likes it. But so far she has resisted, and I am so glad. Evie: I'm sorry I did not put more of your puns in.

Finally, I doubt I would ever have become any sort of writer without the encouragement of my parents, or my grandmother Shirley, who gave her grandchildren copies of her own books—printed and bound by the local stationery shop, several of them individually edited for each grandchild—every Christmas and birthday. I keep them on my bookshelves.

INDEX

Abraham, Reuben, 84–86
advertisements, 30–31, 135–36, 147, 152, 224
Africa, 6–8, 12–13, 19, 86–88, 113, 157–58, 179, 187
Amsterdam, Netherlands, 10, 17–18, 73, 177
Apple, 124, 141, 165
Arab oil embargo, 153, 176
Arizona, 104–5, 112, 133–36, 138–39
asthma, 134–35, 137, 140–42
Atlanta, Georgia, 62–63, 210, 212, 219

bankruptcy, 11, 32, 54–55, 60, 65, 143
batteries, 12–13, 91–92
Benz, Karl, 4, 61
bicycles, 7, 10, 39, 46–47, 105, 169–72, 188, 228

electric, 171, 173–74, 181–83
lanes, 17, 60, 173–85, 187, 205–6, 232
safety, 178–85, 224–25
sharing programs, 177, 179, 183
Biden, Joe, 154, 232–33
Birmingham, England, 4–6, 44, 46, 117, 155, 181, 201, 211, 215, 232
BMW, 136–37, 184, 192, 227
bridges, 74, 110, 116–17
Buchanan, Colin, 42–45
buses, 47–49, 83, 85, 110, 123–24, 222
lanes for, 203, 209–10

carbon dioxide (CO_2) emissions, 4, 8–9, 12–13, 16, 84, 89, 97–99, 134–35, 148–49
car crashes, 7–9, 26, 28, 158–61, 164–65

car manufacturers, 4, 10, 20, 39–40, 53–54, 153–54, 227
   corruption, 13, 18–19, 94–96, 133–39
   on deaths, 164–65
   on electric vehicles, 92–93
   lobbying by, 6, 27, 30–32, 87–88, 133–34, 143–44, 206
   scandals, 133–44
car ownership, 3, 18, 22, 27–28, 87–89, 174, 211, 217–24
   costs of, 20, 191–92, 195–96
   Indian, 80–84, 86
   mass, 44–46, 79, 100
   subsidies for, 12, 152–54, 191
   US, 51–52, 88–89
Centers for Disease Control, US, 158–60, 184
Chevrolet, 148–49, 153
Chicago, Illinois, 1–5, 179–84, 209–10, 222
children, 9, 29, 34, 73, 96, 140, 151
China, 10, 18, 86, 91–96, 195–96
cities, 10, 20, 33, 40–41, 175, 197–98, 217–20, 230–34
   free parking impacting, 124–25
   public transportation in, 22–23, 64–65, 217
   rebuilding, 3, 27, 35–36, 43, 45, 63, 69, 71, 99, 189
   sprawl in, 12, 15–16, 25–26, 212–13
   traffic in, 117–19, 203–4
   US, 9, 15, 31, 51–53, 56–61, 210, 221–22

city/urban planners, 3, 11–12, 33, 40, 43–45, 57–58, 119
   free parking and, 124–27
   Jacobs on, 69–72, 76–77
   postwar, 41–42, 122, 204–5
   traffic and, 35–37, 42–44
Clean Air Act, US, 72, 74, 138
climate change, 4, 11–12, 84, 130, 138, 142, 154, 234
coal, 12–13, 19, 71, 84, 98–99, 128, 218
cobalt, 12–13, 91–97
Cobbs, Courtney, 179
commutes, 10–11, 82–83, 87, 215–16
computers, 103–104, 203, 228
congestion charges, 22, 49, 73–74, 99, 181, 194–95, 231
Copenhagen, Denmark, 176–77, 233–34
copper, 92–93, 96
Corporate Average Fuel Economy, US, 153–54
corruption, 13, 18–19, 94–96, 133–39
costs, 7–8, 21, 27, 46, 108–11, 138–39, 142–43, 230
   car ownership, 20, 191–92, 195–96
   gasoline, 126–27, 178, 212–13
   housing, 82, 120, 122–23, 127, 219–20
   of living, 128, 197, 219–20
   parking, 23, 126–27, 191–92, 195, 207

INDEX

public transportation, 20–21, 208–11
road, 20, 82–84, 115–20, 192–93
Coventry, England, 4, 10, 39–43, 52–53, 56, 172, 208
COVID-19 pandemic, 5, 88, 191–92, 218–19, 221, 227–28
crimes, 30–31, 54, 58, 61, 64–65, 139, 164
Crossrail, 108, 126

danger, 9, 96, 110–11, 150–51, 162–67, 178–80, 224
Dearborn, Michigan, 53–54, 146
deaths, 8–9, 17, 88, 96, 140, 143, 180–81
deaths, vehicular, 26–27, 105, 146, 150–51, 158, 164–65, 177
US, 8–9, 11, 28–29, 159–61, 163–65
debts, 54, 117, 193, 211–12
decline
  population, 2–3, 64–65, 119
  transportation, 5, 46–47, 54–61, 141, 217–19
Delanoë, Bertrand, 170
demand, 98, 149, 227–28
  for parking, 125–26, 128
  for roads, 71, 115–20
Democratic Republic of Congo, 12–13, 91–97
Democrats, 75, 154, 212
Department for Transport, UK, 5, 15, 47–48, 115, 161–62, 184

Department of Energy, US, 5, 18, 88–89, 98
Department of Transportation, US, 17, 224
Detroit, Michigan, 31, 52–60, 64–65, 119, 146–47
developing countries, 6, 23, 82, 86–89, 158–61, 233–34
diesel, 18–19, 102, 133–39, 140–41
Disney, Walt, 34, 234–35
Driscoll, Bridget, 26–27
drivers/chauffeurs, 79–83, 157
drivers' licenses, 26, 160, 215–17
drunk driving, 159–61

Edsell, Arthur, 26
Eisenhower, Dwight, 53, 56, 113
Eisenhower Expressway, 1–5, 7
electric bicycles, 171, 173–74, 181–83
electric vehicles, 91, 97, 100 196, 101–3, 153, 232
  CO_2 emissions and, 12–13, 98–99, 149
  Tesla, 8, 92–93, 99, 105–9
employment, 12, 16, 54, 60, 94, 139, 155, 197, 212, 218
engines, 71, 98–99, 134, 136–38
  internal combustion, 4, 26–27, 33, 97, 100, 102
England, 33–34, 76, 103, 108, 126, 201–6
  See also specific cities
Environmental Protection Agency (EPA), US, 136, 138

ethanol, 144, 230
Europe, 18, 45, 76, 92, 131, 135, 153, 227
European Research Group on Environment and Health (EUGT), 133–35
European Union, 19, 87, 98, 148, 153, 166
Experimental Prototype Community of Tomorrow (EPCOT), 34
exports, 52, 88–89, 93, 189
expressways, 64, 67–68, 70, 176, 192–93

factories, 31, 41, 52–54, 59–60, 141–43, 146–47, 155
Faulkner, William, 52–53
federal government, US, 57–59, 68, 176
fines, 30, 191, 204, 210
Fitzgerald, F. Scott, 34
Ford, Henry, 31, 52–53, 142–44
Ford Motor Company, 27, 31, 52, 142–43, 146–49, 151
France, 19, 149, 158–59, 231, 249
  Paris, 3, 15, 17, 35, 45, 63–64, 169–76, 231
free parking, 5, 22–23, 122–28, 130, 198, 207–8, 232
fuel-efficiency, 9, 134, 149, 153
funding, 32, 192–93, 208, 210, 235

gasoline, 92, 97, 134, 141–44, 218
  cost of, 126–27, 178, 212–13
  prices, 49, 59, 149–50, 176, 227–28, 232
  taxes, 19, 152–53, 191, 232
gender, 26–27, 159–60, 179, 218–19, 222–23
General Motors (GM), 6, 32, 35, 92, 142–43, 147
gentrification, 2, 70–71, 75
Germany, 19, 53, 98, 134–35
Gibson, Donald, 40–41, 70
Glencore (firm), 91–94, 96
governments, 4, 32–33, 37, 40, 45, 55, 92, 99–100, 210
  Parliament, UK, 26–28, 102–3
  US, 57–59, 72, 176, 178, 228
Govind (driver), 79–83
Grahame, Kenneth, 25–26
Great Depression, 32–33, 141–42
The Great Gatsby (Fitzgerald), 34, 166–67
Greenwich Village, New York, 67, 70, 72, 75
gridlock traffic, 49, 62, 73–74, 106
gross domestic product (GDP), 19, 53, 93, 101, 139, 196
growth, 20, 40, 47–48, 92–93, 197–98, 229

health, 9–11, 33, 96, 133–43, 170, 184–85, 202
Hidalgo, Anne, 17, 170–71, 174
high-speed trains, 76, 103, 108, 162, 193, 196–97
highways/freeways, 1, 3, 6–7, 43, 51, 62, 68, 125, 161–63, 192–93, 233

INDEX

Detroit, 56, 58–59
   protests against, 72–76
   relocating population, 2, 64
   Vancouver, 204–5
   See also specific highways
Hitler, Adolf, 133, 143
Hong Kong, 159, 194–97
horses, 71–72, 102
housing/houses, 1–2, 16, 21–22, 33, 57–58, 82, 198, 205
   costs of, 82, 120, 122–23, 127, 219–20
   "dingbats," 121–23
   parking and, 206–7
   public, 58, 64, 215
Houston, Texas, 15–17, 22, 85
Howard, Ebenezer, 22, 40
HS2 railway, 76, 103, 108, 126
hybrid vehicles, 98–99

imports, car, 83, 86–88
incentives, 49, 99–100, 115, 198, 207–8, 231
incomes/wages, 11, 54, 55, 61, 82, 88, 141, 143, 178, 219
India, 9, 18, 79–86
inequality, 27–28, 59–60, 81, 233–34
infrastructure, 20, 45–46, 184, 192–93, 232–33
Institute of Transportation Engineers, 124–25, 127, 130
insurance, 10, 126–27, 152, 217
internal combustion engines, 4, 26–27, 33, 97, 100, 102

International Energy Agency, 83, 89, 149

Jacobs, Jane, 68–72, 75–77
jaywalking, 30–31, 164
Jeep, 147–48
Jim Crow Laws, 57, 62–63

Katy Freeway, 15, 17, 85
Kennedy Expressway, 1, 4–5
Kentucky, 98–99, 116, 119
Kenya, 6–8, 19, 86–88
King, David, 135–36, 139–40
Kolwezi, Democratic Republic of Congo, 91–97

land, 5–6, 20–22, 41, 91–93, 192
Las Vegas, Nevada, 109–10
Lawson, Henry John, 40
leaded gasoline, 141–44, 218
Lean NOx Trap (LNT), 135–36
Le Corbusier (architect), 6, 35, 71–72
Levitt, William J., 34
light rail, 16, 47, 60, 110, 124, 126, 198, 208–9
Lindsay, John, 72, 74–75, 114
loans, 11, 13, 83, 193, 211–12
lobbying, 6, 27, 30–32, 87–88, 133–34, 143–44, 206
London, England, 9, 26, 44–47, 55, 73, 180–85, 218, 222–23, 233
   congestion charges in, 22, 99, 231
   public transportation in, 48–49, 211

London Underground, 21, 33, 84, 120, 196
Los Angeles, California, 30–31, 32, 121–24, 138, 203
  public transportation in, 123–24, 126, 128, 198, 208–9, 222
Lower Manhattan Expressway (LOMEX), 67–68, 70, 72
low-traffic neighborhoods (LTNs), 201–6
Lyft, 12, 104–5, 219

Macmillan, Harold, 43–44
Macron, Emmanuel, 177, 232
Manning Thomas, June, 56–57
Merkel, Angela, 19, 138–39
middle class, 1, 6, 23, 52, 54, 69, 81, 86
millennials, 218–19, 221
mines, 12–13, 91–97, 98
Model T (Ford), 27, 31, 52, 142–43
modernism, 35, 37, 45, 85, 89
monkey gassing, 133–36, 138–39
Moses, Robert, 6, 35, 63–65, 67–68, 70, 113
motorcycles, 55, 81, 83, 86, 91
Motor Mania (cartoon), 234–35
Moynihan, Patrick, 74–75
Mumbai, India, 79–86
Mumford, Lewis, 40, 70, 72
Musk, Elon, 92–93, 100, 103, 106–7, 109–11, 119, 153–54, 233

Nairobi, Kenya, 6–8, 86–87
Najdovski, Christophe, 175–77, 182, 224–25

National Transportation Safety Board, US, 104, 150
natural gas, 98, 228
Netherlands, 10, 17–18, 73, 158, 176–77, 231
New Jersey, 34, 61, 68, 142, 204
New York, New York, 5–6, 29, 31, 52, 73–74, 99, 115, 163, 209, 233
  bicycling in, 178–79, 182, 185
  Greenwich Village, 67, 70, 72, 75
  Moses developing, 35, 63–65, 67
  subway, 64, 108–9
  West Side highway, 113–14 116, 120
New York Times, 29, 113, 133–34, 174
NIMBYism (Not In My Backyard), 75–76, 198–99, 206, 220–21
nitrogen oxides (NOx) pollution, 134–37, 141–42, 153
Norton, Peter, 29–32
Norway, 159, 206

Obama, Barack, 154, 175
oil industry, 15–16, 18, 48, 98, 142, 144, 153, 166, 176, 219, 227–28
Orwell, George, 33–34

Paris, France, 3, 15, 17, 35, 45, 63–64, 169–76, 231
parking, 10, 17, 20–21, 195, 206, 212
  costs of, 23, 126–27, 191–92, 195, 207
  free, 5, 22–23, 122–28, 130, 198, 207–8, 232

parking lots, 2–3, 11–12, 51, 72, 129, 207, 212
Parliament, UK, 26–28, 102–3
pedestrians, 17–18, 52, 80–81, 164, 170–71, 188, 231
   segregation, 30–31, 34, 72, 158, 164
Pennsylvania, 51, 69
Phoenix, Arizona, 104–5, 112
poisoning, 8, 18–19, 96, 138, 142–44
pollution, 7, 10, 33, 42, 84, 97–98, 130
   air, 8–9, 88, 130, 139–40, 170–71, 174, 190
   leaded gasoline, 141–43, 218
   NOx, 134–37, 141–42, 153
   by Volkswagen, 18–19, 133–39
   See also carbon dioxide (CO_2) emissions
population, 7, 52–54, 68, 80–82, 91, 93, 96, 159
   decline, 2–3, 64–65, 119
   density, 35, 55, 60, 75–76, 79
poverty, 48, 61, 80–83, 95, 97, 211–12, 234
   in Detroit, 54–55, 58
prices, 52, 93, 120, 138–39, 219–20
   gasoline, 49, 59, 149–50, 176, 227–28, 232
   oil, 176, 219, 227–28
Priestley, J. B., 39–40
profits, 13, 45, 92, 104–5, 141, 143, 151–54
property development, 33, 43, 56–59, 63, 192, 198

protests, 29, 31, 72–76, 86, 144, 176, 202–4, 232, 235
public policy, 47, 128, 206–8, 224, 232–33
public transportation, 12, 16, 27, 60, 62–63, 108, 174, 211, 228, 235
   buses, 47–49, 83, 85, 110, 123–24, 203, 209–10, 222
   in cities, 22–23, 64–65, 217
   in India, 81–82, 84–86
   in Japan, 188–89, 192, 194
   in London, 48–49, 211
   Los Angeles, 123–24, 126, 128, 198, 208–9, 222
   Musk on, 100, 110–11
   subsidies, 48, 126, 194

race, 55–59, 61–63, 72–75, 179, 183–84
real estate, 1–2, 20–21, 194, 230
redlining new roads, 58, 73
registration, car, 5, 18, 81, 149, 195, 231
Republicans, 74, 154, 170, 212
rickshaws, 9, 80, 82–83
ride-sharing services, 12–13, 104–6, 219
ring roads, 4, 41–42, 44–45, 86
road building, 1–3, 7–8, 45–48, 58, 61–62, 83–85, 87, 194, 213, 232
Rothstein, Richard, 57–58

safety, 7, 10, 27, 29, 31, 36, 79–82, 104–5, 164–67, 219–20
   bicycle, 178–85, 224–25

San Francisco, California, 13, 204, 213, 220
Saumarez Smith, Otto, 43, 45
scandals, 133–44
Schwartz, Sam, 73–74, 106, 212, 1114
Sea Link (toll road), 82, 85
segregation, 58, 61–62
   pedestrian, 30–31, 34, 72, 158, 164
"self-driving" cars, 103–7, 228, 233
Shoup, Donald, 123–26, 128, 130, 207
Shuto Kōsoku-dōro Kabushiki-gaisha (Metropolitan Expressway Company), 193
Singapore, 125, 172, 181, 194–97, 231
size, car, 9, 145–52, 154, 191, 193, 195
skyscrapers, 15, 35, 60, 68, 72, 114, 138
"slums," 41, 44, 58–59, 67, 69–70
The Slums of Beverly Hills (film), 121–22
solar power, 89, 98
Sorensen, Andre, 190–93
South Side Chicago, 3, 180, 183–84
Speck, Jeff, 119, 161, 163
speed cameras, 160, 163
speed limits, 1, 26–29, 31, 224
sprawl, 20, 22, 34, 63, 128, 208
   in cities, 12, 15–16, 25–26, 212–13
Standard Oil, 32, 142–43
steam engines, 26, 71
streetcars, 21, 32, 126

streets/roads, 44, 85, 91, 161–63, 169–71, 232–33
   costs of, 20, 82–84, 115–20, 192–93
   demand for, 71, 115–20
   residential, 188, 198, 201, 203–4
   ring, 4, 41–42, 44–45, 86
   subsidies, 19–20, 44–45, 56, 115–20, 174, 176, 232
   car ownership, 12, 152–54, 191
   public transportation, 48, 126, 194
   suburbs, 56–58, 230–31
suburbs, 2–3, 33–34, 52, 68, 218–20, 228, 234–35
   sprawl in, 22, 63
   subsidies for, 56–58, 230–31
   white flight and, 55–59
subway systems, 1, 64, 108–9, 196
SUVs, 9, 19, 147–49, 151, 154

taxes, 10, 56, 60, 63, 86–87, 139–40, 149–51, 182–83, 191–93, 195, 208
   French, 231, 249
   gasoline, 19, 152–53, 191, 232
taxis, 7, 9, 104–5, 192, 223–24
technology, 6, 29, 33, 101, 103, 117, 135–36, 171–72, 195–96
   electronic vehicles, 91–93, 97
   internal combustion engine, 27, 102
   ride-sharing services, 12–13, 104–6, 219
Tesla, 8, 92–93, 99, 105–10, 153–54

Texas, 15–17, 22, 126, 232–33
Toderian, Brent, 127, 204–6
Tokyo, Japan, 10, 187, 197–98, 231
tolls, 74–75, 82, 85, 116–18, 193, 212
Toyota, 80, 136, 141, 147–48, 152, 158, 189
traffic, 1, 3–7, 18, 42–43, 53, 56, 62, 79–85, 166, 169–70, 187–88
  accidents, 26, 28, 159–60, 164–65
  in cities, 117–19, 203–4
  city planning and, 35–37, 42–44
  gridlock, 49, 62, 73–74, 106
  Jacobs on, 71–72
  lanes, 42, 63, 113, 115–20, 161–62, 173
  New York, 64–65, 113–15
  ride-sharing services increasing, 13, 219
  segregation, 30–31, 34, 55, 164
  trams impacted by, 32, 45–46
traffic engineers, 30, 44, 62, 71, 114, 117–19, 127, 163–64
trains/rail lines, 11, 20–22, 83, 98, 222, 232–33
  high-speed, 76, 103, 108, 162, 193, 196–97
  HS2, 76, 103, 108, 126
  Japanese, 10, 193–94
  nationalized, 46–47, 193
trams, 32, 45–46, 126, 208
trucks, 54, 145–52, 154, 212
tunnels, 107–10, 233
Turbocharged Direct Injection (TDI) engines, 134, 136

Uber, 12–13, 104–5, 203–4, 219
United Kingdom (UK), 18, 49, 97–98, 117–18, 125, 148, 158–60, 163, 182, 208
  car ownership, 22, 26–28, 222–23
  Department for Transport, 5, 15, 47–48, 115, 161–62, 184
  Parliament, 26–28, 102–3
United States (US), 1, 94–95, 117, 134, 136, 138, 146–47, 218–19
  car ownership, 51–52, 88–89
  cars per capita, 5, 13, 211
  cities, 9, 15, 31, 51–53, 56–61, 210, 221–22
  Department of Energy, 5, 18, 88–89, 98
  Department of Transportation, 17, 224
  free parking in, 22–23, 122–28, 130, 198, 207, 232
  government, 57–59, 72, 176, 178, 228
  National Transportation Safety Board, 104, 150
  oil industry in, 15–16, 18, 142
  vehicular deaths, 8–9, 11, 28–29, 159–61, 163–65

Vancouver, Canada, 204–5
Victorian era, 1, 32–33, 35, 44–45, 76, 94, 102, 121
Voie Georges-Pompidou, 169–71
Volkswagen, 18–19, 133–39, 142–44

walking, 7, 52, 84–85, 125, 184, 188–89, 220–21, 224
Washington, D.C., 59, 67, 73, 76, 126, 149, 207, 216, 238
Watkins, Ralph J., 192–93
Waymo, 104–5
Waze app, 203–4
wealth, 22, 27–28, 48, 53, 80–83, 89, 93–97, 233–34
weather, 16–17, 46–47, 175–77, 179
weight, car, 136, 148–50, 153, 231
West Side highway (NY), 113–14, 116, 120
white flight, 55–59, 62

Wilson, S. S., 172–73
wind power, 89, 98–99
women, 26–27, 55, 179, 218–19, 222–23
working-class, 12, 52, 72–73
World Health Organization, 88, 135, 142
World's Fair (1939), 6, 36
World War I, 28–29, 40, 172
World War II, 4, 18, 37, 40–41, 55, 133, 143–44, 146–47, 172–73

zoning, 22, 123, 126, 198

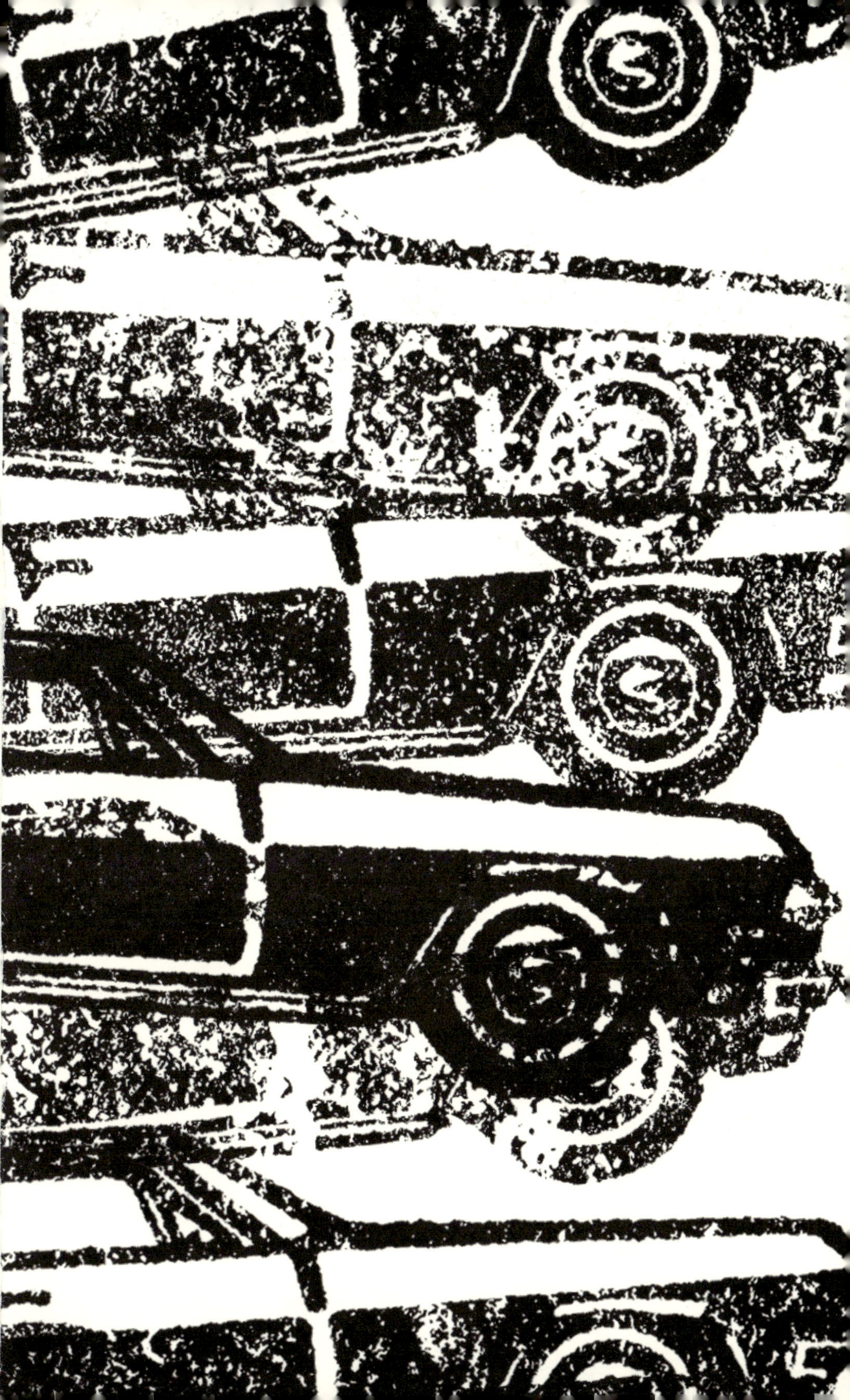

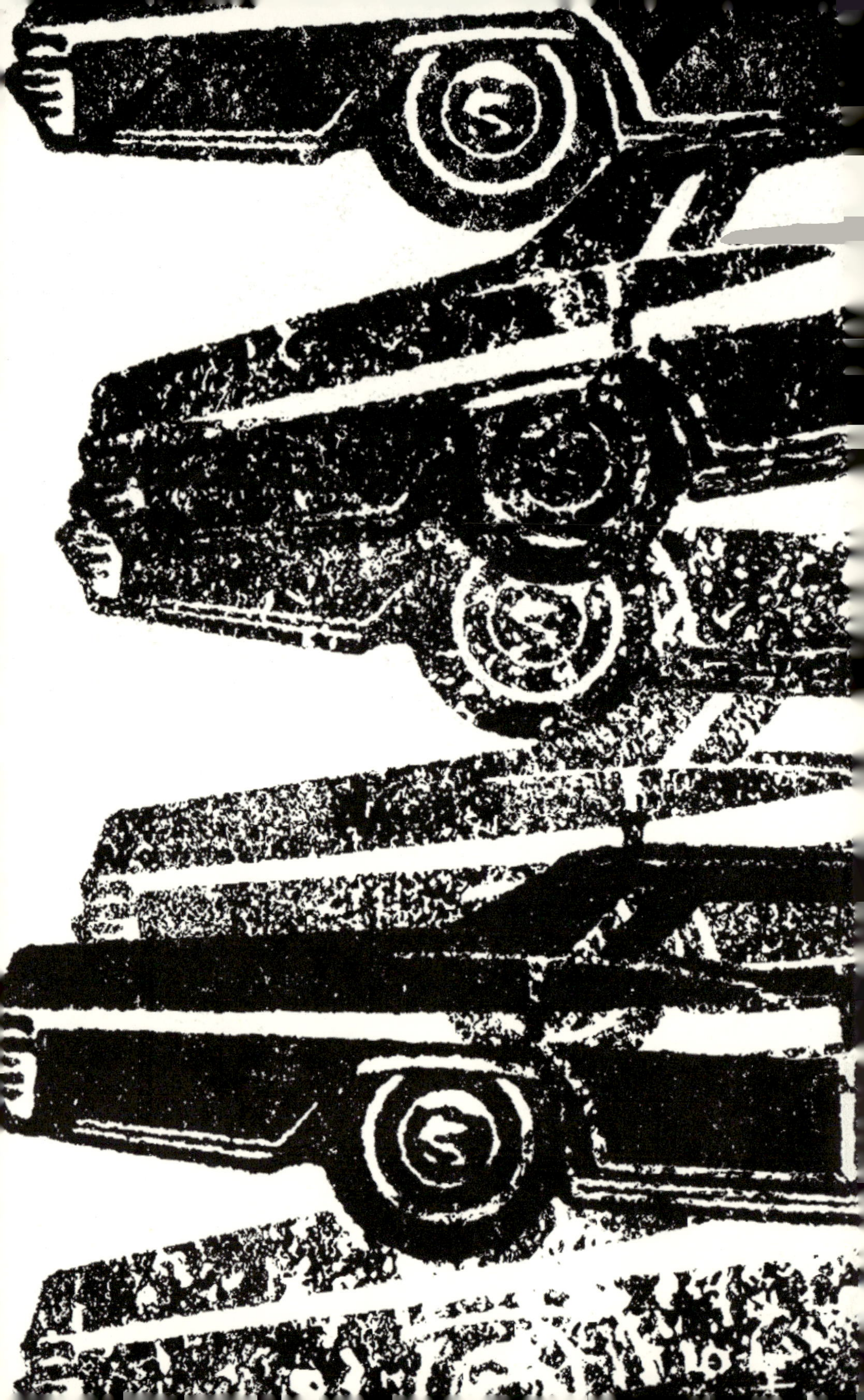